Geography and the Integrated Curriculum

A Reader

Edited by

Michael Williams

Department of Education, University of Manchester

 Heinemann Educational Books

Heinemann Educational Books Ltd
LONDON EDINBURGH MELBOURNE AUCKLAND TORONTO
HONG KONG SINGAPORE KUALA LUMPUR
IBADAN NAIROBI JOHANNESBURG
LUSAKA NEW DELHI

ISBN 0 435 35730 1 (Cased)
ISBN 0 435 35731 X (Paper)

375.91
G-29
127002
Dec. 1983

Published by Heinemann Educational Books Ltd.,
48 Charles Street, London W1X 8AH
Set in IBM Century by Preface Limited, Salisbury
Printed in Great Britain by Morrison and Gibb Ltd.,
London and Edinburgh

Contents

III. INTEGRATION: COMTEMPORARY PRACTICE

Acknowledgements

The essays contained in this book originally appeared in the journals and books listed below, and the author and publishers are grateful to the following for permission to reproduce them:

H. J. Mackinder and the Geographical Association for 'The Teaching of Geography and History as a Combined Subject', *Geography Teacher*, 7, 35, 1913, pp. 4—9.

W. Maclean Carey and the Geographical Association for 'The Correlation of Instruction in Physics and Geography', *Geographical Teacher*, 5, 25, 1909, pp. 148—153.

The Council of the Geographical Association for 'The Position of Geography', *Geography Teacher*, 10, 55, 1919, pp. 91—93.

The Controller of Her Majesty's Stationery Office for 'Suggestions on Teaching: Geography', from the Board of Education Consultative Committee Report *The Education of the Adolescent* (Hadow Report), H.M.S.O., 1927, pp. 203—210.

F. C. Happold for 'Heritage and Environment', from *Citizens in the Making*, Christophers, 1935, pp. 67—78.

The Controller of Her Majesty's Stationery Office for 'The Principles of the Curriculum', from the Board of Education's *Report of the Consultative Committee on Secondary Education* (Spens Report), H.M.S.O., 1938, pp. 152—161.

The Controller of Her Majesty's Stationery Office for 'Geography', from the Board of Education's *Curriculum and Examinations in Secondary Schools*, Report of the Secondary Schools Examinations Council (Norwood Report), H.M.S.O., 1943, pp. 101—104.

The Council for Curriculum Reform and University of London Press for 'The Social Sciences: Social Studies', from *The Content of Education*, 1945, pp. 147—162.

The Controller of Her Majesty's Stationery Office for 'The Study and Practice of Citizenship in Schools', from the Ministry of Education's Pamphlet No. 16, *Citizens Growing Up*, H.M.S.O., 1949, pp. 20—25.

E. L. Fereday and *The Journal of Education* for 'Social Studies in the Secondary Modern School', November 1950, pp. 597—598.

J. Dray and D. Jordan and Methuen and Company for 'The Scope of Social Studies', from *A Handbook of Social Studies*, 1950, pp. 22—38.

The Royal Geographical Society for 'Geography and "Social Studies" in Schools', a memorandum prepared for Council of the Royal Geographical Society by its Education Committee, June 1950, pp. 181—185.

R. C. Honeybone and the Geographical Association for 'Balance in Geography and Education', *Geography*, 34, 184, 1954, pp. 91—101.

The Controller of Her Majesty's Stationery Office for 'The Proper Study of Mankind', from the Ministry of Education's *Half Our Future*, Report of the Central Advisory Council for Education (England) (Newsom Report), H.M.S.O., 1963, pp. 163—169.

C. Cannon and *Educational Review* for 'Social Studies in Secondary Schools', *Educational Review*, 17, 1, 1964, pp. 18—30.

R. Pring for 'Curriculum Integration', *University of London Institute of Education Bulletin*, Spring 1970, pp. 4—8.

M. Skilbeck and the General Studies Association for 'Forms of Curriculum Integration', *General Education*, 18, 1972, pp. 7—13.

F. Musgrove and Wm. Collins Sons and Company for 'Power and the Integrated Curriculum', *Journal of Curriculum Studies*, 5, 1, 1973, pp. 3—12.

N. Graves and the Royal Geographical Society for 'Geography, Social Science and Inter-disciplinary Enquiry', *Geographical Journal*, 134, 1968, pp. 390—394.

D. W. Bolam and Georg Westermann Verlag for 'Intergrating the Curriculum — A Case Study in the Humanities', *Paedagogica Europaea*, *1970/1971*, pp. 157—171.

G. G. Elliott and the General Studies Association for 'Integrated Studies — Some Problems and Possibilities for the Geographer', *General Education*, 23, 1974, pp. 28—34.

A. Williams and *Forum* for 'Integrated Studies Project', *Forum*, 16, 1, 1973, pp. 12—14.

M. Hewlett and the General Studies Association for 'Urban Environmental Studies', *General Education*, 16, 1971, pp. 26—34.

P. Mitchell and *Forum* for 'The Humanities Programme in Thomas Bennett School', *Forum*, 15, 1, 1972, pp. 10—12.

J. Sealey and *Forum* for 'Inter-disciplinary Studies', *Forum*, 13, 2, 1971, pp. 61—63.

D. Hogan and the General Studies Association for 'World Studies at Walworth Comprehensive School', *General Education*, 18, 1972, pp. 38—41.

M. T. Williams and Pergamon Press for 'Modern Studies: a Growth Area in the Curriculum of Scottish Secondary Schools', *Education and Social Science*, 1, 1970, pp. 151—157.

C. V. James and the Centre for Information on Language Teaching and Research for 'European Studies and the Study of Europe', June 1973, pp. 42—52.

Introduction

The geography teacher in a British secondary school may be compared with a rider on a fairground roundabout; he is subjected to centripetal and centrifugal forces simultaneously. He is pulled inwards to an intensive enquiry into the nature of his subject, the content and methodology of geography in a state of dynamism; he is pulled outwards beyond the confines of his academic subject into a consideration of the relationship between geography and other subjects in school curricula. Geography teachers differ in their responses to these forces but in the contemporary school situation it is difficult to escape them.

It could be argued that when secondary schools were small and selective the situation was simpler: they were not involved in the current controversy surrounding proposals for organizing teaching through mixed ability groups, for establishing team teaching schemes, for introducing alternative examination structures, for devising patterns of child-centred learning. There are some teachers who look back to a time when there appeared to be an equilibrium situation, when homogeneous ability groups were taught in preparation for a single, formal external examination, when subjects were clearly demarcated and specialists knew what and how to teach. However, the literature relating to the teaching of geography during this century does not suggest that an equilibrium position existed at any time. On the contrary, the history of geographical education is dominated by the debate over the respective places of physical and human geography in school courses and the links between geography and other courses.

While this collection of articles and extracts is focused upon the latter part of this debate, it is obvious that the more one explores the relationship between geography and other school subjects the more one defines school geography on the one hand, and the more one defines the curriculum appropriate for school children on the other. A critical evaluation of the relationship between geography and other school subjects should lead to improved geography teaching and, it is hoped, to a better education for pupils. That these two potential achievements are not identical is a fundamental component in the unceasing debate about the value of geography in the education of children.

So far the expression 'relationship between geography and other school subjects' has been employed to envelop all those formal and informal school arrangements in which teachers, pupils and subjects interact. In seeking to define this relationship more clearly it is difficult to avoid introducing a number of terms all of which share a common feature in their lack of commonly accepted definitions. 'Co-operation', 'correlation', 'combined subjects', 'inter-disciplinary courses', 'non-disciplinary courses', 'integrated courses', are frequently encountered terms. Although often used as synonyms, these terms do have particular meanings and as one reads through this collection of readings it is clear that although attempts have been made to bring order out of the semantic confusion, as yet these efforts have not been particularly successful. In a recent publication the authors comment:

> There would seem to be a difference between *inter-disciplinary enquiry* (in which a number of disciplines contribute to a particular topic investigation at various times), and *integrated work*, in which subject-specialists may actually work alongside each other in the same lesson, or in which there may be no conscious 'subject contribution'. But it must be fairly said that many teachers use the terms interchangeably. The semantics of the situation are unclear (Bale *et al.* 1973).

To the difficulty of defining the word 'relationship' must be added the lack of generally accepted meanings for titles of courses. In a system of education which permits individual schools to design their own curricula and to initiate new courses we ought not to be surprised that new courses carry titles which are meaningful only in the context of particular schools. Thus expressions commonly encountered in popular educational literature, such as 'social studies', 'environmental studies', 'general studies' and 'European studies' are almost meaningless unless one knows something about the person employing the expression and the particular school situations which he describes. If geographers divide over definitions of 'geography' and 'school geography' it is not surprising that when geography is allied with other subjects the problem of definition of terms is almost insoluble. A further complication arises from the nature of geography itself. Because geography can be divided into physical and human components, in integrated courses it may sometimes be allied with other subjects with a human bias, as in some social studies courses, and at other times it may be allied with science subjects, as in some environmental studies courses. The transition from social studies to social science and from environmental studies to environmental science illustrates some of the attempts made to clear up definitional problems by introducing new terms which are supposedly more precise and more easily defined.

Although the early attempts at introducing integrated courses stemmed from the struggle to introduce geography into secondary schools it quickly became obvious that no sooner had geography taken its place as an accepted part of school curricula than it was subjected to pressures to relate more closely to other subjects. In particular the link between history and geography was much publicized and this principally because of the influence of an active pressure group whose slogan was 'Education for Citizenship'. Spear-headed by the Association for Education in Citizenship, this pressure group had an important influence on the authors of government reports and on teachers in schools. Co-operation between geography and history teachers was seen as a contribution not only to civic education in a narrow, national-political sense (courses of Civics and Current Affairs were products of this thinking), but also to courses which were designed to promote international understanding. Experimentation which started in the pre-1939 inter-war period was to bear fruit in the so-called 'social studies movement'. This movement was distinguished by new courses and 'a flood of books, articles and Ministry reports' (Lawton and Dufour 1973).

While this flood of publications died down in the late 1950s, course experimentation continued: certainly in 1963 the social studies movement was still alive (Williams 1963). It is clear that the 1960s and early 1970s have seen a re-vitalization in the debate about the secondary school curriculum. Projects sponsored by the Schools Council have contributed much to the quickened activity. New courses such as politics, social science, environmental studies and European studies have been promoted by other agencies. This curricular activity has been subjected to scrutiny not only by teachers and subject activists in teachers' professional associations but also by academic educationalists, most notably philosophers and sociologists interested in curriculum theory and practice.

For geography teachers the fundamental questions persist: Can a convincing case be made for the inclusion of geography as a separate subject in the curriculum of *all* pupils of particular ages in secondary schools? If the answer to this question is positive then for what age group or age groups would this be appropriate, and at what point would pupils following specialist geography courses best divide from those following integrated courses? To which integrated courses can geography make a meaningful contribution? What criteria should be employed in determining which pupils should follow integrated courses and what are the characteristics necessary for geography teachers who may be allocated to the teaching of integrated courses? It is not suggested that at the end of this collection of readings geography teachers will feel confident to answer these questions but it is hoped that sufficient guidance will be provided to assist in reaching conclusions on the basis of an accumulation of varying opinions and viewpoints. As yet there is insufficient evidence to answer what many teachers consider the most vital question: do integrated courses in secondary schools create more problems than they solve?

II

The collection of readings is divided into three sections. In the first section the discussion of the place of geography in integrated courses is traced historically from the opening of this century to the early 1950s. It is appropriate to open with an article by Halford Mackinder (Reading 1), the doyen of British school and university geography, not only because the views he expressed were significant at the time of their publication, but also because the arguments he developed have persisted to the present time. For

Mackinder the possible *combination* of geography and history was the central concern, but a reminder of the scientific bias in geography is provided in Maclean Carey's article (Reading 2) where he illustrates how geography may be *correlated* with physics. The Council of the Geographical Association asserted emphatically the unity of geography and is unambiguous in its statement that while geography has been grouped with other subjects in various ways 'into none of them will geography fit quite satisfactorily' (Reading 3). But in the same extract, attention is drawn to the value of geography in citizenship and this introduces a theme which recurs in many of the other readings.

Intermingled with statements affirming the identity of geography as a separate school subject (Readings 4 and 6) are provocative and influential expositions of course arrangements of an integrated kind (Readings 5, 8, 9, 10, and 11). In the inter-war years the debate must be considered against a background in which the changing educational scene, the domestic economic crisis and the deepening international conflict were essential components. The Spens (Reading 6) and Norwood Reports (Reading 7) heralded the post-war reform of secondary school organization which was to witness curricular experimentation including the social studies movement. Fereday's article (Reading 10) includes an interesting example of a secondary modern school course organized along lines proposed by Dray and Jordan (Reading 11). To counter the social studies movement, the Education Committee of the Royal Geographical Society published a blunt memorandum (Reading 12) and this was soon followed by the article by Honeybone (Reading 13) which contained more thorough analyses of the place of geography in the curricula of secondary schools in the decade following the end of World War II.

The Education Committee of the Royal Geographical Society attributed the emergence of social studies to a number of forces, placing the influence of American theories first in their list. The reader will have noticed that the readings in this collection are drawn from British sources. This exclusion of foreign sources is partly motivated by a search for simplicity but more importantly by the editor's conviction that whereas current movements in British geographic education, especially those encompassed in the expression 'new geography', owe much to the stimulus afforded by the materials and methodology of the American High School Geography Project, the relationship between geography and integrated courses is a much more indigenous issue. Britain has a distinctive tradition in school geography and international influences are apparent only in very recent developments. This generalization applies as much to experimentation in integration as to changes within the subject geography as taught in secondary schools.

In the second section the first two readings lay the foundations for two growth areas which were to emerge in the curriculum in the latter half of the 1960s. The Newsom Report (Reading 14) heralds the humanities and the possibility of religious education allying itself with history and geography, and Cannon (Reading 15) looks back at the weaknesses of social studies and forward to the introduction of social science courses. Articles by Pring (Reading 16) and Skilbeck (Reading 17) are of importance for their theoretical insights since they seek to define more closely the concept of integration and in so doing give a new perspective to the place of geography in integrated courses. For Musgrove (Reading 18), integration poses questions about power structures in schools. His article is a valuable reminder that integration goes deeper than the substantive arguments about the relationship of one corpus of knowledge to another; teachers are involved and so are school departments; status, prestige, tradition are important for schools, teachers and pupils as well as for subjects. Finally, Graves reviews the movements towards integration and looks particularly at the place of geography in integrated courses (Reading 19). This article provides a useful bridge to Section III which is composed of eleven articles highlighting types of courses in secondary schools and the articles are valuable either for their case study data or for their review qualities.

The third section begins with descriptions of two Schools Council projects (Readings 20 and 21) and immediately following these there is a description of the work undertaken in a project school associated with the Keele Project (Reading 22). The remaining articles are strongly oriented towards the humanities, and four of them are descriptions of courses in individual schools (Readings 23—26). Williams (Reading 27) examines the place of Modern Studies in the curricula of Scottish secondary schools, demonstrating that the Scottish schools have their own curricular traditions and, as a result, the process of integration has produced distinctive types of courses. The concluding reading by James (Reading 28) introduces a new element — the place of modern languages in integrated courses. European studies is but one of a number of area studies which flourish in some schools. American studies, African studies, Russian studies and Caribbean studies, all have their advocates and, in examining the possible structures in which European studies exists, James indicates principles which are transferable to any of these area studies.

III

At the beginning of this introduction the British geography teacher was compared with a rider on a fairground roundabout. The reader who follows the arguments and counter-arguments for integrating geography with other school subjects to create new courses may appreciate a new dimension to the analogy. Just as the roundabout carries the rider in a circle, returning him to his original starting point, so it would seem that after more than half a century of debate about the place of geography in school curricula the arguments raised by Mackinder in 1913 are still alive today. In the field of curricular integration it is not being over-cynical to suggest that there has been little progress.

Note

No changes have been made to the original texts of the readings except some minor alterations for consistency. Only the most useful references have been retained and these are grouped together alphabetically at the rear of this volume.

I

THE ROOTS OF INTEGRATION

In many respects the curriculum of the Secondary School is traditional; in spite of this, however, it has not remained static but has admitted within itself much change in outlook and method; that further change is desirable we do not deny. It may in the past have been associated with a psychology which is now in some quarters considered to be unsound, but it is not a necessary consequence that the curriculum itself is basically unsound; it may have been the right thing, though for the wrong reason, and the experience of schoolmasters that through it they are doing a good work for their pupils is not lightly to be set on one side (Board of Education, Norwood Report 1943).

The Teaching of Geography and History as a Combined Subject

H. J. MACKINDER, 1913

In this published lecture, Mackinder, who had already achieved so much for the recognition of geography as a reputable subject for study in British universities, argues that in schools the teaching of geography has different purposes according to the pupils who are being taught. The simple distinction he draws is between the few who will be studying geography as a subject which they will continue to study once they have left school, and the majority for whom geography as a specialist subject is of far less importance. This distinction is still of significance today and we find it in Bernstein's definition of the two cultures which a school tries to transmit — the instrumental culture, defined as 'those activities, procedures and judgements involved in the acquisition of specific skills, especially those that are vocationally important'; and the expressive culture, which 'consists of those activities, procedures and judgements involved in the transmission of values and their derived norms' (Bernstein *et al.* 1966). Mackinder's case for unifying the teaching of geography and history for the majority of pupils is argued on the grounds that this arrangement would simplify the curriculum and it would contribute to a 'kind of humane teaching' which would be valuable in a system of national education. This argument has persisted to the present day and it finds expression not only in the institutional form of different examinations, or no examinations, for pupils following courses of geography to the age of sixteen, but also in the proliferation of integrated courses in secondary schools. These integrated courses may be seen as ingredients of the expressive culture, while the specialist geography courses may be considered as parts of the instrumental culture.

I am set down to open a discussion on the teaching of geography and history as a combined subject. This is a practical question. The universities, and this

University, have had for some time in the list of subjects for matriculation and the equivalent school-leaving examination a subject known as history and geography, a combined subject. If I remember correctly this was introduced to meet the requirements of the entrance to the army, and rather brutally the syllabus of the pre-existing history and the pre-existing geography were mutilated, and merely the torsos were put together. The examination is on a single sheet of paper, but it consists of two groups of questions, the one set by the history examiners and the other by the geography examiners, and the two halves, though they do not perhaps war with one another, yet have practically nothing to do with one another, and the whole subject, if you can call it a subject, is incongruous in the highest degree. Your Committee in reply to a communication which they received — I forget whether it was from London University or from some other body — described the present combination as ridiculous. I believe there is an opportunity at the present time of evolving a real combination in the way of syllabus and examination in connection with these two subjects of history and geography, and therefore a discussion to-day from the point of view of the practical teacher will be of great value. At the present moment there is a Sub-Committee sitting of the Committee of your Association which is working at this particular matter, and everything that is said here to-day will be taken note of, and so far as it can maintain itself against criticism, will have its effect upon this definite piece, as I think, of progressive educational work.

You will observe that the title of the subject as set down presents one point that is unfamiliar. I speak of the teaching of geography and history as a combined subject, not of history and geography. After all, alphabetically geography comes before history, and therefore in putting history before geography you must have had a design on the part of those who first did it. The design may have been to pay deference to the greater and more established dignity of history, or it may have been — and this I rather suspect — that those who first put the two words together in connection with education knew some history and knew little or no geography. They thought of geography as merely illustrative of history, and of the geographical element in the combination as quite subsidiary. I protest against that, but I do not wish to be involved in any absurd and odious comparison. We believe that we have vindicated the dignity of geography and we are perfectly ready to admit the dignity of history.

There need be no question of vested interests in connection with the two subjects. Let me be quite plain on that point because it is a practical point. In training colleges, yes, and in some secondary schools, you have history established, if I may so put it; you have teaching posts and tenants of those posts, and I do not wish in the least to threaten those people or to make them combine in opposition to us! There is no idea of attacking the teaching of history as such in training colleges and in similar institutions. It is necessary to mention that, because a great deal of difficulty occurred in the establishment of the modern teaching of geography, a great deal of difficulty was made in the early days — I speak of twenty years ago — by the geologists who thought their interests endangered. They thought that the geographers were making inroads upon their classes, that the necessity for fresh geological posts would be reduced, and that their careers would thus be limited. Well, even scientific folk are human, and such ideas must be taken into account. Therefore, I want to make it perfectly clear that I am not advocating in universities and training colleges, and in regard to higher secondary education, the joint teaching by single teachers of geography and history. To advocate that would be to stultify the endeavour upon which I have spent the greater part of my life. I have asked all along that geography should be taught by trained geographers. In the upper half of elementary education and the lower tiers of secondary education you have, however, to deal with something totally different. There what I suggest is the teaching of a single subject, geography and history. In those stages of education let us have one subject, but let that subject be taught by a teacher who has learnt both geography and history, and learnt them separately.

That is my thesis, and that is the practical problem which is at the present time before us. Can it be solved? You are met with two criticisms. You are told in the first place that you are asking for too much from your teacher, to know both a literary subject like history and a scientific subject such as geography, and you are told also that you are asking too much of the children. I do not believe either of these things. I believe that both those criticisms are based on temporary difficulties, and I say that with the more confidence because I have now for some considerable time experimented both in the direction of writing and in the direction of teaching, and I believe that if we steer our course carefully it is possible to accomplish the things which I have in view.

The previous discussion has shown to you the interest that can be imparted to purely physical geography. It is a great thing to arouse in children an interest in Nature around them, and also to instil the idea that there is order and law in that Nature. By doing so you impart great potentialities of pleasure in later life, and also the power of development, because once you have given the idea of system and law, a child will seek to fit into the law and system all new facts that may come to it. But though all that is true in regard to purely physical geography, it seems to me that in these modern times and in these democratic countries we have far more to do than merely rouse an interest in Nature, and even an interest in the order in Nature. Surely I shall carry you with me in the idea that we have three things to do in our education. We have to teach the three Rs, we have to teach some art which shall enable a livelihood to be earned, and we have to make citizens. If you are to make citizens, and good citizens, you must give — on a low plane, I admit, but in a degree — that sense of proportion, that sense of perspective, that outlook which comes from what is known as the study of humaner letters in a university. It is useless to talk of 'subjects' in regard to children from nine or ten to fourteen or fifteen years old. What we have essentially to remember is that they are going out into the world, and they ought to be sent out *curious* in regard to that world. You cannot have taught them after all very much in the way of facts, but if you send them out into the world curious, seeking to learn, and with an idea that there is order in the world around, and that their experience must fit into a corresponding order in their minds, you have done then all you can hope to do. But it is a great deal to have achieved.

How are the children going to use their curiosity? By taking up a 'subject'? That is an academic idea. A special subject will be taken up by a few scattered people as a hobby, but the vast majority will increase their knowledge not by the study of any definite subject, but by reading this and that cheap book, by reading the newspapers, by talking with friends, and by seeing what they can when travelling. They will accumulate experience and knowledge in the general way that the man of the world accumulates knowledge. Therefore what is important is not to send them out with the rudiments of history as such and the rudiments of geography as such in their minds, but to send them out with some sort of orderly conception of the world around them. Whether a fact is historical or whether it is geographical matters not one straw to them. It does, perhaps, matter to those who are going to increase the knowledge of history or the knowledge of geography, or who are to be specialized teachers of those subjects, or who are going to prepare for examinations in those subjects. But it does not matter to those whose work in life is going to begin at fourteen or fifteen, to the nine out of ten who constitute the mass of the people in our country and carry on its traditions. To those people what matters is an outlook, a sense of proportion, and aroused curiosity in regard to the world around them.

The characteristics of that world are fundamentally time and space. Take an event, such an event as the colossal event that has taken place in the Balkan Peninsula in the last few weeks. That event springs out of the past, has consequences in the future, but to visualize it you must be able to place it in its geographical surroundings. The Bosphorus, the Dardanelles, the Sea of Marmora, the Golden Horn, Adrianople, the Black Sea, the Aegean Islands, even the Suez Canal, and Tripoli — it is necessary for you to have a picture in your mind of those facts, those geographical facts, in order that you may understand the dramatic march of events. But in order that you may understand the causes you must understand also something of the past out of which they come, and in order that you may appreciate their importance you must have got the idea of the development of mankind so that you may project yourself a bit into the future and be able to see the probable or possible outcome. Well now, there are geographical elements that enter into this conception, and there are historical elements, but what matters it to the ordinary person that you should divide them into historical and geographical? Every event takes place in time, and in space. As historians we study records, we fix the sequence of what happened, its causes and results. As geographers we see things from another point of view, from the point of view of climatic and agricultural conditions, perhaps, but we study the same events.

Now what I want to suggest is that it is possible, let us say, between the years of ten and fourteen to do a great deal, provided you know a great deal more than you teach, and provided you select carefully the facts you teach.

Any competent historian, I venture to suggest, would be able to take fifteen or twenty great events, fifteen or twenty of the greatest men, and would be able to show them still continuing, still living in the great contrasts of to-day. Christendom and Islam, the contrast which at the present moment you have at Adrianople, do they not take you back to Christ and Mohammed? To Palestine also and to the Desert? What I am advocating is that you should select the really great facts of the past and present, and teach them not dry-as-dust, but as dramas of life and scenery. Later on they will be generalized into the grand development of human society set in its geographical environment. There is nothing new in this. What is our whole Christian teaching based upon, but upon the historical and geographical description of the life of Christ? Do not vast numbers of children obtain an insight into the very centre of historical and geographical teaching out of their Bible? They hear of the Roman Empire through the Acts of the Apostles. They hear of Palestine in the Gospels. What I suggest is that you may do the equivalent in regard to other places and times. You can make the landscape of Greece vivid — the rainless summer, the clear air, the distant mountain landmarks, the deep blue tideless sea, the olives, the terracing, the crops of wine and wheat and oil, the islands, and the Greek people in the islands. Then you can widen your horizon to Egypt and the Nile Valley, to the coming of the Greeks over the sea, to the march of Alexander, and the foundation of Alexandria. What a difference of meaning the newspaper of the present moment has to the man at the back of whose mind is a picture of the old Greeks in their islands and peninsulas! Your schooling and your newspaper coalesce.

I maintain that it is perfectly possible to carry out this kind of humane teaching. I think that it is essential that it should be carried out. The time was when the village pump was the really important thing to the man in the village. The really important thing to him now is to know something of the place where his wheat is grown on the other side of the world. You may tell me that the man in the village can alter things in the village, but that he cannot alter anything elsewhere. We have to realize that individual men cannot, but that a populace can. What have we dreaded during this controversy of late in Europe, but that the Russian populace, or the Austrian military party, or the Turkish religious fanatics, should bolt from the control of diplomacy? We teachers have not got to think only of the individual in the village; we have to think of the people, who are something more than the sum of the individuals. You have somehow or other to equip the community with a sense of perspective and proportion which will enable it to appreciate its leaders and to throw up the right leaders. I have no illusions as to what is possible in a democracy; but still I believe that the people must and can be sufficiently trained to distinguish clap-trap from reality, so that they may be able to compel their leaders, whether they be newspaper editors or party politicians, to place at any rate rational stuff before them. You cannot select the leaders. You are tempted to think only of the individual, the poor little child in front of you, and of his happiness, and of the village pump he has to work. But I venture to appeal for the larger outlook, for the statesmanship which will remember that a nation is more than the individuals of which it is composed. We have to give a national education, so that the nation may be intolerant of the wrong kind of leader.

I admit that this is a high aim, but I believe I have a perfectly clear view of how we should go to work to achieve it. I ask for something which I know will go to your hearts, I ask for simplification in our curriculum. Instead of two subjects let us have one; but in order that it may be possible to give good teaching of that one subject it is essential that in the training college where our teachers are prepared they shall be taught both history and geography. At the present time those are alternative subjects. How can you hope for complete and balanced teaching in the schools as a result? What I ask is that the Government and the universities shall require both history and geography as separate subjects on the part of those who are going to be teachers in our schools — I am not speaking now of the highest secondary schools — and then that those teachers shall have freedom. Say to them 'Now you have your equipment, throw pedantry on one side; what you have to teach is not history and not geography, but to give an outlook on to this great, richly vital, concrete world into which your students are going out to live their busy lives. Let no examiner sunder your teaching into separate subjects, which exist only in books, and not in the real world.'

The Correlation of Instruction in Physics and Geography

W. MACLEAN CAREY, 1913

The word 'correlation' is rarely used in contemporary discussions about curriculum development. As Maclean Carey shows in this reading it usefully describes the informal network of arrangements which exists between teachers in different subjects whose content or teaching methodology overlap. In the previous reading Mackinder drew attention to the relationship between the subject matter of history and the subject matter of geography. Here the focus is upon the scientific side of geography, in particular the overlap between geography and physics. The article is of interest because it draws attention to a distinctive feature of geography as a subject for study in schools. Without borrowing from the content and methodology of other subjects and disciplines geography could not exist. Maclean Carey reminds readers of Gregory's description of the extension of heuristic methods from the science subjects and mathematics to the teaching of geography. Later in the article he gives examples of this borrowing with regard to the study of meteorology. It is a feature of the new geography that spatial analysis can be undertaken by adapting models and methods, especially heuristic methods, derived from mathematics, science and statistics. Instead of the relatively simple explanation of Boyle's Law, modern geographers are exploring such features as the application of gravity models to geographical problems such as the flow of people and goods between urban centres. There is an increasing awareness of the contribution which other subjects can make to the advancement of geography; and this has led some teachers to assert that one of the distinctive contributions of geography to the school curriculum is to act as a bridging subject between the arts and the sciences, and that because geography is in itself an example of a well-integrated subject, there is no requirement for it to be integrated formally with other subjects to create new courses.

Sir Archibald Geikie gave the teacher of geography some food for thought, when he wrote. 'He (i.e. the teacher) should begin by divesting himself of the common notion that the teaching of geography can be taken up by anybody.

When he has realized what geography in the true sense is, he will recognize that to make satisfactory use of it for purposes of instruction demands qualifications of no mean or ordinary kind.' Again he says of geography: 'Its full value as an instrument of education cannot be obtained except by those who are imbued with the scientific spirit'.

These words were written in 1877, and the past twenty years have furnished abundant proof of their truth. The teaching of geography has made great strides within the last ten years, and is now rapidly taking its place as a definite science.

In his lecture on 'Scientific Method in the Teaching of Geography', Professor Gregory has pointed out how the heuristic methods which have proved so successful in the teaching of chemistry, physics, and mathematics should be extended to geography.

The geography teacher of today finds that he is expected to teach his pupils how to take meteorological observations with the barometer, thermometer, rain gauge and so on. Very precise instructions on these points are given in Mr Marriott's *Hints to Meteorological Observers*, so that to learn the correct method of using these instruments is comparatively simple; but to lead pupils to interpret weather maps and obtain an intelligent understanding of the climatic changes concerned is quite another matter. This at once requires the scientific habit of mind and scientific knowledge. As Professor W. M. Davis has said: 'There are few subjects better adapted to the inculcation of scientific methods than the study of weather changes'.

From a study of the daily weather maps, the pupils should compare and contrast the various weather elements in cyclonic and anti-cyclonic areas, and discover for themselves the eastward progress of these areas and the resulting weather changes.

The active minds in the class will ask the reasons for these regular changes. The necessary explanation involves many physical laws, which need experimental illustration, and the teacher finds himself poorly equipped for his task unless he has a knowledge of physics. If he does not possess this knowledge, he should endeavour to obtain it by attending a suitable course of practical instruction.

If this is impossible, the teacher will be fortunate if the science master works hand in hand with him, and at this stage takes up the subject and in the physics lesson explains the various atmospheric phenomena. The science master has the reward of increased interest on the part of his pupils, when they see the widespread application of the principles which they discover; and the pupils themselves have their breadth of mind and clearness of vision increased by regarding facts from two mental standpoints: the importance of this has been emphasized by Mr Mackinder. Such co-operation, however, demands that the science master should be in sympathy with the requirements of the geography teacher. Correlation will therefore be most successful where the two subjects are taught by the same master.

Attention has been drawn to the fact that the teacher of geography must have a mind that can see the movement of the winds in the cyclone, the movement of the Earth in its orbit, and so on.

The power to visualize is certainly necessary to the teacher of geography, but it cannot be said to be his peculiar qualification. This power may be termed the scientific imagination, and the fact that it is demanded of the teacher of geography is a very strong argument in favour of geography being taught by the chemistry or physics master.

The successful science teacher can see, and make his pupils see, the movements of the atoms and molecules, when, for instance, hydrochloric acid is added to chalk, or again, to choose an instance from physics, can make them see what is going on in a simple voltaic cell.

If this teacher turns his attention to geography he will find no difficulty in developing the imagination of his pupils. Again, the teacher of chemistry or physics who makes his subject truly educational, and keeps the interest of his pupils, is the one who always has in mind the human aspect of his science — its application to everyday affairs, to arts, trades, and inventions. If he takes geography also under his care he will not neglect to emphasize its economic side.

The writer has recently been privileged, through the courtesy of Mr Hay, the headmaster, to inspect the notes made during a five years' course in physiography at Midhurst Grammar School, Sussex. At this school of about seventy boys — which is probably typical of many others — correlation has been successfully carried out by the practical and experimental part of geography being taken in conjunction with elementary physics, and called physiography, so as to count as science in the Board of Education Time Analysis. Geography, which of course still ranks as an English subject under the regulations of the Board, is taught by the same master as the physiography.

The following notes of a lesson on weather, which the writer has frequently given, may serve to show how the application of physical principles helps the solution of geographical problems:

(1) The isobars in a cyclone are seen to resemble the contour lines (or isobaths) of a depression in the ocean.

Treating the cyclone as an actual depression, the barometric curve obtained at any point of observation is seen to be a section of the depression on a plane drawn through that point parallel to the direction of motion of the cyclone, with the difference that the curve is reversed. This may be seen if the weather chart is drawn on squared paper and the section made on tracing paper and then reversed and compared with the barogram. Similarly an anti-cyclone is compared to an elevated area.

(2) The motion of the air from a high pressure to a low pressure area, and the relation between the velocity of the air currents and the steepness of the barometric gradients are deduced from observation of the chart, and are seen to follow the laws which govern the motion of liquids. A simple illustrative experiment may be performed with two tubes containing water at different levels and joined by a clipped rubber tube.

(3) In the case of a cyclone, the upward motion of the air is inferred from the motion towards the centre and the central calm. The effect of elevation in the lowering of the barometric height is deduced from data. Reference is

made to Boyle's Law, and a simple experiment performed. The atmospheric pressure decreases roughly at the rate of one-tenth of an inch for every hundred feet of elevation for some distance above the surface.

(4) The cooling resulting from expansion is next deduced. A cycle-tyre valve opened against the bulb of a thermometer will illustrate this, or a cylinder of carbon dioxide may be opened, if one is available. The solidification of the carbon-dioxide will not be forgotten. The class may be questioned as to the scientific explanation of the cooling produced by blowing with the mouth.

Cooling is also produced by contact with air at higher altitudes. The fact that the temperature falls at the rate of about $1°F.$ for a rise of 300 feet may be obtained from statistics.

(5) Condensation and cloud-formation may be illustrated by attaching a piece of rubber tubing to a damp flask and sucking air from it suddenly, or withdrawing the air by a filter pump.

(6) The central downward motion in an anti-cyclone and the resulting air-compression are discussed in a similar manner. The warming of the air is illustrated in pumping up a cycle tyre. The absence of clouds is inferred and the consequent abnormal loss of heat by radiation at night, with the formation of dew, hoar frost and fog. All these matters are treated very clearly and fully with instructions as to experimental work in Chapter xx of the *Introduction to Practical Geography*, by A. T. Simmons and H. Richardson.

The central calms of local cyclones or anti-cyclones should be compared with the calms of the planetary wind-system.

Mention may be made of a few further points which experience has shown make towards successful correlation of physics and geography.

(1) The barometer and thermometer should be introduced in the first year's course in physics.

(2) The experiments performed for fixing the boiling point and freezing point on a thermometer should not be regarded as merely marking the volume of mercury in the glass, but as forming an introduction to the study of latent heat.

The high latent heat of fusion of ice should be subsequently emphasized. The fact that ice is the most difficult of all substances to melt mainly accounts for the low temperature of polar summers, despite the great amount of insolation received at that season. The effect of the high latent heat of vaporization of water should also be discussed. Usually this is inadequately treated in text books.

The mass of air in a tropical cyclone 100 miles in diameter and a mile deep has been calculated to be equal to that of half a million 6,000-ton ships. Let the class imagine, if they can, this huge mass moving with the speed of a fast train, and deriving its energy mainly from the evolution of latent heat, and they begin to realise the importance of this liberated energy. They might also note that the high latent heat of vaporization of water explains the comparatively low temperature of the tropical oceans and the small daily variation of the temperature of the sea. Again, the warming due to energy liberated during heavy rainfall largely explains the chinook and föhn winds.

Some of the warmth of the Gulf Stream probably reaches our shores in the form of energy liberated during condensation in the rain-bearing westerlies.

Consideration of the variation of the boiling point with the atmospheric pressure should serve as an introduction to the hypsometer for measuring altitudes.

The raising of the boiling point of water produced by increase of pressure leads to the explanation of geyser action. The lowering of the melting point of ice by pressure introduces the phenomenon of regelation and the explanation of glacial motion.

(3) The importance to aquatic life of the maximum density point of water should be noted, and also the disintegration of rocks and soil which results from the sudden expansion of water when freezing.

(4) The high specific heat of water (higher than that of any other substance), should be noted and its effect on climate discussed.

(5) Experiments illustrating convection of heat in liquids should be treated not merely as demonstrating a method of transference of heat, but as bringing out the principle that heat is a form of energy. Consideration of monsoons, land and sea breezes, trade-winds, and ocean currents follows naturally. The difference between convection in liquids and in gases should be discussed. In the case of the latter there are adiabatic changes in temperature resulting from expansion or contraction.

A suggestion made in the *Syllabus of Instruction in Geography* issued by the Royal Geographical Society may be carried out. By arrangement between the geographical and physical teachers an essay might be set involving the explanation of some physical law. For example, the essay might be on the causes which determine the difference between an insular climate, such as that of Liverpool, and a continental climate, such as that of Irkutsk, both places being situated in the same latitude. The subject for the essay might be talked over in class. An examination of isothermal charts shows that over the sea the hot belt is narrowest and the temperature belt widest, while over the land the conditions are reversed. Water is a good reflector of the insolation incident on it; land is a poor one, and therefore has its temperature raised by the absorbed radiant energy. The convection currents set up in the sea tend to make its temperature more uniform throughout its mass. In land there are no convection currents to moderate its temperature. Owing to evaporation from its surface much of the radiant energy absorbed by water disappears in the form of latent heat, and there is a consequent lowering of temperature. Water has a high specific heat and land a low one. Land is a good absorber of heat, and water a poor one.

All these causes tend to make the continental climate one of extremes. The effect of rainfall and water vapour on temperature must also be considered in this connection.

It will be found of educational value, and moreover a great saving of time to the teacher who still has to prepare pupils for examinations, to correlate several geographical problems, and set an essay on the physical law on which they depend. Remarks previously made in this paper will show how the subject of latent heat may be treated in this way.

An essay might be set on the effect on insolation of the presence of water vapour in the atmosphere. A comparison of the rainfall charts and isothermal charts of the world brings out the fact that the regions of great range of temperature are those which have a low rainfall.

The action of water vapour in trapping insolation may be compared to that of the glass of a greenhouse. During questions on this subject in class a pupil of the writer spontaneously compared it to a free-wheel clutch. It has also been compared to a barb.

The explanation of the coldness of mountain tops might be argued out, and a typical desert climate such as that of the Sahara accounted for.

The presence in the tropics of columns of heated air unable to part with their heat owing to aqueous vapour in the atmosphere above, sometimes results in cyclones, typhoons, or tornadoes.

The rotary nature of these wind systems may be compared with the circumpolar whirl. We have to consider, too, the effect of latent heat in increasing their intensity. Though the Earth would be too cold to be habitable if deprived for a single night of its water vapour, yet the presence of this water vapour largely accounts for these violent storms.

The subject of heat has been dealt with at some length on account of its importance in the consideration of causes which determine climate and the consequent vegetation and industries. Light, electricity, and magnetism are capable of similar treatment, though they have less direct bearing on the science of geography. For instance, the theory of the sextant and the explanation of twilight and the mirage follow easily from a study of the laws of reflection and refraction. Terrestial magnetism, the compass, and atmospheric electricity may be introduced early into a course of elementary physics.

In conclusion, one might suggest that a course of lectures on 'Physics, as applied to Geographical Problems', if available, would prove useful to teachers.

The Position of Geography

COUNCIL OF THE GEOGRAPHICAL ASSOCIATION, 1919

In this article the Council of the Geographical Association asserts that 'Geography is a balanced subject with a unity of its own'. The structure of the Public Examinations threatened to split geography into its scientific and human sides. It has been a continuing feature of British geography in schools that the unity of the subject has been reinforced. By contrast, in the United States geography has been effectively subdivided into courses of Earth Science and World Geography, a division between the scientific and human approaches. In British secondary schools the division takes on significance at the end of the first two years of schooling when pupils begin to make choices of the courses they will follow. For the pupils destined to take GCE O level and later A level courses, the nature of the choices made at the age of thirteen may determine the subjects they will eventually offer for examination in the sixth form. By placing geography against science in the optional groupings a pupil may study geography for GCE O level and find himself steered towards the Arts sixth. There is evidence that the traditional A level combination of history, geography and English is less commonly found, especially as teachers become more aware that a combination which includes mathematics, physics, geology or economics is a better preparation for pupils who intend to enter university geography departments.

It is interesting to find, in the concluding sentence, a reference to the term 'Modern Studies', a term which was to be revived more than forty years later to label an integrated course in Scotland (see Reading 27).

The question of the position of geography in the curricula of schools and universities is a fundamental one at the present time, and much depends on the way in which it is answered. Here an attempt is made to state the case and to indicate the lines along which action should be taken.

It is first necessary to understand what is meant by geography and the reasons why it is studied. Among many of those who have not followed closely the recent development of geographical study an impression prevails that there are important divergences of opinion on these points, that different authorities hold different and conflicting conceptions even of the content of the subject. But a more careful scrutiny reveals the fact that a close agreement in essentials is being steadily reached. The Geographical Association has a membership of over 2,000, and includes practically all the recognized teachers of geography in England and many in Scotland and Ireland. It was possible for this Association to issue a manifesto on the subject, which has met with practically universal acceptance. In this the aims of teachers of geography are explicitly stated and the content of the subject implied: 'In teaching geography in schools we seek to train future citizens to imagine accurately the interaction of human activities and their topographical conditions. As these conditions have been established partly by natural forces and partly by human effort, any discussion of the correlation of various conditions must be both scientific and humanistic. The mind of the citizen must have a topographical background if he is to keep order in the mass of information which he accumulates in the course of his life, and in these days the background must extend over the whole world.'

There have been different conceptions of geography in the past. As the veteran French geographer, Vidal la Blache, said in 1913: '*Nous avons connu longtemps la géographie incertaine de son objet et de ses méthodes, oscillant entre la géologie et l'histoire.*' He was however careful to add, '*Ces temps sont passés.*' Even this oscillation was only the result of incomplete and possibly biased views of the contents of the subject. These and similar views are neither untrue nor incompatible. They arise from the fact that geography, while it is a unity and while it presents many different facets to different students, yet has two distinct sides — scientific and humane. Therein lies at once the difficulty of adequately presenting it, and its special value as a mental training.

The world must be studied as a whole. It is not the world as a mere aggregation of parts or elements that geography has to study. It is the organic unity of the world on which man 'lives, moves and has his being' that geography has primarily to investigate. This is no mere academic study at the present time, when men are saddled with the solution of problems, individual and social, which demand a knowledge of affairs all over the world. Nor will a knowledge of isolated facts suffice. We must try to understand the world relations which give those facts meaning.

Geography then deals with the real world, the world of which one learns best through one's boot soles or bare feet, or by means of trains, vessels, motor cars or aeroplanes, and only as a makeshift by description, pictorial or otherwise. But it does not end with a study of the externals thus presented. It deals with the reasons why the material world — regarded as a whole and made up of related parts — has come to be what it is. This involves relations with the natural sciences. It deals with the way in which this material world has influenced man, and in turn has been modified, altered and adapted by human action.

There are then certain conditions to be satisfied if geography is to perform its true function in education. Unless the subject matter is felt to be real it is of little value. Unless a study of the world is based on a knowledge of the actual physical facts it supplies no sound basis for future activities. Unless the relationship of man as a reasoning and purposeful being to this world of physical facts is considered and realized, geography is deprived of its chief objective.

This tripartite geography, real, scientific and human, takes a necessary place in education, valuable as culture, valuable as supplying knowledge of facts useful in everyday affairs, valuable and even necessary for the citizen in order that he may understand his duties.

Thus viewed, geography has a unity of its own, but is related to two groups of studies which have been called the arts, or humanities, and the natural sciences, and it is this relationship which is at once the root of its cultural strength and its weakness as a mere subject of examination.

Geography is scientific not merely in the sense that history or Latin is scientific. It deals with natural phenomena in a way in which the humane subjects do not deal with them, and it has definite relations with the natural sciences rather in the way in which natural sciences have relations with each other. It has relations with meteorology in the same way as meteorology has relations with physics or physics with mathematics; it has relations with botany in the same way as botany has relations with chemistry. In these cases some definite knowledge of the one science is necessary for a student of the other. The student does not require to have an exceedingly deep acquaintance with those natural sciences which geography touches, but he does require to know more than is necessary for a general education. He requires not merely to have general ideas but to have some accurate knowledge of scientific facts. It is in this sense that geography is specially related to the natural sciences.

On the other hand, geography has relations with the humane subjects not shared by the natural sciences. These latter, it is true, are not wholly divorced from humane associations. But geography deals directly with human beings, with the results of their actions, with the results of their thoughts; the object of the study is to understand conditions under which men think and act in the varying circumstances of the various regions of the world. Geography is thus essentially concerned with the manifold diversity of man and of his problems and opportunities. It may thus claim to contribute in a unique fashion to an education which aims at the appreciative interpretation of the modern world. In this it is specially aided by history. Geography is essential in the study of the past, but it is more important to realize that history is an aid to geography in the interpretation of the present. Based on the bed-rock of physical facts, geography rears its head into the region of human endeavour. It is a well-balanced subject.

But this relation of geography to the humanities and to the natural sciences has introduced difficulties in connection with the examination of students. It does not fit easily into the examinations of the Faculties of Arts or of Science, or indeed of any other group. No one of the Faculties can claim geography as peculiarly its own. There has been a tendency to solve the difficulty by excluding it from all the Faculties. It is evident from what has been said that the true solution is to include geography, pass and honours; in both Arts and Science, as has been done by the University of Wales.

In the school examinations lately reorganized geography has had to face the same difficulties. Subjects have been grouped in various ways: these groups are convenient perhaps on the whole, but into none of them will geography fit quite satisfactorily. In particular, the 'Arts' and 'Science' classification tends to reappear in some form or other under the influence of the university tradition, with the result that geography is placed sometimes in one and sometimes in another group.

It is however evident that no system of examination is even approximately satisfactory that does not allow geography to be taken with either group of subjects with which it is specially related.

Even this solution is not ideal. Geography is a balanced subject with a unity of its own. It is not predominantly either scientific or humanistic, and it should be possible to arrange schemes of examination such that this unity is not destroyed.

We therefore urge that—

(1) *At the Universities*

Geography should be included as a subject of examination in both Arts and Science Faculties. In the Pass courses it should be related either with Science or with Arts subjects. In the Honours course it should be studied as a balanced subject, with perhaps a slight bias given by the choice of a subsidiary subject.

(2) *In the Second Public Examination*

(*a*) Geography should be included in the groups, both of Modern Studies and of sciences, in order to allow schools which specialize in either group to select geography.

(*b*) A special group should be instituted in which geography would be studied along with a science on the one hand and a humane subject, such as history, on the other.

(3) *In the First Public Examination*

Geography should appear in both the Modern Studies group and the science group, and arrangements should be made so that it is possible to take history, geography and a science.

Suggestions on Teaching: Geography

BOARD OF EDUCATION (HADOW REPORT), 1927

The Hadow Report was published in 1927 by the Consultative Committee of the Board of Education and its terms of reference were:

(i) To consider and report upon the organization, objective and curriculum of courses of study suitable for children who will remain in full-time attendance at schools, other than Secondary Schools, up to the age of 15, regard being had on the one hand to the requirements of a good general education and the desirability of providing a reasonable variety of curriculum, so far as is practicable, for children of varying tastes and abilities, and on the other to the probable occupations of the pupils in commerce, industry and agriculture.

(ii) Incidentally, thereto, to advise as to the arrangements which should be made (a) for testing the attainments of the pupils at the end of their course; (b) for facilitating in suitable cases the transfer of individual pupils to Secondary Schools at an age above the normal age of admission.

In considering the principles upon which the curriculum of the adolescent should be based the authors of the Report comment:

If, on the one hand, the education of older pupils be kept too general in the supposed interests of individual development, the pupil is apt to find himself ill-equipped on leaving school to cope with the demands of modern life. If, on the other hand, undue stress be laid in the school course on the needs of later life, and the training of the pupil be made too specific, the individual man or woman may be sacrificed to the workman or citizen. A well-balanced educational system must combine these two ideals in the single conception of social individuality. The general aim should therefore be to offer the fullest possible scope to individuality, while keeping steadily in view the claims and needs of the society in which every individual citizen must live.

More specifically it is later argued that three requirements should be borne in mind by those planning curricula for Modern Schools and Senior Classes:

(1) The curriculum should be planned as a whole in order to avoid overcrowding;
(2) it should be planned with a view to arousing interest and at the same time ensuring a proper degree of accuracy;
(3) it should be planned with a due regard to local conditions, and to the desirability of stimulating the pupil's capacities through a liberal provision of opportunities for practical work.

In the planning of individual syllabuses 'each subject should be regarded as a whole'. Certainly in the description of geography in the Report there is a total absence of any consideration of geography as a subject which may be combined or correlated with any other school subject.

The importance of geography as a subject in the curriculum for all types of post-primary education needs little arguing. Travel and correspondence have now become general; the British dominions are to be found in every clime; and these facts alone are sufficient to ensure that the subject shall have an important place in every school time-table. But these utilitarian reasons are not the only ones that make its claims to inclusion in the time-table incontrovertible; and, from some points of view they are not even the most important. For however useful geographical information may be its value must rest, for the purpose of our reference, on its use as an instrument of education, i.e., as a means of developing the growing interest of the pupils. In this connection, it has proved itself to be a subject which, when well taught, makes a very strong appeal to them. As a consequence, it should occupy no subsidiary or doubtful place, but should be one of the principal items in the curriculum. During the last twenty-five years the method of teaching geography has noticeably changed; perhaps no subject has made a more general advance, and the main principles are now widely known. Nevertheless, it may be of value to set them forth briefly here. The main objective in good geographical teaching is to develop, as in the case of history, an attitude of mind and a mode of thought characteristic of the subject. In the study of any one region the following elements are involved: (i) the physical and climatic conditions that go to form the region: (ii) the characteristics of the inhabitants; and (iii) the conditions and effects of their work. The objective which we have stated requires as an essential principle that these three elements should be viewed habitually together and their relationship and interaction thus constantly studied.

The extent to which this principle can be satisfactorily carried out must depend primarily upon the training and qualifications of the teacher. For it is fatally easy to make false deductions on unsatisfactory or insufficient data, and to learn striking-generalizations without any conception of the materials from which they should be formed. Moreover, the increase in the facilities for more rapid and general communications, the wider dissemination of knowledge, the opening up of fresh natural resources, the development of new industries, and the varied rates of growth in the population of different areas make great demands upon the teacher for a constant readjustment of his outlook. It is important, therefore, that, in all Modern Schools and Senior Classes, the teacher in charge of the subject, in addition to his general qualifications and training, should have given, and should be able to give, some special attention to it: and further, that in selective Modern Schools, where the ages of the pupils may range from 11 to 16, it is desirable that he should have had some special geographical training also.

Second only to the qualifications of the teacher is the provision of adequate equipment. In this perhaps some differentiation might be made between the various types of school. In schools where the linguistic attainments of the pupils are high and their background of experience is considerable, a more adequate provision of textbooks, which at the same time will be of a more advanced character, is necessary than in schools where pupils are less advanced in these respects. This more advanced literary material will demand more accommodation and more equipment for practical work, although there will not be so great an amount of the latter. On the other hand, in the other type of school, more provision will be needed for school journeys, educational visits, and for the construction of simple apparatus. Where circumstances permit, and in the planning of new schools, it would be advantageous to equip one classroom, having a southern aspect, as a geography room. If the geographical work of all or most of the classes were taken in this room, the necessity for duplicating larger apparatus, such as wall maps, would be removed. But whatever difference there may be between school and school, much of the equipment will be common to all types. Of this common equipment the first and most important item is a sufficient supply of good atlases to ensure one for each pupil; and in this provision we would urge generosity. An atlas should be the most frequently used volume in the pupil's outfit. All other books he changes from time to time; his atlas must be with him throughout his school career, and it is handled in such a variety of ways that, if used as it should be, its life is inevitably shorter than that of most other books. The atlas should have a good index, and the maps should be artistically produced. There is a great attraction for pupils in the study of good maps; and such is the fascination that they will take up map studies with as much pleasure as they take up recreation. Supplementing the atlases, there should be a supply of wall maps and one or two globes. The wall maps should be of various kinds, not merely physical and political maps; maps showing other distributions, such as rainfall, temperature, vegetation, populations, trade routes, geological conditions, are necessary; and where possible, closely interconnected distributions should be shown on the same map. For observation work, particularly in connection with the study of maps dealing with climate, there should be in every school a barometer, a maximum and minimum thermometer, and a wet and dry bulb thermometer. Apparatus such as a simple plane table and sighting rule, a sundial, and perhaps a simple theodolite, might easily be made in the handwork room, or in the centre for practical instruction.

In the matter of books, some differentiation would be required. For in selective Modern Schools and particularly in schools in which a high standard of work is possible, the content of the syllabuses would be more ambitious and more academic in character, so that in the later years, say from 13 onwards, the type of book in use might be very much on the lines of a good ordinary textbook. On the other hand, in schools where such books are too difficult, textbooks of a semi-descriptive type would be used throughout, although the content of such books would be set out in accordance with the principle governing good geographical teaching. The problem of the style of the books for such schools needs special consideration. The tendency is for the geography of the British Isles to be dealt with on fairly simple lines, and the world as a whole in more technical language. But modern teaching tends to the presentation of some world aspects concurrently with the study of the British Isles, and books dealing with these larger areas in simple language are, as a consequence, very necessary. In addition to the textbooks for use during the course, there should be a supply of works containing good descriptions drawn from the accounts of travellers and explorers.

In addition to books, collections of illustrations typical of scenery and conditions of life in different regions should form a regular part of the school equipment, especially in Senior Classes and in the non-selective Modern School. In this connection, some teachers have themselves formed excellent collections from poster and picture-card advertisements of business firms and railway companies, and from the publications of the Dominion Governments. But only pictures which bring out some special geographical feature, or which illustrate some geographical principle, should be included, and when they are in use, attention should be concentrated on these features. For this reason lantern slides are often a more effective aid because they are usually made with the definite object of illustrating some special point. Moreover, the illustration is sufficiently large to be seen and studied by the whole class under the guidance of the teacher. It is obvious that the portrayal of objects and scenes which involve movement cannot be adequately represented by means of lantern slides. In the illustration of such scenes the use of the cinematograph is most desirable. Beyond this material for the use of children there are certain publications other than textbooks which should be provided, primarily that teachers and pupils in all types of schools may follow the movements of commerce and industry. These are *The Statistical Abstract of Trade, The Labour Gazette, Commercial Intelligence*, the reports of the Board of Agriculture, the publications of the Dominion Governments relative to conditions of life, labour and settlement in the respective Dominions, and a work such as *The Statesman's Year Book* or *Whittaker's Almanack*.

The suitability of the equipment necessarily plays a large part in determining the content and stages of the geography course in the average elementary school; but as there are now at least a few textbooks dealing with all parts of the world in comparatively simple language a variety of alternative schemes is increasingly possible. Whatever course may be taken, however, it will presuppose a certain minimum of preliminary study during the age period from 7 to 11. It is reasonable to assume that under average conditions the average child by the age of 11 will have acquired (i) some simple notions, by direct observations, of the sun, wind and weather, and of the seasons; (ii) simple ideas, again from direct observation of actual scenery or of suitable photographs, of the principal features composing landscapes, and of their representation on maps; (iii) some knowledge of the prominent physical features of the British Isles, of two or three outstanding features of our climate and of the major industries, together with a few of their principal centres; and (iv) some simple ideas, mainly from descriptions and pictures, of the shape of the earth, of the distribution of land and water, and of the clearly defined climatic areas such as the Arctic regions, the desert areas, the Steppe lands, and the forest belts, including the wet tropical lands.

Starting from this basis, in which the general character of the work is descriptive, the course for the senior pupils will require a different treatment. This difference will show itself in three ways: (i) in a systematic study of all kinds of maps so far as they are suitable to the age of the pupils; (ii) in a closer observance of principles, enunciated at the beginning of this section, in their application to regional studies; and (iii) in the more frequent unaided use of the textbook, by the children themselves, for the purpose of extracting information and making summaries.

In the understanding of maps, the educational visit, the school journey, the weather observations and records, and suitable pictures, will all play a very valuable part. All observations, whether of physical features or of weather conditions, should be kept in close relationship with the type of map which represents them. The map of the locality should be thoroughly understood in its relation to the area which it covers, and much attention should be given to the study of contour maps for the purpose of imagining distance, direction and the configuration of the land. By these means, maps begin to suggest to the pupil's mind the concrete ideas which they are intended to convey. Map projections and simple surveying should be reserved for the later stages; but the simple uses of latitude and longitude might be taken at the beginning of the course. It is quite easy for the children to see that latitude and longitude combined give the precise situation of any place; that latitude enables them to find the angle of incidence of the sun's rays at midday in different parts of the world, and also assists in judging distances; and that longitude is specially useful in estimating the hour of the day in different countries. In order that children may appreciate the true comparative sizes of various areas it is desirable that the maps in any particular series should be drawn to the same scale.

But the interpretation of maps is not the only practical value which can be drawn from the thorough study of the locality. The home district, or some easily accessible one, is an essential for the first-hand study of geographical relationships — lines of communication and configuration, sites of castles and defensive features, sites of villages and water supply and drainage, soils, rocks and local industries, vegetation, etc. In this respect rural schools are well served, and we would urge much outdoor study in geography as well as in science in these schools, for in this way geography, even of foreign countries, becomes a much more real thing. In schools situated in the centres of great cities this problem is much more difficult of solution, but every child should have some opportunities of studying, map in hand, the configuration of a district. Consequently, for these, the educational visit and, if possible, the school journey should be as certainly a part of the school timetable as the subjects themselves. On the other side, however, town schools have an advantage over rural schools. The industries, the warehouses, the shops, the railways and the docks can be used, not only to illustrate the interaction of geographical and human elements, but also, to demonstrate the interpendence of the peoples of the world.

Important as this work is it is still only a means to an end. Side by side with this must proceed an ordered study of the geography of the world together with some more detailed study of those regions which directly concern the British boy or girl. In dealing with this, such differentiation as there may be will be determined partly by the length of the course, and partly by the rate at which pupils can assimilate book work. There is much to be said for completing a simple general sketch in the first three years in all types of school. In the senior classes and in some classes of the non-selective Modern School, less geographical detail would be given, and more concrete and experimental work carried out. But apart from this, the regular study of maps, the making of rough sketch maps, the insertion of distributions in outline maps, and the practice of making notes and of writing essays should be general.

Assuming that children by the age of 11 have acquired the body of geographical knowledge mentioned above, *we give a brief indication of the kind of work which a three years' course might cover.* In the work of the children under the age of 11 the British Isles claim the fullest treatment, but this treatment will be largely descriptive. It forms, therefore, a good basis for the work of the first year with senior children. Accompanying this would be the study of some portion of the world which would involve all the main climatic zones. For this purpose, either the Americas or the three southern continents would be suitable. In the second year the remaining portion of the world would be studied, by comparison and contrast, wherever possible, with the parts of the world covered in the first year; this would be supplemented by a short revision of the geography of the British Isles. The third year for the Senior Classes and non-selective Modern School might then be very properly devoted to the British Empire. But even here the geography taken should not be rigidly exclusive of the other parts of the world. Some such scheme as this ensures not only the observance of satisfactory principles in dealing with the subject, but also some geographical knowledge, in proper perspective, of the world as a whole. Moreover, by spacing the work in this way, the amount of detailed knowledge of the different regions will be in proportion to the bearing those regions have upon the lives of the children. Naturally, in covering such a large area the detail will not be great, but the pupil will have acquired the habit of looking at geography geographically, of quick intelligent use of maps and atlases, and of referring to books to obtain the information which he seeks. Nevertheless, essential details should be firmly grasped and the essential names clearly fixed in the memory.

In the selective Modern School where there is a fourth year it might be occupied with a thorough study of the British Isles in their world relations. In the school with an industrial bias some of the greater industries — cotton, wool, steel and so forth — might be studied in detail in connection with (i) areas supplying the raw material, (ii) areas recieving the manufactured articles, and (iii) the competition of areas of other nations carrying on the same industries. On the other hand, schools with a commercial bias might pay special attention to commercial questions including those of transport, distribution, markets and so forth. In both classes of schools this course might be accompanied by a broad study of the great natural regions of the world, with a view to the pupil's understanding the basis of the classification in each case. In rural schools the course, in addition to providing for the same general education in geography, might be arranged to include vegetation and food products, with some reference to the interdependence of industrial and agricultural areas.

Heritage and Environment

F. C. HAPPOLD, 1935

In the writings of Happold we see the English tradition of curriculum development operating in its almost ideal form. An individual teacher develops an idea into a course of study which he convinces his colleagues is a worthy experiment. The course is taught and teaching materials are produced and later published, and finally, the course itself is described and published so that other teachers may benefit from the experiences of the experimental school. Teachers may reject the suggested course or attempt to teach it, introducing their own modifications in the light of their own particular school situations.

In this chapter he describes how geography, history and English were brought together to form social studies. He refers to three constraints which had to be considered before the experimental course was mounted — external examinations, staffing and the availability of suitable textbooks. All secondary school teachers since that time will sympathize with Happold in this. What is remarkable is his final statement in this extract: 'At least our experiment shows that a unified social studies course, designed to give a boy a picture of his heritage and environment is a practical possibility, which, given the desire, is capable of being carried out in any normal school without much difficulty.'

When he writes 'My own experiments have shown that, properly taught, social studies can be used as an excellent medium of training in the art of expression, both verbal and written, in precise, honest and courageous thinking, in the use of books and the handling of material, in short in those abilities and qualities of mind that a boy should acquire during his school career, if it is to be of any real value to him', he succinctly describes some of the qualities required of the teacher who sought, and seeks, to experiment with new arrangements of courses.

If education is to be in any sense a preparation for life it should give the boy as complete a picture as possible of the environment in which he will eventually live. At present English specialists teach boys English, history specialists history, geography specialists geography. Much valuable cultural work is undoubtedly done, but few schools yet attempt to ensure that the boy is given that unified picture which might enable him to understand the world into which he will go. Yet this is one of the most important tasks of the school. It is through studies of this kind that the boy may receive a real training for participating citizenship. The treatment of history, geography, English and economics as separate sections of the curriculum is a natural result of the method in which they have been introduced; each has crept in as a separate subject and as such each has remained. Convenient as they may be for specialists, for the ordinary boy these academic subdivisions are both unnecessary and undesirable. A boy comes to school not to learn geography or history or English but to be trained how to live. The amount and kind of history or geography or English he needs is that which will enable him to live better and more fully.

In the reconstructed curriculum which has been sketched out in the previous chapter the present subject divisions of history and geography and English have disappeared and they have been replaced by what is there called Social Studies, a unified course designed to give the boy a knowledge and understanding of his own age, considered not in isolation but in relation to its origins — that is, a picture both of his environment and his heritage.

There are some educational reformers, particularly in America, who would abolish all studies which are not intimately concerned with the present. To do so, however, would be to prevent the boy from seeing his own age in proper proportion and would, moreover, deny to him that historical sense and enrichment of the mind which an acquaintance with the high thoughts and achievements of the past can give. An introduction to that story of struggle and achievement which is the history of man — whether it be the part played by his own nation in the advance of European culture, whether it be the story of scientific development, of the conquest of the forces of nature and the harnessing of them for the use of man — whatsoever form it may take, it is essential for the full development of both mind and character. But to divorce this study of the past, as is now so often done, from the world in which the boy will live, to make it a tale

> Of sad forgotten far off things
> And battles long ago,

remote from and unconnected with present reality, is to deprive it of its chief value. Not only must the boy be initiated into his past heritage, he must also be given an understanding of his present environment. He must be taught something of the institutions through which both in his own and other countries men are governed, of the arrangements through which he is fed and clothed and the means whereby the products of one part of the world are exchanged for those of another, of the problems, social, economic and political, about which he will soon be called upon to think.

The task of the school, as has already been stressed, is to train the boy's mind effectively as well as to instil into him a given body of knowledge. So while this social studies course will aim at giving him, even though it be in an elementary form, knowledge essential for right citizenship, it will equally aim at giving him, through the process of acquiring that knowledge, a sound mental and emotional training. My own experiments have shown that, properly taught, social studies can be used as an excellent medium of training in the art of expression, both verbal and written, in precise, honest and courageous thinking, in the use of books and the handling of material, in short in those abilities and qualities of mind that a boy should acquire during his school career, if it is to be of any real value to him.

How then should this work in the social studies be organized? Much experimental work will be needed. Not only must we decide what its knowledge-content shall be but also the best way of teaching it, so that through it the boy may be given that training which is desirable. That in the following pages I shall constantly refer to the work done in my own school must not be taken to indicate that I consider that either our syllabus or our methods are the best that can be devised. The general principles which have determined the methods of learning have been worked out and tested with different groups of boys by different masters over a number of years and found to be effective; the knowledge-content is still in a purely experimental stage.

In our work we frankly accept for the present the limitations imposed by the School Certificate Examination, which must be taken at the end of the middle school course. From one point of view these limitations are serious. Some of the work we should wish to do could best be done by boys at the age when the School Certificate is taken. Since many boys, however, leave after passing the School Certificate it must be done before a boy enters the School Certificate Division, which is really too early, or omitted altogether. Moreover, so long as the School Certificate remains in its present form it cannot be regarded as in any real sense an adequate test of either the knowledge or ability gained through a social studies course. Its existence, however, does not prevent an effective social studies curriculum organization throughout the school below the School Certificate stage. Except that it is necessary to ensure that boys who wish to take geography have done sufficient formal work to enable them to tackle successfully the School Certificate geography syllabus, we have found that the demands of the remainder of the Group I subjects can be fully met by boys trained on our methods in the year in which the examination is taken.

In preparing for our experiment in this social studies unification the first problem which had to be faced was that of staffing. Could masters, each one accustomed to teach his own particular subject, be persuaded to attempt a task they had never done before? Any attempt at a complete unification was, at first, neither possible nor indeed desirable. Masters had to become accustomed to looking at the normal subject divisions in a new light; they had to learn how to combine the knowledge-content of each into a reorganized whole; they had to think out how the revised synthesis should be arranged and presented. These considerations, together with such mundane concerns as difficulties of timetable organization, have dictated a policy of caution. The staff, however, accepted the principle that a teacher of English subjects, whether his degree were in English or history or geography, should be prepared, in the forms below the School Certificate, to teach any combination of these three, together with such economics and civics as it was necessary to add to them, in such arrangements as appeared desirable.

It would be tedious to describe the organization in detail; it will be sufficient to indicate certain features of it. For some years it had been our practice to devote the first year history course (average age 11.5) to world history, using my own book, *The Adventure of Man*, as a basis, and taught by methods described in another which has been already mentioned (in an earlier chapter), *The Approach to History* (Happold, 1928). Thus both the historical material to be used and the technique of study and presentation had been worked out and written up. The methods of study employed were, to a great extent, individual. The boys worked up their own material and expressed it in the visual forms of Record and Time Charts. The geography specialist had also worked out and written down a course of elementary world geography to be used side by side with this course of world history and has also carried out experiments in the use of methods of work in the teaching of geography similar to those previously worked out in the teaching of history. Thus it was possible to frame a first year unified course of social studies, designed to give the boy a picture of the history and environment of Man from his beginnings up to the present day, which any competent master could teach without any specialist knowledge. Of the three groups which made up the first year division, one was handed over to a history specialist, one to a geography specialist and one to an English specialist. All have worked in collaboration but different methods and groupings of facts have been tried out by each. It was not considered necessary at this stage to place the teaching of English literature and that of heritage and environment in the hands of the same teacher. While the great stories of the world were included in the literature syllabus, this work together with drama (actual acting of plays on a stage), speech training in the form of lectures given by boys and definite instruction in the writing of prose and verse were divided up among different masters as appeared most convenient from the point of view of timetable organization.

In the work of the second year, in which our own country is studied, various experimental unifications are being tried out. In one set the whole of the historical, geographical, literary (with the exception of drama) and expression work has been combined under one master, a specialist in history; in another the history and geography of England is correlated under a geography specialist; in yet another England's history and literature are taught together by an English specialist. In all these studies much training is given in expression, both logical and imaginative, written and oral, in the individual collection of material, in the building up of note books, in the use of libraries and the production of development charts and elementary theses.

The knowledge-content of this second year course is, however, at present in a particularly experimental state. Ultimately we aim at devising a course showing the development of the British people in relation to their physical and economic background, combined with a study of such English literature as will best illuminate this theme. The course, though primarily concerned with our own nation, would not be insular in outlook; British development would be treated in relation to its European and world background. In order to reduce this course to reasonable proportions one would be forced to concentrate on significant eras and topics, connecting them up by brief summaries. At present we are working out detailed correlations in certain aspects.

In the third year division, from which many, though not all, pass into forms taking the School Certificate, it has been possible to test out a completely unified course, designed to give the boy a picture of the world into which he will pass and how it has evolved. To describe all that is done would demand a small book. It includes a study of human society, what it is, why it is necessary, how it has come about. Forms of government both of the past and of the present, in this country and in foreign lands, are surveyed. The origins of Parliament, its present procedure, the duties of the various government departments and the work done by local government are touched on. Modern economic organization is also included in the course. The boy is taught something of how goods are manufactured and sold, of the function of money and the organization of banking, of the relationship between capital and labour and of the problems of power and transport. Various countries are studied with reference to their geography, recent history and political and economic institutions. For instance, in the study of Russia a general survey of its geography is combined with a brief account of its past history, followed by a more detailed consideration of the rise, character and achievements of Bolshevism. The same method is used in studying Germany, France, Italy, the United States, India and the Far East. Boys also consider such topics as the methods by which newspapers influence opinion and advertisers persuade people to buy goods for which previously they felt no need. The principles governing sound town planning are worked out, the layouts of ideal towns are designed and plans and elevations of the houses, which the inventors would like to build if they could, are drawn. The radio, the cinema and the theatre all come under review. Each week reports are given on current happenings. The acquisition of an epidiascope has made it possible for boys to give lectures, illustrated by pictures and diagrams prepared by themselves, on such topics as the production and selling of milk, the organization of a gas works, the manufacture of radio valves, the cultivation and use of coconuts and present-day methods of farming, to mention but a few recent ones. Opportunities, moreover, are given during the year for work to be done on subjects of the pupil's own choice, the material being collected from a library. For example, during the summer term of 1934 individual boys prepared short treatises on such subjects as the influence of science on modern production, how goods are bought and sold, how money works, how a town is run, etc., as well as on the working of the mind, the development of religious worship and the measurement of time.

Let it not be thought that we regard the work being done in our school as anything but an experimental and tentative approach towards something much bigger and more revolutionary. The right sort of books are often lacking. So far as I know, no one has yet written a satisfactory book on the heritage and environment of the English people, in which the facts are so arranged that the boy can get a clear picture of how the English nation has been made, of how its geography connects up with and has influenced its history and economic development, of its trade and industry, its government and national characteristics. Nor is it possible to get suitable textbooks for our third year work. Larger works there are in abundance but the lack of suitable textbooks means that the master's voice must be heard more than it ought.

Nevertheless, much spade work is being done, masters are learning to regard their task in a different way, sound methods of training are being evolved, an effective knowledge-content is being thought out. Eventually we shall learn how much of the history and geography now taught can be excluded from the unified course and what new elements should be added, how much formal training in expression is essential and how much may be acquired automatically through the work done in social studies, how much English literature should be included, and what parts should be regarded as aesthetics and be either treated separately or linked up with other studies such as music. At least our experiment shows that a unified social studies course, designed to give a boy a picture of his heritage and environment, is a practical possibility, which, given the desire, is capable of being carried out in any normal school without much difficulty.

The Principles of the Curriculum

BOARD OF EDUCATION (SPENS REPORT), 1938

Having reviewed the education of the adolescent (Hadow Report, Reading 4) the Consultative Committee turned their attention to the primary period of education and then, in the Spens Report, examined secondary education. Much of this report is taken up with discussion about the curriculum of grammar schools and this reading is abstracted from Chapter IV. The chapter entitled 'The Curriculum of the Grammar School' has five parts — the need for reconsideration of the curriculum, the principles of the curriculum, the content of the curriculum, the country grammar school and the school as a society. This extract is from the second part and starts with the principle that the curriculum 'should be thought of in terms of activity and experience rather than of knowledge to be acquired and facts to be stored'. Account is taken of the arguments for unifying the teaching of history and geography but the authors question how far geography's 'valuable distinctive character' will be lost by such unification. They suggest that gains may be obtained from 'intimate working alliances between subjects' but for grammar schools the essential autonomy of subjects must be retained. In a single sentence the principles underlying the grammar school are frankly stated: ... the school "subjects" stand for traditions of practical, aesthetic and intellectual activity, each having its own distinctive individuality; and we hold that the profit a pupil derives from them does not come from casual or episodical contacts, but by his being, so to speak, put to school to them, and so getting to make their outstanding characters part of the equipment and habit of his mind.'

We are to legislate for a society and are to indicate the scope and nature of its chief activities. We have agreed that these are to be chosen with a view to the pupils' physical, intellectual, moral and social development and must reflect what is best in the life and traditions of the community. And we have adopted the further principle that, *while studies should not be introduced which are beyond the present comprehension and unrelated to the present experience of pupils, yet, especially towards the end of the course, studies may well be introduced to a limited extent which have a definite bearing on the next stage of their life*, whether that be a future occupation or continued education at a school or university.

We wish to reaffirm a view expressed in our Report on *The Primary School* (Board of Education 1931), in which we urge that *the curriculum 'should be thought of in terms of activity and experience rather than of knowledge to be acquired and facts to be stored'*. Learning in the narrower sense must no doubt fill a larger place in the secondary than in the primary school, but the principle we quote is no less applicable at the later than at the earlier stage. To speak of secondary school studies as 'subjects' is to run some risk of thinking of them as bodies of facts to be stored rather than as modes of activity to be experienced; and while the former aspect must not be ignored or even minimized, it should, in our opinion, be subordinate to the latter. This remark applies most clearly to 'subjects' such as the arts and crafts and music, to which we attach great importance, but which have generally been relegated to an inferior place in the school programme; but upon our view it holds good also of more purely intellectual activities, such as the study of science or mathematics. An unfortunate effect of the present system of public examinations is that it emphasizes, perhaps inevitably, the aspect of school studies which we deem to be the less important.

The intellectual and other activities to be specified are, we have said, to represent or reflect what is of highest and most permanent significance in the life and traditions of the community. By the 'community' we mean here, in the first instance, the national community of whose life the schools are a part. It is true that the elements which have the highest and most permanent significance for our national life are not, in general, things denied to other nations; they have the highest value and significance for the human family as a whole. But for education one needs the influence of a concrete tradition or way of life, and there can hardly be said to be a common human tradition. There is, undoubtedly, a common Western European tradition, derived mainly from the Graeco-Roman civilization as it was transformed by Christianity, and one of the chief functions of secondary teaching is to make boys and girls conscious of it and regard it as something to be reverenced and preserved. But the right way to do this is to begin by making them conscious of that tradition as it exists in their own country. Hence the importance of fostering in our schools the special traits of the English character at its best; of giving English letters a chief place in the studies of youth; and of cherishing English traditions in the arts and crafts, including our once proud art of music. To speak thus is not to accept the ignorant and presumptuous doctrine that we have nothing to gain or to learn from other nations. On the contrary our pupils should discover, as occasion offers, how much our national development owes, in many of its aspects, to the influences of other peoples, should learn to respect great civilizations which are widely different from our own, and should understand how essential international co-operation has become to the progress of science and invention and the applications of knowledge and skill in increasing the health, wealth and convenience of mankind. Nevertheless, *the national tradition in its concrete individuality must, for the reasons adduced, be the basis of an effective education.*

14. A broad survey of the activities of a community shows that they fall roughly into two types, which may be distinguished as *conservative* and *creative*. The former are the multifarious activities which secure the community's continued existence and maintain its 'standards of life'; that is, they are the activities that go on in a myriad factories and offices and households, on farmlands and on the seas. The latter are most clearly exemplified in the activities of poets, of dramatists, of painters, of musicians, of men of science, inventors and the higher classes of administrators and legislators. The difference between them is not ultimate; for the routine performances of today were the creative achievements of yesterday, and may — as in the use of wheels, of weaving, of the fundamental agricultural processes, of writing — have been among the highest creative achievements of all time. It is, indeed, a commonplace that purely creative activities — such as the theories and discoveries of 'pure' science — generally prove sooner or later to have conservative value. Conversely, activities which are conservative in their genesis, such as the vast industrial organizations of today, may have an impressive creative aspect. The antithesis — and the synthesis — of the two types appears in the individual as well as on the large scale in society. We are all, to a considerable degree, creatures of routine, clinging to familiar conditions and sequences, finding a certain satisfaction in their repetition, and prepared to devote energy to their maintenance. It is less obvious that every man is also a creator, yet, if one looks closely enough, the generalization becomes acceptable. For instance, although the use of language as a means of communication — obviously a conservative function — consists of routines learnt in childhood and made habitual by endless repetition, there is yet some intrusion of the creative spirit even into the speech of the stupid: it has been said that no one can begin a sentence with any certainty of what it will become by the time he reaches the end of it. And it is obviously true that the dullest person constantly adjusts the common idioms of his native tongue to the task of reporting events or thoughts or wishes which, at least for him, are new. In poetry this creative spirit, which is scarcely anywhere wholly excluded, takes control of the situation, and the common means of communication becomes material for the highest and most individual art. What we have said about the effect of creative in raising the level of conservative activities does not fail here; for the national idiom has in many cases been greatly indebted for its vigour, beauty and efficiency to great literary artists who have made it their medium of creative expression.

Mutatis mutandis, what we have said about letters may evidently be said about other arts and crafts. It is also true of activities of very different type, such as physical science. The outstanding discoveries and inventions which punctuate the progress of civilization were born in creative moments of which no record remains, except the technical processes derived from them that spread from community to community and were handed down from generation to generation. Many of these involved acute observation and exact knowledge, but they were not science any more than forcible speech is poetry. Science, in the proper sense of the word, appeared only when the creative spirit of man began systematically to seek satisfaction in building up intelligible pictures of nature's intimate ways for the pure purpose of understanding them.

The bearing of these ideas upon our problem is direct and important. In the first place they remind us that a school, if it is to reflect truly the activities of the 'great society', must both give the knowledge and training required for the routine duties of adult life and also foster the creative impulses needed not merely for new enterprises and adventures but even for the daily adaptation of routine and technique to changing situations. Surveying the work of the secondary schools as a whole, we cannot feel that the reminder is unnecessary. In spite of modern advances, didacticism is still overweighted in comparison with originating activity. On the one hand, the pupils assimilate too much and do too little; on the other hand, the schools are inclined to stand too long upon the ancient ways and to be out of touch with the modern movement.

In the second place they suggest that the activities which are the richest in the creative element have the strongest claim for a place in the curriculum. For these spring from the deepest needs of human nature, and represent cultural movements, generally of great antiquity, which have developed characteristic modes of discipline and technique and mark out the main lines of human achievement.

15. It does not follow, because we expect to find both these elements contained in school work and school life, that a recognition of their presence provides any basis for a division into different classes of what are commonly known as school subjects. As we have said already, the difference between the creative and conservative activities of a community is not ultimate. It may be that this difference is particularly hard to distinguish in a community of adolescents, whose capacity both to maintain what is traditional and to create and assimilate what is new is related, no less to their social tendency to learn from and imitate each other, than to their ability as individuals to respond directly to adult teaching and influence. In every subject both elements are present, and the relative prominence of one or other will depend not only upon the content of what is taught but upon the teacher's personality and mode of thinking and even, it may be, upon the actual methods which he employs in the classroom.

In some of the main lines of human thought and feeling with which it is one of the functions of education to make children familiar — in religion, art, morality — it is often impossible to make any valid distinction, and say when they are to be regarded primarily as safeguarding the conditions and maintaining the standard of individual and social life, and when they represent adventures of the human spirit into the previously unknown and unexplored.

We have cited already the use of language as one example of how the two elements are combined almost inevitably in one field of mental and physical processes. An example of a different kind may be found in the actual organization of the school society itself and of those many activities outside the classroom, including the generally accepted school games, which the tradition of the English public school and grammar school has committed, in greater or lesser degree, to the control of boys and girls themselves. The boy who is learning to exercise responsibility, in whatever position may be assigned to him in the structure of the school society, will have continually in mind a tradition to be maintained and strengthened, and a continuity to be preserved. But it is equally important that he should feel that each successive generation may have something of its own which is fresh and useful to contribute to that tradition; and that authority in permitting him to take his part, within carefully considered limits, in the regulation of school life is giving him the opportunity, in co-operation with others, to initiate as well as to conserve, to make precedents as well as to follow them.

Nevertheless we repeat that *both elements must be represented in the curriculum, and that a larger place than hitherto must be found for those activities which we believe opinion would generally agree to call creative.* This consideration does not, however, lead us to any revolutionary conclusion as to the actual content of the curriculum, though it leads us to advocate a rather drastic revision of the allotment of time as between the different activities and courses of instruction. We believe that on the basis of the foregoing considerations there is justification for including in the curriculum of the child during adolescence religious and moral teaching and training in the care of health, bodily efficiency and grace, manners and social organization; and also that time must be found for those lessons which consist to a greater extent of direct teaching. They comprise (I) Letters: that is the use and appreciation of language, including at least some study of the native literature; (II) some forms of art, including music, the most universal of the arts; (III) handicrafts, taught with emphasis either on the aesthetic aspect, as in weaving, carving, handwriting, or on the constructional aspect, as in carpentry and needlecraft; (IV) science, including mathematics as the science of number, time and space. To these must be added history and geography, which appear in two-fold guise. History is in one sense literature and is read for more than the information that it contains. Similarly, geography has a strongly marked scientific side which entitles it to a place in our fourth group. But the two subjects have, taken together, the special function of recording and interpreting the human movement — history explaining the genesis of the present from the past, geography teaching the dependence of men's activities upon the natural environment and their interdependence all over the globe. In these aspects history and geography may be said to be central in the curriculum, and in our opinion are both indispensable.

We believe that of the activities which we have mentioned those associated with moral and physical training in the widest sense are fundamental and should be the concern of all pupils. But it might be contended that differences in *ingenium* sometimes justify choice among the others, though we hold that they should all be represented in the secondary school curriculum. We admit that there are extreme cases: boys and girls who are on general grounds suitable members of a secondary school but who seem to have a 'blind spot' which prevents them from gaining any good from some particular form of instruction. Where these cases are due to absorption in some other line of study for which the pupil discloses a marked talent, they are not much to be regretted: nature's own way of establishing her balance should be accepted. They are, however, much more often due to defects, positive or negative, in the pupil's early training, and may then be curable by patience and understanding. We believe that, speaking generally, the common needs and impulses of human nature are distributed with rough impartiality, and that there are few pupils of normal intelligence whose imagination is not stirred, whose interest is not awakened, and whose powers are not engaged when they are brought, under wisely chosen conditions and by competent teaching, into contact with any of the great cultural traditions. A well-rounded education involves some degree of contact with all of them, although not necessarily contact with all at every stage. It is, in fact, the gravest defect of the present system that a boy or girl may pass through a secondary school having made no contact, or next to none, with one tradition — that of the arts and crafts — which is certainly not the least noble or the least ennobling.

Not to recognize important differences in *ingenium* and ability would, however, be to shut one's eyes to plain facts. While, then, we think that, in principle, every pupil should make acquaintance with all the groups of activities in our second class, yet we also think that, where possible, there should be varied provision for pupils of varying talents and taste. Our group (IV) may be taken as an illustration. Mathematical thought is one of the greatest gifts of the Greek mind to the modern world, and the spirit of natural science the factor which above all others has made that world what it is. Without some acquaintance with these, much that is fundamental in modern life is unintelligible. But although the essential features of mathematical thought and the broad aims and achievements of science are almost universally attractive when properly presented, many minds — and by no means the least bright — are oppressed by the arid technique and the excess of detail with which the teaching of these subjects is too often darkened and encumbered. There is, therefore, a need for courses, both in science and in mathematics, which shall bring out the essential characters of those modes of creative activity and illustrate the part they play in the business of mankind, but shall be, for certain pupils, alternative to the standard courses. And we wish to make it clear that we contemplate a flexibility in the public examinations which would permit these — possibly unexaminable — courses to be taken under proper safeguards by aspirants for a School Certificate.

16. In the foregoing paragraphs we have, for the reasons explained, constantly spoken of 'activities' rather than of 'subjects'. In avoiding the

latter term we do not wish, however, to reject one of its important connotations or implications. Some writers on education maintain that a 'subject', such as history or mathematics, is a kind of museum collection of activities, made after the life has gone out of them, and for that reason is not to be made the basis of school studies. Intellectual growth, it is urged, should be nourished not upon these dead materials docketed and classified in textbooks, but by presenting the scholar with problematic situations to be dealt with by means of ideas and methods which may now have the historical character, now the mathematical, now the physical or biological. These ideas and methods are to be acquired as the need for them emerges, without reference to the logical categories to which they belong. Seductive as this doctrine is, even the authority of Dewey does not make it wholly acceptable. As will be seen below, we attach much importance to the 'problem method' which is akin to the 'project method', and in our Report on *The Primary School* (1931) have stated that in our opinion the 'project method' in the full sense of the term has a very useful place in the teaching of young children. We recognize, moreover, the great value of occasions (the production of a school play or the building of a cricket pavilion are obvious instances) which invite the application and synthesis of a considerable range of acquired knowledge and skill. But our general doctrine forbids us to go much farther than this; for its essence is that the school 'subjects' stand for traditions of practical, aesthetic and intellectual activity, each having its own distinctive individuality; and we hold that the profit a pupil derives from them does not come from casual or episodical contacts, but by his being, so to speak, put to school to them, and so getting to make their outstanding characters part of the equipment and habit of his mind. If this is to happen, the subjects must be pursued as such — though we have urged that they should be pursued actively and not merely be assimilated by memory and understanding.

For these reasons we think that proposals for unifying subjects should be entertained with some caution. There is, for instance, a good deal to be said for unifying history and geography; there would result a useful economy of time, and the topics treated would receive complementary elucidation from two points of view. Is it, however, certain that geography, if combined with history, could retain the valuable distinctive character which it has acquired in the hands of modern scholars and teachers? If not, the apparent gain might actually be a loss. On the other hand, there is everything to be said for intimate working alliances between subjects, provided their essential autonomy is preserved. The teaching of physics and of mathematics — especially, perhaps, of mathematics — suffers much at present from a separation which Newton would have found incomprehensible; and, as some of our witnesses have pointed out, the teaching of history loses a great deal because it neglects the contribution which the teachers of science and art could make to it. Again 'education for citizenship' could be much assisted by a careful planning of syllabuses which would, at suitable times, concentrate upon the relevant topics the light of several subjects.

It is, however, not inconsistent with our position to deprecate the needless subdivision of subjects — a subdivision which in some cases, such as mathematics (e.g. the separation of solid from plane geometry, of elementary calculus from algebra), physics, and biology (e.g. the neglect of zoology in comparison with botany), tends to distort rather than to bring out the characteristic architecture of the subject.

17. The views on the curriculum here set forth may meet with objections or doubts from two directions. There are some critics of school teaching whose simple criterion of its value is its direct usefulness in after-life; to these we shall address ourselves in the next section. There are others, a large body with the support of a long tradition, who think that the school subjects are to be valued for the sake of the special or general training they impart to the mind. There are some who reduce this creed to a single article: 'It does not matter what you teach a boy so long as he dislikes it.' Others, however, express ideas which have been the faith of philosophers and schoolmasters from the time of Aristotle. Modern psychology has attacked them and shown that some of them are indefensible; it has, however, not convinced either experienced teachers or mature students that the faithful study of one of the major subjects does not impart some virtue to the mind. We believe that our view about these subjects makes the nature of that virtue clear. The subjects in question represent, it has been said, typical modes of activity which have been established through the centuries by the labours of a few men of supreme genius, a larger group of practitioners of outstanding talent, and an immense army of journeymen. We are apt to think of them in a too abstract and narrow way, forgetting that for the poet, the craftsman, the scientist, his poetry, his craft, his science is a way of life with ethical as well as intellectual or aesthetic characters. There is a characteristic integrity of the poet, of the musician, of the mathematician, just as there is a characteristic ethical code of the medical man or the seaman. And just as the young doctor or sailor in the making not only acquires certain knowledge, skill and habitual reactions, but also undergoes a special kind of ethical permeation, so the student who is put to school to one of the great cultural traditions acquires something of the ethical as well as the other characteristics that individualize it. We may, then, speak of the 'training' he receives in art or in mathematics, using the word to mean essentially what it means when we speak of the training of the doctor or the seaman. This training may quite properly be described also as 'mental discipline'. For it involves the submission of the pupil to the influences of the great tradition; it is his endeavour to learn to do fine things in the fine way.

18. With regard to the other possible line of criticism, we accept fully the position that school studies should fit boys and girls for the practical affairs of life, and that if they do not do so they must be badly planned or badly conducted. There is, however, in our view no educational heresy so serious as the belief that culture and practical utility are mutually exclusive. We even accept with some reserve the view that education should train for the right use of leisure — sound as the doctrine is — lest it should lead to a dichotomy

between studies important for serious life and those pertinent only to hours of leisure. In brief, we are not prepared to admit that any of the activities of the secondary school, assuming them to be pursued in the spirit we have indicated, are not 'useful' in the sense that they tend to raise the level and quality of life in all its phases and moments.

Geography

BOARD OF EDUCATION (NORWOOD REPORT), 1943

In the Norwood Report it is clear that the authors have sensed that all was not well in geography teaching in secondary schools. We have already noted how the Spens Report affirmed the place of individual subjects in schools. In the section devoted to geography, quoted here in its entirety, geography teachers are warned not to extend their range so widely as to swallow up other subjects for in so doing they may lose their sense of purpose and the virtues inherent in specialist studies. Further, 'in the hands of a poor teacher the subject may become as motley and disintegrated as it is sometimes thought to be'.

Generally, the Norwood Report is far more tolerant of working relationships between subjects in the school curriculum than the Spens Report. It condemns the competitiveness which exists between subjects in these terms:

> In the first place, subjects have tended to become preserves belonging to specialist teachers; barriers have been erected between them, and teachers have felt unqualified or not free to trespass upon the dominions of other teachers. The specific values of each subject have been pressed to the neglect of values common to several or all. The school course has come to resemble the 'hundred yards' course, each subject following a track marked off from the others by a tape. In the meantime, we feel, the child is apt to be forgotten.
>
> In the second place, a certain sameness in the curricula of schools seems to have resulted from the double necessity of finding a place for the many subjects competing for time in the curriculum and the need to teach those subjects in such a way and to such a standard as will ensure success in the School Certificate examination. Under these necessities the curriculum has settled down into an uneasy equilibrium, the demands of specialists and subjects and examinations being nicely adjusted and compensated.

While acknowledging that specialism has certain strengths the authors urge that the common ground of subjects, 'the seed-bed of sound learning', should not be neglected. In this extract it appears that some geography teachers have defined the 'common ground' to be their own domain.

Without attempt at precise definition it may be said that geography is the study of man and his environment from selected points of view. Yet natural science, economics, history, the study of local conditions as regards industry or agriculture might also be said to be concerned with environment. For this reason geography is a good school subject, since it finds it easy to make contact with other subjects; for environment is a term which is easily expanded to cover every condition and every phase of activity which make up normal everyday experience. This expansiveness of geography carries with it an advantage and a temptation; the advantage is that geography at many points invites other subjects to join with it in a concerted attack upon the same topic from various points of departure, and in so doing calls attention to the common purposes and utilities of those subjects. On the other hand enthusiasts for geography may be inclined sometimes to extend their range so widely as to swallow up other subjects; in so doing they widen their boundaries so vaguely that definition of purpose is lost, and the distinctive virtues inherent in other studies closely pursued are ignored in a general survey of wide horizons. Such virtues cannot be ignored without loss.

Again, geography as the study of environment, proceeds from immediate surroundings to more remote surroundings. From the nature of its own subject-matter, therefore, it finds it easy to obey the precept that the enlargement of experience at which the study of school subjects aims should take place from what is familiar and concrete towards the less familiar and the abstract.

These then are reasons why we urge that geography should be a compulsory subject in the early stages of the school course; they are not, however, such as to preclude it from a place among advanced studies.

From what has been said it is clear that as regards geography perhaps more than any other subject the planning of the course of work must be closely related to the circumstances of the school, and among these circumstances must be included not only the physical environment of the school, but also the nature of the other subjects undertaken there and the gifts and sympathies of teachers concerned with those subjects no less than of those concerned with geography. That geography in a given school should take into account the physical surroundings of that school is familiar enough; it is equally important that it should consciously relate itself to the other studies pursued at that school and to the particular aims and scope of those studies. This does not mean that geography is placed in a subordinate position as a handmaid to other subjects; it means only that geography should be wise enough to understand its own advantages, and in that understanding to realize its own specific aims in close association with other subjects.

No general report therefore can attempt to discuss in detail the course of work which schools might undertake; for the scope and range of the geography syllabus is peculiarly dependent on special circumstances. We would confine ourselves therefore to two points.

(*a*) The course of geography in schools might reasonably be expected to include:

    (i) the elements of physical geography;

    (ii) studies on various scales (e.g. world, continent, region, parish);

(iii) training in such skills as map-reading, the use of atlases and of books of reference;

(iv) fieldwork and first-hand knowledge of town and country and of life in town and country;

(v) opportunities for the study of the geographical aspects of ventures which challenge or inspire human effort as, for example, exploration, mountaineering, flying.

A framework such as this can ensure no doubt a reasonable body of general knowledge and of facts and their relations, but we would emphasize at this point the importance of a good grasp of facts; sometimes modern geography teaching, we think, is inclined to forget it, and some of our evidence bears this out. We would draw special attention, however, to the value of fieldwork, for it is in such work that we find a point of departure for broader studies which will give opportunity for co-ordination of subject-matter and co-operative effort by teachers; these studies perhaps approximate most nearly in the secondary sphere to the 'project' of primary education, and offer means to derive first-hand knowledge from immediate experience of data ready to hand.

We would urge that such fieldwork, or local survey, should find a place in every syllabus. Admittedly timetable arrangements, co-operation among teachers, the time needed for preparation of suitable schemes may present difficulties; but in our opinion every effort should be made to surmount them, and to make way for a type of work which holds out great promise as an introduction to practical citizenship and as a means of bringing about the unified approach to different fields of learning which we have desired.

The value of setting aside a single room for the teaching of geography has already been proved by experience. The room must be of good size, conveniently placed and large enough to allow for the ready use of the various aids to teaching — maps, pictures, models and the like — and for the tables which are more convenient than desks in the teaching of this subject.

(*b*) Geography is a subject which in conjunction with such subjects as modern languages, history, economics, public affairs, statistics makes up a course of studies in the sixth form particularly suitable for pupils who will read economics or history at the university or will go on to posts of an administrative nature in business or public concerns. Such courses tried in different quarters have proved their value; geography, broadly interpreted, has offered a framework or provided a cement which has held together other subjects and given unity to the course.

It is not realized even now as widely as it should be that the advance in geographical knowledge has been so great that general truths have been established for which the evidence two generations ago simply did not exist. No one can realize more vividly than the trained geographer that the great regions of the earth are interdependent, and no one can base the approach to world harmony on sounder foundations than he. The advanced study of geography is not only of economic but of high political value, and, though it makes use of the contributions of several sciences which for its purposes are ancillary, it imposes its own unity upon them. For that unity is imposed by nature itself; it is the unity of the region which is the subject of study. It may be that physics and chemistry, botany and biology, geology and meteorology may all in turn be called into conference, and in the hands of a poor teacher the subject may become as motley and disintegrated as it is sometimes thought to be. But in the hands of a good teacher it will not be so. He will use the study to bring out all the facts that nature has given, and to establish the vital truth that, while there is much in nature which governs man inevitably, on the basis of that knowledge and that knowledge alone man can proceed to the discovery that there is much in nature which he in turn can govern and direct. Without this firm basis in geography we cannot proceed with confidence to the planning of the economic or the political design of the future world. It is for this reason that the subject is a good foundation for enlightened citizenship, that it is good material for sixth form study, and will in our opinion hold a place of increasing importance in the future. Whether we look to the town, country and regional planning which must have place in this country or to the much greater task of planning in interdependence the industrial and agricultural regions of Europe and the world, whether we consider the problem of developing colonies without exploitation or directing rightly the growth of primitive populations and the supply of raw materials, it is geography which will give the basic knowledge and remind us continually that the world is not only one but extremely diverse. It is hoped that in the future geographers trained in this full sense will not be so rare as they are today.

The Social Sciences: Social Studies

COUNCIL FOR CURRICULUM REFORM, 1945

In the introduction to the book from which this reading has been extracted the Norwood Report is criticized in these terms:

> Without being suspect of *parti-pris* or of lack of charity, one may express the view that this report is not a very satisfactory piece of work. It has been received by teachers without enthusiasm. It fails either to give a lead or to examine in a philosophic way the bases of the curriculum and the principles which should guide the curriculum designer.

The Council for Curriculum Reform had been formed in 1940 by a small group of teachers and educationists, led by Mrs E. M. Hubback of the Association for Education in Citizenship and Dr P. Volkov of the New Education Fellowship, who discussed in their initial meeting 'both the qualities and capacities which should be fostered in all citizens and the characteristics of the new society which is in the process of formation'. Calling themselves initially the Committee for Curriculum Reform they changed their name in 1941 to the Council for Curriculum Reform.

This extract from the chapter entitled 'The Social Sciences' is indexed in the book as 'Geography'. Its content must be viewed against a summary of the 'formidable array of criticism' of the secondary school curriculum which appears in an earlier chapter. It reads:

1. This curriculum is still essentially a collection of subjects, largely unrelated and taught in airtight compartments.
2. These subjects are too formal and academic to meet the needs of the majority of children who do not go on to higher studies.
3. School-leaving examinations dominate choice of subjects and methods of study.
4. Practical and aesthetic subjects are therefore not given sufficient time or attention.
5. In most subjects the stress is on what was rather than what is.

6. Hence what he does in school neither satisfies the developing needs of the child as a child, nor prepares him adequately for the world he will live in as an adult.

Realizing how chaotic are the values of a modern industrial society, how depersonalized are its social processes, and, above all, realising how our urban life has obscured the foundations of a vital society, many social thinkers and educationists are turning, like Rousseau, to contemplate afresh the 'noble savage' in order to clarify the issues of the building of a 'new' society. As T. S. Eliot says, in *The Idea of a Christian Society*: 'And without sentimentalizing the life of the savage, we might practice the humility to observe, in some of the societies upon which we look down as primitive or backward, the operation of a social-religious-artistic complex which we should emulate on a higher plane'. It is the cohesion of a primitive society, the vitality of its way of life, and the relations of work and culture, though limited in range and in depth, that is so striking, so refreshing, and so revealing to the modern mind in search of the basic conditions of community. And what is most important, these 'primitives' present a clear picture of elements of society and their interplay that are lost to view in the modern mass industrial society.

Social Initiation

As a result of his study of primitive civilization Herbert Read, as one would expect from a loyal disciple of Kropotkin, has also caught a truth of some significance for educationists; in one of his essays he reminds us that in the life of primitive societies instead of 'education we find certain rites of initiation — a drawing of the individual into society to merge him with the group.' It is a significant idea: it defines the purpose of social studies in schools — the purpose is social initiation, or the development of social character by drawing the individual into the community, making him aware of its collective life and collective ideals.

If we are to understand this process of social initiation in terms of our current needs, it is essential briefly to examine its character. It is obvious that the process of social initiation will vary with the character of the society in which the child lives. As is well known, fascist societies have mobilized this process for their own social ends and by methods characteristic of their ideologies. These methods have been marked by a kind of compulsion we would reject. In a democratic society social initiation cannot be a coercive process. It is rather a process of discovery, the discovery of the social world in experience; it is emergent, and it arises with experience, as a result of interaction of the individual and the vast array of social situations. Hence in this bi-polar process, the selection of social experiences to be explored needs to be socially worth while and appropriate to the stage of the child's development. But to select these social experiences for exploration we need to be aware of the way the cultural conditions interact with human nature at its early stages of development. For example, even at an early age children realize that they do not simply eat, but eat certain things, in certain ways, and at certain times, and that these meals and habits change from district to district and from country to country. At the perceptual level young children are interested in these social differences, derived as they are from differences in social milieu. At the conceptual level with older children the dietary of the Hampstead child may be compared with that of the Bermondsey child, or a comparison of the dietary of the Bengali peasant and a Californian fruit grower may be drawn, and as a result the social problems involved and the whole problem of minimum standards of nutrition and their relation to agriculture of our own islands and of the world as a whole may be studied.

Social Understanding and Geographical Place

From this example there is raised, not only the question of the subject-matter of social studies appropriate to the stage of the child's development, but also the important matter of growth of the social understanding, from the perceptual to conceptional levels with\the associated maturing of social attitudes and evaluation. Unfortunately social psychologists can tell us little concerning the charting of the stages of a child's voyage of discovery of his social world in its 'public' aspects; by 'public' is denoted all those social experiences that are shared in common — the habits, customs, the folk ways and institutional ways, and so forth, common to the social world, of which the child is a member and is to become a citizen.

It is an accepted sociological fact that social character has a territorial basis. For many reasons geographical place is one of the most powerful factors that gives coherence to social character; place acts as a catalyst of sentiments, values, and loyalties; and this social experience of belonging to a community and to a place is the fundament of the whole structure of social character. The boundaries of community and place expand — from home to neighbourhood, from neighbourhood to region, from region to nation, from nation to the world. But unfortunately social psychologists can give us little guidance concerning the expansion of social character in relation to place. Piaget, Susan Isaacs, and other child psychologists, with penetrating brilliance, have illumined the subtleties of the social development of the child; but their work is largely limited to the personal relationship of child and child, of the child to the small group in the classroom, and of the child to parents. Work of equal insight needs to be done on the growth of the social character in its 'public' aspects. For example, how does a child grow in loyalty to a neighbourhood, whether it is a village with a distinctive natural and cultural feature, or a patch of built-up area in a London borough with a drab pattern of streets, shops, and factories? By what processes and by way of what symbols does the youth of Tyneside or South Wales identify themselves with the region? How do they absorb the regional experience that characterizes South Wales or Tyneside? What guidance can we obtain on the growth of national sentiment? What degree of intelligence is essential for a comprehensive social awareness and understanding of our national life? And there is the training of awareness of world relationships, training in world citizenship — a formidable task unless we are content with a vague emotionalism as a substitute for an ordered intelligent comprehension, rooted in a social character that has been well based in local and national understanding.

Nevertheless, from the anthropologist and the geographer we do gain guidance which confirms our empirical leadings, and we are sure that the heart of the problem of social initiation lies in the discovery of belonging to a community and to a place. Here I need only state, without further elaboration, that it is accepted that we are concerned with initiation into a democratic way of life, the qualities of which have already been described (in an earlier chapter). But I wish to stress the territorial basis of this initiation, and to do so I would direct attention to the results of recent investigations into democratic society by such social observers as G. D. H. Cole, who are stressing afresh the importance of a small group life for social living.

It is an obvious fact that the growth of a mass society has increasingly taken away the basis of a common neighbourhood and smothered the social impulses of the masses. But war conditions have released afresh the spirit of social service, and, what is important, the war-time social services were organized spontaneously on a basis of neighbourhood. The people in the cities and countryside were faced with the common needs of fire-watching and fire fighting, shelter organization, communal feeding, and so forth, and in the solution of their problems and the choosing of their leaders the people rediscovered the meaning of neighbourhood, and felt the social satisfaction of living democratically in a small unit of group life which they could comprehend. But it has been discovered that these neighbourhoods do not correspond with administrative units, such as wards and parishes and boroughs; the truth is that prevailing administrative units may have little meaning for social living. We need a redemarcation not only of new regional units but neighbourhoods and local communities. This is a controversial matter, but town planners have reached a fair unanimity on the question of the establishment of neighbourhoods, however much they may disagree about the larger regional units.

In the quest for guidance on the aims and content of social studies in schools, it is clear from the above considerations that schools should base their social studies in the first stage on the neighbourhood and not necessarily on an administrative unit that may have little relation to the social life of the local inhabitants. This neighbourhood may be a collection of streets in the city or a rural area with a village at its centre. This is not the place to discuss the criteria of the delimination of neighbourhoods in detail. A clue to the solution of the matter is given by Mumford when he says: 'A neighbourhood should be an area within the scope and interest of a pre-adolescent child such that the daily life can have unity and significance for him,' and 'its size is determined by the walking distance between the farthest house and the school'.

Awareness of a Common Life

And now I come to a more important point. The purpose of this local initiation is to arouse an awareness of its common life, its needs and problems, and so foster the spirit of neighbourhood and local fellowship. It is in the initiation into his home locality that the growing child discovers his social roots. It is here that he is initiated into the first stage of his development in social awareness and understanding. I agree with G. D. H. Cole when he says: 'I do not believe that any state or society can be effectively democratic in great affairs — in national or international affairs, or in the government of its great cities and country areas — unless it is so organized as to be democratic in small things, and to give the small groups, of which the great society is made up, real opportunities for democratic action.' Such an idea should be an inspiration to local study in schools. The rediscovery of neighbourhood is vital for true democratic living.

Local Survey and Economic Life

Much could be written about the content and methods of study of local survey in schools. Their most serious fault is the lack of any central theme, with the result that most surveys are a loose assemblage of unco-ordinated detail. For the process of social initiation a central co-ordinating theme, defining purpose and content, and if possible allowing for participation in social activities, is essential. It must cover a range of social experiences intrinsically interesting to the child, and as the awareness and understanding grow the process of initiation should be progressively involved. It is suggested that such an integrating theme is 'work', using the word in the widest sense to include the whole range of cultural phenomena usually associated with the term 'economy'. For our purpose the emphasis will be upon the modes of livelihood and their direct and indirect consequences. Justification for this idea may be made from many other points of view. To mention but one such point of view — it is important to remember that an individual's work is the chief way in which he makes contact with society as a whole, and assures himself of having a function and being wanted. For the great mass of humanity it is in work for the community that they feel significant, and inevitably they strive for the social and economic conditions to secure the fullest social recognition of their daily toil, so that work may be a way of life productive of the highest cultural satisfaction.

In every neighbourhood there are a large number of workers concerned with food and supplies, with transport and communications, with social and civic services, and with production. These workers serve the common life of the neighbourhood. By the study of their jobs, both in their present actualities and past evolution, children are initiated into the meaning of community in terms of work. Often to the workers their jobs fill their imagination and become a way of life, and children catch the spirit of a new valuation of work. Moreover, if the schools adopt the right methods of study the schools can help in heightening the feeling of neighbourhood. But let us not examine the workers' jobs like specimens in a museum; let the children interview them, and let the workers feel the co-operation between the school and themselves. Thus the school will become an integrating force in the neighbourhood, bringing together work and culture. Indeed, from the drama and adventure of worker's lives as realized by the children and from the information gained about the details of their jobs, there will spring the social consciousness of a common culture rooted in the work that maintains the life of the community.

Many social and economic changes must be instituted before the use value of labour is substituted for money value, and public service for private profit. But the schools as a social force must point the way to the democratic way of life, where work and culture are no longer divorced and where through their work, executed well and accepted socially, men and women feel they belong to a place where they obtain social satisfaction in the personal contacts of a life shared in common.

To facilitate this initiation into the life and work of a neighbourhood, the disciplines of the subjects need to be used according to the age and ability of the children. Many social surveys done by schools illustrate the way in which the content and methods of study of such subjects as history, geography, economics, and social science have been unified in their exploration of a locality. Here we need no discussion of these contributions. All we need to remind ourselves of is not to be satisfied with any arid academic assemblage of lifeless material.

Social Values for Older Children

For older pupils the study of neighbourhood will come within the larger economic unit of which the neighbourhood is an integral part. This economic unit may be an urban settlement, such as Leicester or Nottingham; a rural district focused upon a small market town or large-urbanized village; or it may be a borough in London. Usually such economic units are identical with administrative areas under local government, and youth's initiation into this wider community becomes also the problem of training in local citizenship. Relationship to the local community has been at best narrowly conceived, but more often it has been ignored and neutralized because of the academic idealism of the school and the accepted divorce of school from community. But initiation into citizenship cannot be left to a haphazard growth of a local sentiment. Local sentiment of late years has been losing vigour and has tended to degenerate into a mere emotional embroidery of frustrated citizenship, woefully apathetic towards local affairs and alarmingly careless of its rights and duties. To stem this apathy and to reawaken a vigorous local citizenship is the vital need of our democratic life to-day. This can be achieved only by fostering a local sentiment well based on civic knowledge and civic idealism. This is the task of education for democracy in its local dimension.

Fortunately under the influence of the idea of planning there are promising signs of a recrudescence of vigorous local town and country planning. Planning embodies much of the idealism emerging from the chaos of this war, and by its emphasis on change, and action to secure the betterment of our collective life, it makes a strong appeal to youth. Our schools need to educate for local planning, initiating our young people into a more dynamic relationship with their town and district, stimulating them to know both its physical and cultural landscape more intimately, to study its functions and economic activities more systematically, to appreciate the drama of its civic life and to see the town as a humanized landscape, man-made and shaped, an expression of human associations that have excellencies to be enjoyed and encouraged, and deficiences to be deplored and eradicated. In a word, our schools should be not only the transmitters of a local culture and heritage, but creators of a new idealism of local planning and local citizenship.

For the senior pupils the analysis of the local community needs to be systematic. The mapping and statistical techniques of the geographer and the social planner should be employed, and then the physical, social, and economic components of the community revealed in map and diagram may be critically examined from the point of view of the ideal standards of a balanced community. The town or district as an organization for collective living will be assessed; housing, cultural needs, location of industry, socio-economic zoning, and so forth will be critically discussed; and the merits and defects of the local planning will be realized and understood. At the same time, the powers and procedure of local government will be examined and the services for which it is responsible will be learnt. Comparative studies of different kinds of neighbourhoods — the rural and urban; 'building estate' neighbourhood, and the slum neighbourhood — and also of different types of towns and districts should be made. Such studies will demand a historical background involving the perspective of the evolution of our administrative areas and the growth of urbanism in relation to the development of our economy; they will demand a knowledge of geographical factors and of the techniques of study included in modern urban geography; many economic facts will need to be elucidated, and the social implications of modern technology cannot be ignored.

This course of social studies is intimately related to each stage of the social survey, and cannot be developed in its contemporary setting without reference to the planning movement that has gripped the progressive minds of to-day. It is envisaged that each town or region will establish a planning centre whose planning officers would invite schools to co-operate in the solution of real planning problems. Undoubtedly youth in these social studies would desire to do some real work for the local community, and one such form of work might be some practical diagnostic work of local conditions undertaken for the local planning centre in some such way as was done in the preparation of the Land Utilization Survey under the direction of Dr Dudley Stamp.

Social initiation into a complex modern society at its local level cannot be confined to some dramatic ritualistic episode of a visit to a stage-managed council meeting, nor limited to a month's course after the School Certificate examination. The process demands a graded course of social studies associated with social survey and based on the ideas already discussed. The social world is not a series of chapters in a textbook, it is a world to be discovered in experience. Social curiosity, the mainspring of activity in the young social discoverer, will be touched into liveliness and maintained in intensity only by contact with the actualities of the social world, and to avoid academic aridity and the degeneration of this work into a mere assemblage of bits and pieces of maps and other lifeless material, it needs to be vitalized by the breath of actuality. This can be achieved in no small measure by methods of interviews and so forth already indicated in the study of the neighbourhood. But undoubtedly it can best be achieved by spells of actual employment on real jobs. It is through real experience of the work of the community that youth can be truly initiated into the local social and economic life. These spells of work should not be narrowly limited to work in local industries and commercial offices, but should cover the public utilities of water, gas, and electricity, the social services of refuse disposal and sewerage, the work of medical services, and so forth.

For the Young People's Colleges the linking of vocational initiation with social survey and social studies for the purpose of training in citizenship should present no difficulty provided that education and industry are united in a common idealism for youth's development both as a citizen and as a worker. Even for the modern and secondary school some kind of occupational initiation would be highly valuable for giving the touch of experience of life that would make the social survey and studies come alive. In war-time, spells of potato picking and harvesting have been successfully organized, and surely it is not beyond the powers of the organizers to arrange for spells of work in engineering shops, in commercial offices, and in those types of work that are significant to the community. It would need to be planned and placed under educational control, so that its social significance would not be perverted by crude economic purposes. Our prime purpose is the initation of youth into a new valuation of his local community, its life and work, so that he will feel a concern for the good life of the community, moved to think and to act in the best interest of its corporate life. And to that end let us keep in mind what Whitehead said about the study of a factory, and apply it to the world process of initiation; these are his illuminating words: 'A factory, with its machinery, its community of operatives, its social service to the general population, its dependence upon organizing and designing genius, its potentialities as a source of wealth to the holders of its stock, is an organism exhibiting a variety of vivid values'. Herein lies the germ of cultural initiation and the birth of a culture that springs from work. It is the discovery of these values that will give meaning to daily work and awaken the sensibility from which will grow a democratic culture based on a new vision of work and community. But this vision waits upon a new social order in which work is not conceived merely in official terms as 'gainful employment' but as a service and a way of life, giving dignity and significance to the individual worker however humble his job.

The Region

Beyond the town or district there is a wider territory, usually called a region. The concept of a region is derived mainly from geographical thought, and there is much controversy concerning its essential characters; but however defined and demarcated, regional consciousness is a reality. The Tynesider, for example, is proud of his regional affinity as expressed in a common outlook, customs, speech, and work, and the Teesider is equally loyal to his regional area and life. No one can be unaware of this regionalism in Great Britain who passes from South Wales to North Wales, or from the Lake District to South Lancashire; indeed, Great Britain is a mosaic of areas to which the people feel they belong and express their loyalty. Regional experience is therefore an important aspect of our social life. It may be best understood as a product of the interaction of place, folk, and work; it is a blending of the physical landscape and the works of man, a synthesis of earth and man endowed with a kind of personality that possesses cohesion of sentiment and social unity.

In our national planning, especially during the war, for many social and economic purposes, areas of administration have become larger, and have somewhat fortuitously and haphazardly reflected the regional pattern of our cultural life. For our future planning of the many social services and cultural facilities many believe that regional organization must prevail, and some kind of regional democracy will need to be established to ensure proper public interest and control. Examination of the political means to this end of reorganization of local and regional government would take us beyond our purpose, but it needs to be emphasized that no regional democracy can be established without a more developed and more articulated regional life than exists at the present time. Therefore, both for the purpose of political revival of regional life, for the spreading and deepening of social roots, and for the sake of our cultural diversity, the next stage of our social growth is the initiating of youth into regional consciousness, well based in regional experience and knowledge.

This study of a region would flow inevitably from the social survey and studies of the smaller economic unit of town or district. In the investigation of the influence of routes and circulation on the growth of a town and its functions, regional relationships cannot be ignored; in the discussion of the town as a centre of public services and cultural facilities regional connections would necessarily be considered; and in any work on town planning it would be realized that town and regional planning cannot be separated. Hence the study of a region would be a natural development of the previous work already described and discussed.

The basic principle of regional initiation is again the empirical approach. Before the physical and cultural landscape of the region, its activities and functions, are treated as abstract subjects, they should be felt and lived through as concrete experiences. The quest of these experiences and their organization can be best achieved by regional survey, and since the unit of study in geography is a region, necessarily we must seek guidance from the geographers and apply their methods of regional analysis and synthesis. For this purpose our schools must become mobile, and from field centres or school camps, established in the region, exploratory expeditions should be conducted to gain first-hand impressions of the physical and cultural landscape; to appreciate its distinctive scenery, both rural and urban; to investigate the characteristic modes of livelihood; to visit the places of historical significance; and in general to absorb the common feeling of the regional life. In this exploratory work the pupils will see and feel the regional landscape and the way in which man reacts to the regional resources. Then by map and diagram and a supporting course of regional studies, the appropriate depth and range could be given to the work.

The central theme is the study of human economies — the dominant means of livelihood in the region, both agricultural and industrial. It will be so easy for this regional study to become a static accumulation of facts about the hills, rivers, valleys, soils, minerals, and place names, because so often is the region conceived as a convenient apparatus for assembling geographical facts rather than as an organization maintained by work and integrated by arteries of circulation along which goods, services, people, and ideas move between village and town and city. As a result, the region has a certain coherence, balance, and integration arising from a dynamic relationship of man and earth. Let us see the region in terms of movement both in space and in time. The present actualities and the future planning of a region cannot be intelligently understood without historical perspective, and therefore it is essential that the history of the dominant economies of the region be introduced at the appropriate stage. The idea of regional planning of services, of location of industry, and of settlement will be inevitably discussed by the older pupils, and through an intelligent regionalism we may broaden and deepen the social roots of our future citizens.

The Country

Just as we cannot get a satisfactory definition of neighbourhood, town, or region without reference to place, so no definition of nation can be valid without reference to the country. This place, of whatever size — local, regional, or national — should be understood, not as a mere neutral extent of territory, but in terms of human ecology, with man in relation to the earth through his mobilization of its resources and its forces for his social needs. Through man's interaction with the earth it is transformed into landscape in which the physical and cultural are intimately fused. Our country is a blending of natural features and man's work, about which cluster emotions to form a national sentiment. So our love of country and pride in our distinctive cultural heritage must spring from concrete experiences of our island home.

At this initiatory stage of entry into national heritage, youth needs to see and feel the grand variety of our physical and cultural landscape; he needs to see and feel the lonely expanses of the Highlands of Scotland, the Cheviots, the Pennines, the Welsh Hills, and Dartmoor where shepherds herd sheep; he needs to see and feel how the soil responds to the farmer's effort season by season, from region to region; and he needs to see and feel the industrial drama in the mine, the shipyard, and the cotton mill.

It will be realized that from region to region the physical and cultural pattern changes, and to be drawn truly into the inward meaning of our country we need to have in our mind's eye the distinctive quality emerging from the whole assemblage of the experiences of our regions, the common feeling of country that binds us together into a nation.

Towards the end of his *Tractate on Education* Milton, with great insight, suggests that towards the close of their career at his academy youth should be encouraged 'to ride out in companies with prudent and staid guides to all quarters of the land; learning and observing all places of strength, all commodities of building and of soil, for towns and village, harbours and ports for trade'. Youth today also needs to enlarge their experience of their country, and it cannot be beyond our powers of organization to see that our young people are afforded opportunities in school journeys and other means to explore the face of Britain and learn the distinctive features and qualities of her landscapes; such expeditions could be arranged in school time and in holidays, or, as Milton wrote: 'In those vernal seasons of the year when the air is calm and pleasant it were an injury and sullenness against nature not to go out and see her riches and partake in her rejoicing with heaven and earth.' Then our youth may be introduced to a great truth that the landscape of Britain is the most humanized in the world, the most friendly and intimate — truly a homeland.

This exploration of Britain beyond the local region will necessarily be limited in range, since all the different regions cannot possibly be visited during the adolescent period. For example, owing to distance, a visit to the Cheviots may prove impossible to arrange for schools in the south. But some imaginative introduction to that region can still be given through the power and intimacy of film, and for this purpose there is Basil Wright's film, *O'er Hill and Dale*. For this purpose of extending youth's experience of the scenic and cultural heritage of Britain, the number of good films available is unfortunately small. In the training of its young technicians and promising aspirants to direction, the British film industry might well arrange for some of its cameras to capture and interpret the life and work of Britain in all its regional variety. It would be a service both to the film industry and to social education.

National sentiment is a complex growth fertilized by many cultural conditions, of which 'love of country' is but one energizing ingredient. As is well known, national sentiment may deteriorate into a vague emotionalism, easily manipulated and exploited, unless its core is progressively sustained and vitalized by social purpose and social knowledge. And so it is hoped that these experiences will, not only stimulate the feelings of 'belonging' to a distinctive homeland, but also will arouse a wider sweep of curiosity and interest in social and economic conditions of our national domain.

As a result of the experiences of evacuation and the needs of war industry, it has been realized that before the war one half of Britain did not know how the other half lives and works. This state of social and regional cleavage has revealed the need of a new sense of interdependence of town and country, of region and region, of the local area and the national whole, and it has also revealed the need of a vision of the national pattern of an integrated economy that sees and feels the needs of our communal life as a whole without in the least underestimating the distinctive needs of the local and regional areas.

Our schools should reflect this vision and provide the initiatory experiences and social knowledge. With this aim in mind the social studies in their national dimension will demand a new orientation. We cannot resurrect a fresh social purpose and galvanize our maturing boys and girls into a lively interest in social affairs merely from a study of the dead bones of factual material, usually embedded in the lifeless pages of our school textbooks of geography, history, and civics. They lose all interest in the academic intricacies of the structure, and leave school without the awakening of the social mind that sees the main contours of the build of the contemporary world, and something of its inner social, economic, and political forces and tensions.

Our plan of social studies therefore must be founded upon experiences extending their horizons progressively from neighbourhood to town, from town to region, and from region to the nation as a whole. The associated course of studies at this national stage should consist in a linking of these extending territories, or in other words should consist in a cross section through the different levels of the social and economic pattern, showing the continuity and integration, so that the life and work of locality, region, and nation are seen to be organically related. Thus this stage is essentially marked by inter-dependent thinking, which links local and regional economy with national economy; local and regional services with the national services; local and regional cultural conditions with those of the nation as a whole. All the details of linkage need to be selected to suit the interests and the social needs of maturing boys and girls. It is this selection that is so obviously important. With the principles of selection that we have discussed hitherto and with this idea of linkage in mind, it will not be difficult to frame a syllabus in the concentric pattern recommended that will cover the main aspects of our social and economic life, both in present actualities and its historical evolution, and at the same time pointing to the future ideas of planning.

The World

The final stage of initiation into the sociological way of thinking encompasses the global earth. Or, in other words, it may be said that to think in terms of terrestrial unity is the final synthesis of the course in social studies. An informed world outlook that is fully aware of the intricate cross currents of national policies and interests is the product of a life-time of experience and thought. In order to avoid the precocious youth who can talk the language of internationalism, imputing motives rather too glibly and offering political solutions with little knowledge, we need to keep our schemes of work and selection of topics within the limits of the guiding idea of initiation. The foundations of the international mind can and should be well and truly laid; the idea of the world community and the need for world planning introduced; and the ideal of a common humanity evoked by progressive opening of the eye of faith through experience and knowledge of world unity. Something can be done both at the primary and post-primary stages if we keep in mind that we are concerned with the *growth* of awareness, and that we should confine ourselves to the fields of experience of the contemporary world that come within the comprehension of our maturing boys and girls.

An example perhaps will help to clarify the point of view and scope of work intended, and incidentally demonstrate the linkage of locality, region, nation, and the world. The food quest and rationing is a primary interest in our contemporary world, and the problem of our food supplies is a topic that should come within the course of social studies. At the primary stage the distribution of shops in the neighbourhood and the life and work of the baker, milkman, butcher, and other workers concerned with food supplies, their sale and distribution, can be studied by methods that are fully described in *Actuality in Schools*. Then in descriptive terms, aided by visual material of all kinds, including films, the sources of our main foods — milk, bread, and so forth — can be appreciated by a lively treatment of particular farms in Britain and overseas. But at the post-primary stage this simple descriptive treatment, referred to in the chapter on the Junior School, of the food quest extending the range of interest in a widening pattern of locality, nation, and world must be more carefully articulated, with greater detail both in range and depth. In addition to a close study of the production and distribution of foods, the older pupils will need to be introduced to the new science of nutrition, and its relation to a revived agriculture both in Great Britain and the rest of the world. Their attention throughout the course should be called to many striking facts: that we have an authoritative standard of diet for health; that children born of poor parents in poor districts are of poorer physique, suffer from more disease, and have a lower expectation of life than children born of well-to-do parents, and the main cause of this grave social injustice is inadequate diet; that through adequate dietary mankind can be freed from much of the burden of disease and the resulting suffering. Having introduced these facts, illustrated with examples drawn from local experience, it may be established that we need a food policy based on nutritional needs. Then it can be readily shown that we cannot achieve an adequate dietary for ourselves without endeavouring to secure it for all the other peoples of the world. A world food policy, based on human needs, would involve a great increase in agricultural production. This world need for increased production would bring world-wide prosperity to agriculture. The introduction to these ideas would arise from the careful study of regional pattern of our own agriculture, our different types of farming, and the suggested plans for the future of British agriculture, and also from the study of the granaries of the world, the dairy producing areas, fruit-growing areas, and of the possibility of the extension of the growing of wheat, maize, and so forth.

The climax of the study of our food supplies would come in the reference to future planning. The United Nations have declared for a world food policy based on human needs, and at the Conference held at Hot Springs formulated general principles of great significance for implementing the 'freedom from want' clause of the Atlantic Charter. The section reports of this conference should be available for the older pupils, and certainly they should examine the Scott Report. It may be — this is a matter of faith — that from these studies of food supplies there will spring a new moral value, namely that the right of every individual to the means of attaining his full inherited capacity for health and physical fitness should rank equal with his right to religious and political freedom.

Many other such topics — world communications, the world's petroleum resources, and so forth — will come readily to mind, and can be treated with similar emphasis on inter-relationships and the emergent new values.

In addition to these general topics of world significance, there would be needed systematic studies of those countries with which we are in close relationship and with whom we shall be intimately concerned for the future planning of the world; the countries are the United States of America, Soviet Russia, and China, and those occupied countries whose destiny is bound up with the new Europe. Also our own British Commonwealth of Nations and Colonial Empire demands careful study in its world relationships. It is obvious that these world studies will require careful planning in order to link them with the previous work.

In this brief conspectus of social studies three foci of coherence have been briefly examined, and the integrating lines of development tentatively traced out to provide a pattern of social studies that reflect both the needs of our maturing boys and girls and the needs of a changing democratic order. The three instruments of coherence are: (1) the territorial basis on which is focused the feeling of 'belonging'; (2) the economic basis or work in its cultural manifestations; and (3) planning, which term embodies the spirit of social and economic change of our times. These focal points also provide view-points from which the initiation of our boys and girls into their complex society may be surveyed and the lay-out of studies planned with due regard to the integration of the contributing disciplines of such subjects as history, geography, economics, and social science. Finally, we would emphasize this is but a first sketch drawn from experience of teaching of social studies in many types of schools.

The Study and Practice of Citizenship in the Schools

MINISTRY OF EDUCATION, 1949

From time to time in British education arguments are promulgated for the permeation of the whole secondary school curriculum by some principles or other. Hence at the time of writing suggestions are being made for giving all the subjects in the curriculum a 'European dimension' (see Reading 28). In this extract from a Ministry of Education pamphlet the introductory paragraph suggests that 'the study of man in society should permeate the matter of all organized studies and should constitute a unifying factor in the curriculum'. Later in the extract consideration is given to the special place which geography has in the task of citizenship education. A distinction is made between the traditional region-bound geography teacher and the 'realistic' teacher. The emphasis upon realism, which is taken to be synonymous with the study of contemporary phenomena, is made on the dubious assumption that only the here and now is seen to be relevant by school pupils. The popularity of social and environmental studies in the late 1940s is noted and this pamphlet is concerned to see them as a 'branch of social training'. This comment on training echoes a statement by the Secretary of the Association for Education in Citizenship: 'It has become increasingly recognized that in order for the citizens of this country to form an effective and critical public opinion and to be capable of intelligent and independent judgement, a specific training is necessary (Hubback 1936).' But, as Livingstone commented: 'We must not make the error of Socrates and think that Knowledge is virtue, or that duties are performed because they are known (Livingstone 1943).'

10. General and Special Opportunities in the Curriculum

There is wide agreement in this country that one essential purpose of education is to nurture the development of the future democratic citizen. But there is less agreement about the proportions which education of this kind should assume, and the methods which it should employ. There are those who fear that citizenship may come to be the sole aim of education. There are also some who suspect that the purpose is to 'condition' the pupil so that, when he is mature, he shall serve the purpose of the state. Those who share these fears and suspicions are inclined to join forces with those who argue that social studies are essentially adult, and to urge that 'politics should be kept out of the schools'.

These criticisms are certainly not uppermost in the minds of most of us today. What is conspicuous at the present time is the strong and growing feeling that education in citizenship is necessary. But it would be unwise to ignore the suspicions or the fears which such education is liable to provoke. In this field of study we are concerned with man in his political and social relationship, rather than as an independent individual or as a spiritual being answerable to God or to his conscience. There is also a real danger lest we become so preoccupied with the problems that confront our society today, both at home and abroad, that we carry with us into the classroom matters which are beyond the understanding, and fail to arouse the interest of children. There has always been a temptation to introduce too early to children what preoccupies ourselves, and the danger is no less today merely because we have abandoned the dogmatic controversies which interested pedants in earlier ages and perplexed their pupils, and have put in their place economic and political problems which may seem to us of greater relevance, but may be equally beyond the range and interest of children.

These dangers should be recognized. But after recognizing them, let us recognize also that teachers, on the whole, have nevertheless come to feel that we cannot and should not ignore in our education the political and social environment of today, for the compelling reasons that we have evolved a society which needs the co-operation of all of us, and in which a share in controlling our fate belongs to each one of us. No realistic education which seeks to secure some relation between school and the needs of adult life can any longer ignore these things. It would be as unreasonable as it would be unwise to exclude today from the school curriculum information about these institutions, local and national, through which we govern ourselves, earn our living, and manage our affairs. And so we find that secondary schools today very generally recognize a need for introducing at least their older pupils to the political, social and economic life of our times and to the institutions through which that life finds expression; while adult education, in all its forms, is very naturally even more deeply concerned with these things.

Clearly we are concerned with out-of-school activities as well as with formal instruction: these are further discussed (in later Sections). Similarly, since it is a matter of influence and example, citizenship is bound up with the characters of teachers and taught, and with the tone of school life. It is really an integral part of the whole underlying purpose of education. It would not be correct to draw any sharp distinction in respect of it between the formal 'subjects' of education and out-of-school activities. The good student, who applies himself, is likely also to become the useful citizen. And each 'subject' contains within itself its own 'discipline' and thus contributes to the development of character and intellect and to the widening of the understanding. It was, for long, the legitimate boast of the old classical studies that by their very nature they trained a man for the wide and varied responsibilities of later life — a boast which the careers and achievements of many great figures in our national history, brought up on the classics, went far to justify. The classics play a smaller part in education to-day, but newer subjects, such as English, modern languages and history, make something of the same claim, while the sciences and mathematics — most evidently mental 'disciplines' in the traditional sense of that word — are not without similar apologists. All school subjects should contribute to developing the character as well as the intellect, and should thus indirectly prepare for citizenship. There are no water-tight compartments in education, and least of all can citizenship, which rests upon character, be prepared for by one means alone.

Recognizing this, we should no doubt also be cautious in suggesting that any one of the traditional subjects ought so to adapt itself to prepare directly and consciously for civic responsibility, thereby assuming a purely didactic role. There are always dangers besetting these attempts and reference was made at the beginning of this chapter to some of them. A selection, for example, of literature for school reading which is made solely with the purpose of portraying social or patriotic virtue will soon defeat its purpose by provoking the opposite reaction to that intended. And the same may be said of a history syllabus which is so preoccupied with explaining the social, political and economic set-up of the present day that it ignores the fact that history is a story. The main branches of human study will not bear distortion of this kind; moreover, to attempt it is to thwart the true purpose of a liberal education which must concern itself with the individual child and with his spiritual, imaginative and intellectual welfare, and must not push prematurely before his eyes social concepts for which he is unready.

But to say this is not to say that in planning the ordinary work of the school teachers should eschew the inclusion, within the different 'subjects', of material which will lead to some understanding of contemporary life. Indeed, it is likely that more can be accomplished by awareness, on the part of the whole staff in their teaching, of the claims of citizenship, than can be accomplished by the isolated weekly lesson in public affairs taken by one particular teacher. In several of the normal school subjects it is possible for the teacher to include material with a practical bearing upon citizenship, and to do so logically and naturally with no distortion. It is, after all, necessary for a teacher to consider many different values in selecting the materials of his syllabus. He will no doubt have in mind his pupils' natural interests, the logical progression and build-up of the work from term to term and from year to year, and the value of the work selected in advancing his pupils' mental development. But one, at least, of the values he will want to consider is whether the work selected is going to improve his pupils' understanding of their own neighbourhood, of their own country, and of the role which one day they will play in both as citizens.

There are, for example, in English literature, many different children's tastes to cater for, and much treasure to be extracted from a mine of wonderful wealth and variety. But amongst the many benefits which children derive from reading and from being read to, one of the richest is an ennobling of the sentiments of loyalty and service which are latent within them. Literature does not cease to be literature because it was written or spoken with this purpose and because it has had this effect. Whether the educational value of reading of this kind should be described as literary or whether as a 'training in civic virtue' is, no doubt, a nice point, but it is one in which close definition seems unprofitable. And the same is true of other subjects in which the aesthetic or spiritual element is predominant; of art, of music, or of religious instruction. It is unwise and often impossible to 'separate off' the social value in this education, or to obtrude it upon the children's attention; that value is certainly present, even though the material must be chosen and treated for its aesthetic or spiritual worth.

But it is the work in geography and in history (or the local study and project work which combines these subjects) which gives the most direct opportunity for providing the future citizen with the information and understanding he should possess. It is here that the pupil will find the subject matter which needs to be explored; for, while in his school life as a whole and in his home life he will develop the qualities of character without which knowledge is either useless or dangerous, it is more particularly through his work in history and geography that he will acquire the knowledge itself. This is widely recognized by the teachers of these subjects. In many schools they combine their efforts to enable children to discover the character of the life of their locality and of the nation into which they have been born. The work takes a number of different forms, but the local study, which has won much favour, may be taken as exemplifying it. In one of its most fruitful forms this work proceeds by encouraging each child to find out all he can about some particular aspect of the neighbourhood — its roads, its architecture, its local industry or agriculture, its sanitation system, its church — and to proceed by a chain of questions and answers until, between them, the children have built up a real picture of the life of their locality. They will not have failed to map it, or to trace its history. But no locality — especially to-day — is self-contained. At many points (the election of Trade Union representatives, the election of Members of Parliament) the enquiry will have led on to the central organs of the nation. The roads and railways are obviously parts of a national system of transport. The products of local industry or agriculture are being transported elsewhere — where? and why? What is being brought into the locality in exchange, and where is it coming from?

In history and geography, broadly understood, is to be found the answer to the how and the why of the local corporate life and of the national corporate life which is the subject matter of citizenship. The question which teachers of these subjects have to ask themselves to-day is how far they will make this civic value their sole value and criterion in their syllabus and presentation. Many history and geography teachers have taken up advanced positions in this respect, and the older subject names have sometimes in such cases given place to 'social studies' — an indication of the change in point of view. But others are reluctant to allow the illumination of the contemporary scene to become the sole purpose in this range of work, and hold to the more traditional approach which proceeds historically through the centuries and geographically through the regions of the world. Between these two extremes lie many different methods, governed by many different purposes.

It is not the intention here to recommend a specific method in the teaching of history or geography. Most teachers of these subjects feel that to them belongs the task of introducing the pupil to the political, economic and social life in which he is about to share. Many find this duty so compelling, that, abandoning traditions, they seize firmly upon those local realities which are within children's own experience, or to which they can easily introduce them, and from these work outwards in space and backwards in time in their attempt to explain the less known and the less obvious. Such is usually the method of those who favour local studies or projects of various kinds. But those who prefer to adopt a more formal or traditional approach need not, for that reason, divorce this work from the purpose of explaining contemporary life, and it is quite possible for them to feel as strongly as their 'realistic' colleagues the important duty which they have in throwing light upon the local and central institutions of our life to-day. We may take, as an example, the role of the more traditional history teacher who feels, not without justice, that history, like all good stories, moves forward rather than backwards, and who is determined to show its development by pursuing it chronologically rather than by making a series of plunges back in order to explain a series of contemporary phenomena. His method of explaining our life to-day will not be to wait until his story has reached the eighteen-eighties before he discusses the county councils, or the Act of 1911 and the Bill of 1947 before he discusses the modern powers of the House of Lords. Nor will he wait till he reaches recent times in order to discuss trade unions or nationalization. He will be discussing trade unions when he is discussing their medieval equivalent, the guilds, by constant comparison, back and forth, which will serve to illuminate both — the past throwing light upon the present and the present throwing light upon the past. He will discuss nationalization when he is discussing the medieval Statute of Labourers, and again when he is discussing Queen Elizabeth's or Cromwell's economic legislation, and again — by contrast — when he is discussing the unchecked individualism of the Industrial Revolution. Whatever approach he chooses to adopt, if he feels he has a conspicuous duty in the field of citizenship, then it is not necessary that he should pursue one method rather than another; the light which he wants to shed upon the present he will shed.

Something has been said already of the danger of trying to introduce adult concepts into children's education, and there is much in our modern political, and still more in our modern economic machinery, which is neither interesting nor digestible for children, though it may be suitable for students in institutions of further education. But there is one positive asset which is always available to the teacher who seeks to explain the present: he is talking about something the children already know something about. Whether he starts with the trains and the trolley-buses or with the cows and the cabbages; with the latest news-reel or with the latest talk in Children's Hour, he can start with something that is within his pupil's experience. And as he moves on to what is not within their present experiences he can at least show them that he is talking about what will, in due course, become their life, and that, again, is a real asset. He can always be sure, if he is at all wise in his selection, that he will meet with a response, and that he will fulfil a great purpose.

Social Studies in the Secondary Modern School

ERNEST L. FEREDAY, 1950

The November 1950 issue of the *Journal of Education* was given over to a series of articles concerned with the teaching of social studies. Fereday's article is one of these and he suggests some of the difficulties encountered in introducing social studies in secondary modern schools. These schools accommodated the majority of British secondary school pupils in the decade after 1945 and these were the pupils described by Mackinder (Reading 1) as 'those whose work in life is going to begin at fourteen or fifteen ... the nine out of ten who constitute the mass of the people in our country and carry on its traditions'. These are the pupils described in *Half Our Future* (Reading 14) and about whose curriculum Musgrove wrote: 'The curriculum to which educationists have ascribed a variety of subtle objectives has been a structure of activity designed to fill the time. Pupils have often been only too aware that they were digging holes in order to fill them up again (Musgrove 1968).'

Initially it was hoped that the curriculum of the secondary modern school should not be a weak imitation of the traditional grammar school curriculum, and the introduction of integrated courses was a reflection of this intention. A subjectless curriculum without external examinations was seen as a distinctive contribution to the education of adolescents. However courses have become subjects and examinations were designed to match these courses. The Certificate of Secondary Education provided a vehicle for the examination of integrated courses and, where Mode 3 courses have been introduced, distinctive course arrangements suitable for particular pupils in particular schools have been planned.

The characteristics of this work in secondary modern schools are the recurring special needs of those who find reading and writing difficult, and the widely diverging topics which they will choose if given genuine opportunities to follow their own individual interests. Many theorists have naïvely stated that the local industry, parents' occupations, easily accessible historical remains, local land utilization, modern transport, any classic work of literature currently filmed, or contemporary discoveries and developments in science widely publicized in the popular press, to take a few random examples, will be 'familiar' and of 'live interest'. Many experienced teachers who have tried the social studies approach would contest the validity of such assumptions. They would say that in so far as such things are familiar they do not excite interest; where they arouse interest it is because they are far from well known.

Some results of experiments with these topics suggest that to the young people concerned they were neither interesting nor familiar. One educational writer has said that young people who live inland have little notion of our shores, ships, and seas. This may appear to be merely an academic glimpse of the obvious, but it is important for our purpose to recognize that such youngsters often have an avid interest in these topics and have been known to convert a seaside holiday into a vital educational experience rather than a spell of conventional relaxation. Even more important is it to realize that ignorance of these three things exists also among children who live in Brighton, Southend, Weymouth, and Portsmouth.

It is much to be regretted that 'social studies' has come to be regarded as a 'subject' when its development has gradually come about from tendencies whose common origin was the desire of educationists to move as far as possible away from the very idea of subject divisions in the curriculum. At least one member of the Inspectorate has looked at a school's syllabuses and commented 'Social studies in the fourth and fifth years, but none in the first, second, and third years', in face of syllabuses in history, geography, science, literature, and so on, each of which clearly indicated appropriate regard for the social significances of both content and method and for the integration of the balanced development of each pupil. To regard 'social studies' as a '*new* subject' is to confess a quite disastrous failure to give unprejudiced consideration to the declared purposes of those doing this work.

Recently the Education Committee of the Royal Geographical Society abandoned its traditional scientific and objective approach to theories of education and dismissed social studies as 'an amorphous hotchpotch of geography, history, and civics'. Any highly regarded textbook of geography affords ample evidence that school geography is a brilliant reconciliation of the carefully selected essentials of several specialized sciences. Most of us owe so much to those clear-thinking teachers of geography in the last generation who patiently and purposefully expounded such well-ordered symposia to us that we should at once condemn as unkind any one who could characterize such work as an 'amorphous hotchpotch'.

The metaphor in another part of the Committee's memorandum, however, reveals a surer touch, for the most ardent advocate of social studies could hardly better their image of the 'squeezed lemon'. The result of combining different modes of approach to a topic is, they suggest, 'exactly what happens when a lemon is squeezed: the juice is removed and only the useless rind and fibres remain'. It would appear to be most desirable that solutions to the urgent problem of selecting the materials of study from a widely increased range of possibilities should retain the nourishing and necessary while rejecting the noxious, the nebulous, and the nugatory!

Criticisms more clearly founded upon actual classroom experience of both types of curriculum show a growing conviction that the methods used in social studies have too suddenly and too completely abandoned the 'plain story simply told'. Teachers have generally had to give much more detailed guidance than the theorists have suggested. It is so easy to overestimate the capabilities of young people whose attention has been stimulated by a novel introduction to a fresh 'centre of interest'. So many of them are, as it were, 'trailer-minded': but the trailer is not the film nor the blurb the book. The real problem of guidance in this is to ensure that the later stages of a project are well provided for. It is for teachers of social studies in secondary modern schools to evolve methods of integrating unrelated ideas and information on a variety of facets of the topic selected, even though the selection may have been made by the individual child or group concerned.

This means more and not less preparation, a good deal of which may not be immediately used. It is unnecessary to console such teachers by reminding them that in the past and with traditional 'subjects' much preparation has often been abortive, but it seems necessary to remind some critics of social studies of that simple truth. Many discussions which have ranged round this controversy seem to suggest that the choice is between a class-room situation where interest in the topic is evinced by the teacher but by none of the pupils, and one where each youngster has a different interest in the topic but the teacher, possibly for want of a textbook, is merely bewildered. It is fashionable to underestimate the abiding value of competent narrative discreetly and sparingly used. Schemes which start at the age of 11 with the child itself, and are neatly planned to work ever outward until the wide world is encompassed, sacrifice the absorbing interests of 'far away' and 'long ago'. The general appeal of the B.B.C.'s 'How Things Began' Series is widely attested by teachers, and those who are fortunate enough to be able to use the services of educational museums like that at Tottenham find the same keen curiosity.

Returning from journeys, despite assiduous work in preparation by teachers and pupils, the young people tend to report experiences rather than observations under 'headings' suggested or in reply to questions set out in advance. Effective guidance can be given only in 'follow-up' work. In few connexions will they successfully distinguish the transitory from the permanent. The 'activity' advocates tend to be overcritical of a situation where the young people are not 'fussing about', but physical passivity may indicate mental activity and emotional receptivity. Just as leisured observation and unhurried thought are the prerequisites of speed, precision, and purpose in fine writing which is to be efficient, so for the making of an effective social study there may well be a quiet gathering of impressions for a long time before the expression work.

There is general agreement among teachers in secondary modern schools, and frequent comment from His Majesty's Inspectors, that even fourth-year pupils lack understanding of their own bodily structure and functions. Yet it is normally true that the young people are interested in the way their bodies work, and from the beginning of their school lives hygiene will have had an important place in the curriculum. Talk of proceeding systematically from the child himself to the uttermost ends of the earth in a scheme of studies has possibly been a little glib.

In many instances work in health education has been stultified by isolation. Varied experiment is urgently needed in weaving health education into projects primarily conceived as historical, geographical, or more generally scientific. It is being given a fair place in most 'civics' schemes, generally with good results.

Any school curriculum is inescapably conditioned by the nature of the society which it is to serve. The special contribution of historical study is its approach to each age and historical figure on the basis of such standards as prevailed at the given time, consciously checking hasty conclusions founded on our own contemporary values. The essential is to stress in every sub-topic the slow evolutionary growth of all our political machinery and legal conventions to serve the ultimate purpose of individual freedom. It is not necessary to disguise that this freedom involves the control of individual caprice. The amalgam of ideas and institutions from Western Europe's inescapable past is meaningless until studied in the light of history.

To prepare a rising public opinion for the friendly and peaceful settlement of disputes between nations, predisposing the minds of a new generation to the democratic defence of international good order, is a task which would appear to involve us whether we like it or not in an 'amorphous hotchpotch'. The challenge which confronts us is to develop social studies interesting in themselves and significant beyond themselves.

The Scope of Social Studies

J. DRAY AND D. JORDAN, 1950

Between 1949 and 1953 several important books on the teaching of social studies were published in Britain. All carried the same message expressed forthrightly in this chapter from Dray and Jordan's book (1950): 'Social Studies should be social education in direct terms'. The case for introducing specially designed courses labelled Social Studies was argued on the grounds that the lessons learned from these courses were better taught than caught. Thus Hemming (1949) writes:

> All subjects can be used to develop social awareness and responsibility by including whatever social content is appropriate to them. But the effects will be relatively patchy and scrappy unless all the partial contributions are unified within a course specifically designed to build up the social understanding of the child.

And in similar vein Nicholson and Wright (1953) argue:

> If our contemporary predicament demands from us more knowledge of social behaviour and greater social awareness than were ever before required of adult citizens it follows that Social Studies constitute an essential need for future citizens . . . . For here is a whole fertile field of studies . . . . A topic or theme in Social Studies is not merely an adding together of subjects; it is a growing point of a body of social knowledge to which various distinct 'ologies' may have contributed.

In defining the scope of social studies, Dray and Jordan explore the social environment of the child and seek to synthesize this with 'four statements of human experience' which they have abstracted from a 'wheel of knowledge' — a pattern of 'important subjects to which man has devoted his thought and imagination' — which significantly excludes mathematics and history, but includes geography. Though crude by comparison with more recent epistemological studies, such as those of Phenix (1964) and Hirst (1965), this study by Dray and Jordan does represent a serious attempt to inject some theoretical unity into the body of practical pragmatic experimentation.

One of the first problems to be dealt with is how Social Studies is to be fitted into our present crowded timetable. There is very little room for an extra subject. Some schools fit in a current-events or a world-affairs programme once a week, particularly in upper forms. That may be a very useful addition; but it is not Social Studies in the sense in which we understand it. Current events provide useful material for supporting social studies, but are too haphazard and not sufficient in themselves to form a sound basis from which to start. They must be subservient to a broader plan. Social Studies should be an integral part of the curriculum, not an 'extra' introduced at the top end of the school.

Social Studies or Socializing Subjects

If there is not room in the timetable for an extra subject (and the compilers of the Norwood Report could find little space for one) Social Studies must either be incorporated into the work of existing subjects or it must replace them. We have shown in the first chapter how most knowledge, and certainly most thinking, is apt to become an unreal abstraction unless it is expressed in terms of human experience: indeed for the majority of us, unless it is expressed in terms of familiar *human* experience, preferably our own.

It has become a commonplace in educational parlance that we should begin with the child's own experience. But somehow this has not, in general, become part of our educational practice. Why not? Because we have not planned our curriculum in those terms. Most of us choose the old subject categories and try to provide some link between everyday life and history, geography, biology, or whatever the subject may be. Admittedly it is useful to give such subjects a social bias: this may greatly increase their interest and effectiveness. But that does not really solve our problem. The stress is still on specialized departments of knowledge. Instead of relating our work in these subjects to everyday life why not take everyday life as our starting point and view it from as many standpoints as we can? Too diverse, too rambling, some may say. Too trivial, or, too transient, say others. Nevertheless it is possible to take this fascinating jumble of everyday experience and discover in it significance, beauty, use, and a great stimulus to further thinking and better living.

Every topic can be viewed in the perpendicular of time or the horizontal of space. Every topic has problems of dimension or finance, of human need and control. Each can be studied, that is, in terms of history, geography, mathematics, economics, civics and sociology. It is not the purpose of Social Studies to ensure a thorough knowledge of any of these fields, though such knowledge may result from the course. The purpose of Social Studies from the point of view of the teacher is to provide the child with the opportunity, incentive and equipment to ask questions about life and find as many and varied answers as possible. Social Studies should be social education in direct terms. It should mean something happening to pupils and teachers and not merely something studied by them. Education is derived quite as much from the process of discovery as from the information found.

So what we need is a general outline of generous proportions to allow for a wide selection and variation within its bounds. Spare us from any precise agreed syllabus! The best way to draw up a plan is for the various members of staff concerned to meet and agree upon an outline. In Oregon, U.S.A., all the schools in Eugène met together and agreed upon a Democratic Living Programme which covered all grades from the youngest child to the college entrant, so that the main part of the curriculum was co-ordinated in all school work from primary to high school.

If there are enough teachers with sufficient enthusiasm and drive surely we could do that in some districts here. At least it ought to be possible within one school to draw up such a scheme. The task is really to look at life and see it not in terms of subjects but in terms of social values.

Begin with the Individual
The next problem then is: Where should we begin? What ground should we attempt to cover?

The beginning, as we have already suggested, should be our own particular Here and Now. First of all, ourselves. A great deal of our living is rightly and inevitably concerned with ourselves; our health, our survival, outlets for our propensities, opportunities for satisfying emotions, talents, bodily needs, for giving vent to our ideas and feelings. The individual is the fundamental unit in social problems, as the cell is in biology, the element in chemistry, the atom in physics. Yet the individual is hardly ever made the subject of study in school. We do not study ourselves except privately, unless we qualify for some course in higher education and follow a course in psychology. Yet this fascinating topic has many aspects which are of real and vital interest to children and which generally they have very little chance to discuss.

When we study history we take a particular patch of time and study what happened then. We may or may not find out how men lived in those days; we probably discover where they fought and what laws they made. We do not begin by studying men; we begin by studying a period. When we study geography we take a particular patch of space. We may or may not find out how men live in those parts; we probably discover how they travel and what work they do. We do not begin by studying men; we begin by studying the environment. When we study biology we usually take the anatomical structure of some animal which may or may not be man. We study the skeleton, the muscular, nervous, circulatory and reproductive systems. But we do not begin or end by studying the human being in all his aspects, the complete man.

So with psychology. So with economics. We begin with a certain body of knowledge and relate it more or less to human life. We do not begin with the human being himself.

Suppose we were to change all this and begin with a human being. What is a human being? Bones, flesh and blood. Yes. A seeing, hearing, feeling, tasting creature. A thinker too. A growing organism who gradually learns physical control, who teaches himself the difficult art of balancing on two legs and propelling himself in this fashion. An expanding mind, that discovers, stores and relates a fascinating jumble of knowledge. A developing personality learning a psychological control more difficult than the physical; adapting himself to people and situations, but retaining, for all his diversity, his own integrity.

How much one human being is like another. There is far greater physical variation among dogs than among men. How similar men are the world over in their emotions, ambitions, talents, as well as in their physical needs. Groups of men may organize themselves into different social patterns, but the essential unit in human society — man himself — is remarkably true to type.

An Individual Belongs to Many Social Groups

When we have discovered something about what we mean by a human being let us see how much human beings are modified or changed by being grouped together and by living in different environments. First of all let us look at a very natural human group, the family. Families exist elsewhere in nature; in the animal kingdom at all events. We use the word family with regard to plants and other phenomena; but merely to indicate relatedness, not in a social sense. The remarkable and interesting thing about human families is that no two individuals have quite the same function or status. Individual differences become strongly apparent within the common environment of this limited social group. A family needs to live together to be a real family; it needs some kind of common dwelling-place, some form of wealth; some form of social control, partly traditional, partly self-devised, by which its various members can live together and make their particular contribution to family life. What is the particular function of the father, the mother, the daughter of fifteen, the son of eleven, the baby in its pram? By what stages do the growing members become independent of the family and finally break away from it — physically and economically at all events?

Then consider the school. This is a social group of a very different kind. Here the child finds that instead of being unique in age and status as he is at home, he is with many others of much the same age and ability who have similar rights and responsibilities. Here he learns his first notions of abstract justice. Two kinds of adaption are demanded of him. He has to adjust himself to his school work, and he has to adapt himself to living in the school community. The school is a human institution; we do not find its counterpart elsewhere in the animal kingdom. The nearest approach to anything of the sort would seem to be in the communities of ants and bees.

The factory, farm, office or shop, like the school, has its own particular form of organization and allots its different tasks among people of various aptitudes. The incentives may be very different from those of the school, and the system of justice based on a different sense of values. Here is an important and much neglected field of study and investigation.

The home, the school, the work group and the various leisure groups. These make up a part of a much wider group — the neighbourhood — a more impersonal and yet a more familiar field to many of us in school. This is the realm in which environmental study usually begins, and pioneers have already blazed trails for us. But the true use and value of a study of a local environment is dependent upon an understanding of the needs, ambitions and necessary adaptations of the individuals living within it.

Widening Circles

Study of the local environment may begin with town or village. We consider its geographical features, its natural resources, trades and occupations, its social organizations. From such considerations we should turn to the wider region of the Highlands, the Midlands, the Home Counties, Greater London or whatever our setting may be. Such a setting should be compared with another of a different character.

The next important social group is the nation. This may mean England, or Great Britain or the United Kingdom. We should try to assess the implications of nationality, though probably we need to go abroad before we realize at all vividly the real characteristics of our own national way of life. We should try to realize that we are where we are historically because we are where we are geographically. If we can realize that for ourselves, in our own country, then we can look at the Arab, the Zulu, the Chinaman, and discover what he is like and why, in similar terms. How is he different from us? And more important still: how much like us is he as an individual, beset by the same human needs, gifted with many of the same human talents, filled with the same individual aspirations, even though his social aims may be different from ours.

So we come to the larger groupings in the world, in terms of natural regions, social civilizations, political organizations, racial affiliations or military conquests. It is instructive to consider how the world may be divided in these larger groups; they indicate the nature of world problems.

Finally we come to the full outer circle of the world itself and the social needs and interests of the millions of individuals who inhabit it. Food, for instance, should be thought of as something to eat and drink, something that keeps human beings alive and in good health, and not merely as a commodity to be bought and sold. Science, art, literature and music have to some extent already become an international heritage, and in a lesser degree so have religion and philosophy; but the material goods of the world have still to be shared. While people are starving in one continent wheat is burned in another. If we are to realize that our largest and greatest loyalty is owed to this all-embracing social group — the human race — we must understand it in terms of individuals like our own selves, as well as in terms of caste, creed or colour. These aspects of social life may perhaps be best represented as a series of concentric circles, the inmost one being the individual and the outermost the world (Fig. 1). The astronomer and some religious thinkers may wish to add yet another and include the universe itself.

The social groups described by these circles will be a sufficient guide to some teachers who wish to plan a course of social study. Others will like to have a clearer indication of what to include in the study of each group and of how to incorporate some important contributions made by more familiar subjects such as geography, biology and economics. For this purpose we give

Fig. 1   Widening social groups

four useful statements that may be borne in mind in studying any social group. These have been arrived at by considering the field covered by subjects of all kinds (Fig. 2) and then eliminating the multitude of subject names and replacing them by four simple statements about human experience which sum up their scope (Fig. 3).

The Wheel of Knowledge

Fig. 2 shows a wheel which indicates some of the important subjects to which man has devoted his thought and imagination; and shows them in a pattern in which each bears some relation to the one that comes before and the one that follows it. Many more subjects could be inserted. The order of many might be changed. Two are significantly missing — history and mathematics — because these, we would suggest, are not subjects in the same sense as other areas of knowledge. History is a dimension, a measuring of things in time; eveything has its history, and the facts and assumptions usually studied as history are a somewhat fortuitous choice of constitutional, military, and political happenings of the past. Mathematics is a skill rather than a science; one of the skills of communication. Some problems and solutions are best expressed in words, others in figures and symbols. The logic of the argument about them may be communicated in sentences or in algebraic equations. But words and figures, though both may be cunningly juggled with for their own sakes, really serve to express that body of knowledge that is observed, analyzed and synthesized in other subject areas.

Some subjects have obvious links with each other. We may group together the sciences and the arts. This diagram, however, is designed to show how we may map out the field of human knowledge in a complete pattern. It is only

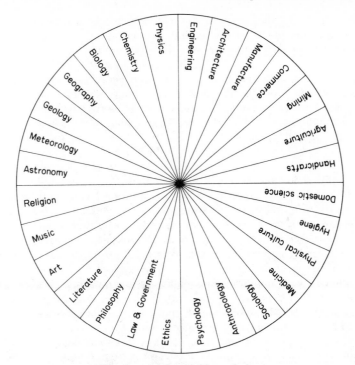

Fig. 2   A wheel of knowledge

one of many possible ways, but it is designed to show the relation of many, if not all, subjects to one another.

Suppose we begin with astronomy, the study of heavenly bodies. Very closely related to this is meteorology: the study of the atmosphere, the science of weather on which the sun and moon have considerable effect. Descending through the atmosphere we come to the study of the earth's crust — geology — which naturally leads us on to a description of the earth's surface — geography — both in terms of physical relief and in terms of vegetation. Here we enter the realm of biology, the study of life in all its forms, life considered in terms of cells. Closely linked to it is chemistry, in which the unit is not the living cell but the chemical elements of which things are composed: hydrogen, carbon, etc. It is next door to physics in which the atom or the electron is the unit of analysis in the study of properties and the inter-relation of matter and energy. The application of physics to practical processes is seen clearly in mechanics, the science of machinery allied to engineering. Problems of engineering are involved in the science of architecture. The line between art and science is difficult to draw and may be unreal; the scientifically sound often leads to the artistically true. From building to manufacture — the production of new substances — from these to commerce, the buying and selling of goods so produced. On the other side of commerce from production is the supply of raw materials; mining, agriculture. These in their origin are closely concerned with the deftness of manual skill; from them arise handicrafts. The latter brings us to the realm of domestic science. Out of this arises a concern for health and bodily welfare manifested in the study of hygiene, the active practice of promoting good health in the study of physical activity — the theory of physical training. Thence to the remedial aspect, medicine and surgery. And as medicine concerns itself more and more with environment — witness the Peckham Experiment — so we come to sociology. Inevitably bound up with the study of man in his social setting is the whole study of man, anthropology, which includes in its range the study of his mind, psychology. From a consideration of man's behaviour we come to a consideration of the moral code that has arisen from his habits of behaviour, ethics — from ethics to the constitutional establishment of this code in the form of Law and Government. The pattern of government is determined partly by a traditional moral code, partly by the impact of new ideas shaping themselves into a philosophy. Before these philosophic concepts become generally accepted and lead to outward reformation they generally find their expression in literature, in art. The spirit of the age leads to a new translation in contemporary terms of the ageless pursuit of beauty, truth, goodness in all forms of art, including music. Music is perhaps the most perfect vehicle for the expression of spiritual experience because it has no need to resort to the debased coinage of words. From music thus to religion; not in the sense of ethics, but in the sense of the exploration of a primary human experience. So we come full circle; for religion leads us to consider the stars: the measure of our external universe widens the horizons of our inward being. 'When I consider the heavens, the work of thy hands. What is man that thou art mindful of him?'

Subjects Translated into Statements about Human Experience

The somewhat phenomenal task now before us is to summarize this vast range of human knowledge so that we can deal with it within the general limits of our purpose. It is important that this summary should be in terms of human experience and not in abstract terms. A simple classification appears in Fig. 3, where this wheel of studies is divided into four main sectors: man explores his world; man uses natural resources; man struggles to survive; man shapes his destiny. Let us state at once that this is only one of many ways of classifying the field of human knowledge, and enterprising teachers will of course work out their own survey and summary. It is appended for those who would like some help in reassessing the areas of factual information and possible research in school work. Let us glance at these four sectors and note some of the implications:

Man explores his world. First with ears, eyes, nose and finger-tips: then with microscopes, telescopes, stethoscopes, barometers, thermometers and so forth. Man's mastery of the world as a frail member of the animal kingdom is due not a little to his sensitive finger-tips, unhampered by claws, his keenness of sight in observing what he feels, and his power to remember what he has

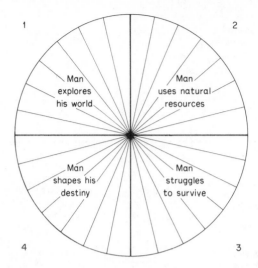

Fig. 3   Four statements about human experience

observed and felt. And finally his power not only to remember but to compare and perceive relationships and principles. From observation and discovery comes the perception of relationships and from this the invention of new forms and mixtures and combinations. So we come to the second sector—

Man uses natural resources. In primitive conditions he uses his muscular strength and the skill of his hands to shape wood, flint, stone and clay to his purpose. Then he harnesses the power of fire, water and wind to serve his needs. Finally he devises machinery to execute labours beyond his own strength and skill; by touching a lever he releases forces that wreck a city, or he establishes almost instantaneous communication with his fellow-men in the antipodes. Even so—

Man struggles to survive. However observant and inventive he may be he has certain humble bodily needs in common with all creatures, and these needs must be supplied if he is to live. He must have food, shelter, exercise, fresh air, rest, and if he is to invent and create he must be able to have these things securely, without a full day's struggle for them. 'The simple life' is a full time programme of hunting, tilling, fishing. But man at his best has an urge to do more than satisfy the bare needs of his nature—

Man shapes his destiny. He wants not only physical security as a chance for physical survival; he wants a field for adventure, for experiment in ideas, in feeling, in experience beyond his senses. So he learns to govern himself; to live in a community; to communicate to his fellows his experience in language, painting, sound. He beholds an increasingly splendid vision of the possibilities of human life.

To take one aspect of each of these sectors as represented by a subject

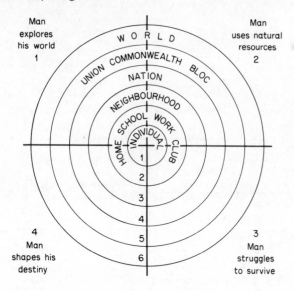

Fig. 4   Social groups and human experience (see Figs. 1 and 3)

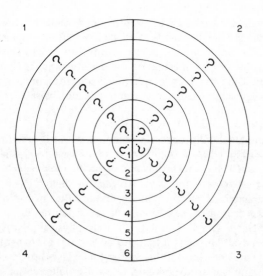

Fig. 5   Asking questions. For example, circle 2, sector 4 — What qualities in mother, father, children make for happy home life? What are the advantages of being one of a large family?

does not really throw into relief the remarkable contours of each of these regions of experience, any more than studying one peak makes you familiar with a whole range of mountains. How are we to set about gaining a useful general survey of the whole range of human endeavour? How can we make a map that will show the vast areas of human knowledge related to the various aspects of social life? We attempt to do this by placing Fig. 3 upon Fig. 1.

How does this give us a plan for social studies? In the next chapter we draw attention to the need for asking questions, and not merely repeating other people's answers. Here is where our questions begin: If we ask the relevant questions about each of the little sections into which our circles are now divided we shall be asking the most important questions about the life of the individual as well as about human destiny (see Fig. 5). Having asked the questions, what then? How can we find the answers?

Geography and Social Studies in Schools

ROYAL GEOGRAPHICAL SOCIETY, 1950

The two school subjects most affected by proposals for introducing social studies into schools were history and geography. In the light of suggestions made by educationists, authors of Ministry publications and the experiments conducted in schools some response was needed from the professional associations of teachers of history and geography. The geographers responded first and in the Memorandum quoted here a scathing attack is made upon the 'amorphous hotch-potch of geography, history and "civics"'. This latter expression is a modification of a comment published more than thirty years earlier: 'nor should we be over-particular if the geographer tells us that what we propose to teach is not geography but a 'hodge-podge' of geography, history, politics, economics, military strategy and the like. We take no account of the scholastic pedantry of names and subjects; what matters is to give our pupils an outlook, a sense of proportion, and aroused curiosity in the world around them and this is not history, or geography, or economics, or politics, but something whose texture contains them all' (Welton 1914). Historians, too, took exception to the inroads which Social Studies was making into the established place of their subject in schools. Burston, in a leaflet published by the Historical Association argued that there was no evidence to show that a child can understand what is contemporary, and 'perhaps what is in front of him better than he can understand the past which he must imagine' (Burston 1954). It is in publications of this kind that we see the power of subjects which Musgrove has commented upon (see Reading 18).

The term 'social studies' is used nowadays in two senses: to denote a certain advanced discipline at some of our universities, and to indicate a subject recently introduced into the curricula of schools, particularly in Modern Schools and in training colleges preparing teachers for them. It is with the latter sense that this memorandum deals. So understood, 'social studies' represent an attempt to compress several branches of learning into one. The result is exactly what happens when a lemon is squeezed: the juice is removed, and only the useless ring and fibres remain. The attempt may be attributed, first, to the influence of American theories, which, however, have since lost ground in the United States and also in Canada; secondly, to the pressure of subjects in school curricula; thirdly, to a new and rather dangerous conception of education; and, fourthly, to the necessity for training teachers quickly. It is felt that 'social studies' will destroy the value of geography as an important medium of education, and the Education Committee is concerned at its spread in the schools.

The Present Position
Most teachers of geography in primary and secondary modern schools come from the two-year training colleges, where far-reaching changes are taking place in the curriculum. One major change in particular requires careful attention. This is the substitution, in most colleges, of a course in 'environmental studies' for the ordinary courses in geography, history, biology, and the physical sciences. The aim is said to be to enrich personal experience and widen the social outlook of the student. The course is usually compulsory for all students: it may last for six or more weeks, or be spread over the whole two years. As a result, the number of teachers-in-training who study geography beyond the stage they reached at school is reduced to the small percentage taking 'advanced' geography. There is also the danger that student-teachers may misunderstand the special purpose of this course of 'environmental studies' in their own training, and regard it as another 'subject' suitable for the primary or secondary modern school.

In fact, under the name of 'social studies' this new subject is being increasingly taught in schools, especially secondary modern schools, where it displaces geography and history as separate subjects in the timetable. It is difficult to estimate precisely how far this elimination of geography as an ordered study has proceeded. There is, however, much evidence of a strong tendency to 'break down the barriers between subjects' (an explanation given for the change) and to teach an amorphous hotch-potch of geography, history and 'civics' under the heading of 'social studies'. The contents of the courses varies considerably from school to school; most contain a little geography, but in a disjointed and attenuated form, insufficient to preserve the characteristic outlook and discipline of the subject, which in recent years have come to be regarded as indispensable in the education of citizens.

Moreover, in many schools geography, influenced by the new trends, has become largely a superficial study of a series of social and economic topics, to the almost total exclusion of the physical basis. Thus, though still called geography on the time-table, it is scarcely distinguishable from the 'social studies' mentioned in the preceding paragraph. There has also been much emphasis on a type of local study, which consists of scraps of social survey leading to an acquaintance with the civic services of local government. Again, it has been an easy step to change the name to 'social studies' and to omit aspects of local study that the geographer regards as essential in any school geography course.

These developments are in part due to a new attitude to educational theory and practice which is exercising an increasing influence in the schools. Its adherents regard education as the adjustment of the child to its social environment, and not as the development of the child's individual potentialities within the environment. From this point of view education is a social process, which the child acquires through experience and activities related to the contemporary world. The curriculum therefore ceases to contain separate subjects on traditional lines: these are replaced by 'projects' centred on social topics and by 'activity methods' of study.

These changes are also related to views on the capabilities of pupils in the secondary modern schools which include 70 to 80 per cent of our children from eleven to fifteen years of age. The Norwood Report characterizes the secondary modern type of child in the following words: 'He is interested in things as they are; he finds little attraction in the past or the slow disentanglement of causes or movements. . . . Because he is interested only in the movement he may be incapable of a long series of connected steps; relevance to present concerns is the only way of awakening interest, abstractions mean little to him.' Even if this were true of all secondary modern school pupils, and it is certainly not, it points to a more realistic and less academic presentation of geography for some pupils, and not to its submergence in social studies. It must be repeated that if such a submergence occurs, this branch of learning cannot make its characteristic contribution to education.

The Dangers of Teaching 'Social Studies' in Schools

These developments must impair the standards of instruction in geography. An attempt to study a group of subjects together introduces such complexity that children cannot see any general pattern or gain a clear and memorable educational experience. The geographer is well aware that knowledge is whole, but makes no apology for dividing it into separate subjects for the purpose of learning. History and geography, for example, are distinct branches of study, and each is recognized as having a unique contribution to make to the intellectual equipment of the educated citizen of to-day. But these contributions are different, and cannot be made unless the recognized content and characteristic method of presentation of each subject are preserved. This is impossible if the two, with others, are merged into a single subject, 'social studies'.

Local studies are usually stressed in schemes of 'social studies'. They are undoubtedly an essential part of a good geography course, but local studies in a geographical setting are very different from local studies in a 'social studies' course. In the former setting they are, or should be, related to a larger whole, first the homeland, and then the world, and in these relationships lies their chief value. If the locality is studied in great detail, down to its very trams, rates and sewers, then the time left for the great countries of the world is likely to be inadequate. Which is more desirable — that a child should know the number and dispositions of all the hospital beds in the borough or that he should have some idea of the broad geographical features of the principal countries of the globe? This is in fact the kind of alternative presented in some schools at the present time. It is not true that a child is ordinarily interested for long periods of time in the myriad details of the life of his own locality. Boredom usually sets in before a full term is out. The strange and unfamiliar can always command his attention and stimulate his imagination. A sound geographical approach continually links aspects of the local area with the geography of more distant lands and imparts a fair and realistic idea of the home country and of the broad natural and human features of the continents. In the study of distant lands it is their geography — that is, their present reality as the home of man — which is essential.

The emphasis placed in 'social studies' on human affairs and the complexity of this subject matter lead to a neglect of the natural environment in which man lives. It is the geographer's aim to balance these two aspects, the natural and the human, and an essential contribution of geography to education is the appreciation of the relationship between man and his environment throughout the world. So much damage has already been caused by neglect of this relationship that the omission of this theme from education would be disastrous.

The Place of Geography in Education

The Committee considers that the present unsatisfactory position of geography in the curricula of schools which have adopted the new 'social studies' is largely due to failure to understand the nature of geography. A re-statement of its content, suited to the education of the city child, should remove much of the present misunderstanding. Its subject matter — the earth as the home of man — must give it an important place in education.

The geographer, like workers in other fields, draws some of his factual material from other branches of knowledge — the natural sciences on the one hand and the humanities on the other. His primary interest is in the distribution of these data, and he employs his particular technique, map making and map reading, with other visual and verbal methods, to analyse, describe, and relate them. His aim is then to perceive and understand the inter-relationships of these facts. In school this usually becomes a study of man and his activities in the natural environment. The degree to which the complex relationships are studied will be adjusted to the ages, aptitudes, and abilities of the pupils. With senior pupils the emphasis will be on this inter-relation, and it is this training which forms the main contribution of geography to education.

Geography is a vital link between the natural sciences and the humanities, and, in fact, brings out the essential unity of these two spheres of knowledge. It is upon this position that its claim to importance is based. Hence, the place of the geographer in the fields of knowledge and education is vital even in schools.

The importance of geography at all levels of education is urged not only by geographers, but by many educationists of standing and experience. 'I therefore want you to make the bold claim,' said Sir Cyril Norwood, 'that geography is an essential part of education whatever forms education may take, and that there can be no question of dropping it in any considered course of study: it is in my opinion more important than a foreign language or a science, highly important as these are, for the simple reason . . . that the intelligent person must understand something about the world and the country and the district in which he is set to live his life.' The steadily increased importance of geography in the grammar schools is reflected by the numbers of those offering the subject in public examinations. Up to the present, 'social studies' have not made much headway in these schools, and it is hoped that any pressure in favour of the innovation will be resisted.

The progress of geography in the grammar schools has been paralleled by the increased attention given to it in the Universities, where the number of professorial chairs has increased by eleven since 1939, so that geography now ranks as one of the major advanced studies.

Conclusion

The intellectual power and habit of mind afforded by a sound geographical training, with the factual content of the subject, are vital and unique contributions to the educational equipment of future citizens, and cannot be omitted without grave loss to their education. The essentials of a school geography course are:

(a) a training in the use of maps;
(b) an appreciation of the orderly grouping of significant facts, physical and human, leading to a balanced conception of the neighbourhood and its setting in the home country, and of the major varieties of natural environment and human activity in the world;
(c) some understanding of the relation between man's activities and his natural environment.

The organized presentation in school of the significant facts and the gradual emergence of coherent geographical unities are of high educational importance. Upon this basis boys and girls can be trained to be intelligent and enlightened citizens. Social studies alone, even with a geographical bias, can never yield a comparable result.

Balance in Geography and Education

R. G. HONEYBONE, 1954

This article by Honeybone is closely linked to the Memorandum of the Royal Geographical Society (Reading 12). Honeybone looks back to 1939 by which time 'geography had become grievously out of balance; the geographical synthesis had been abandoned; and the unique educational value of the subject lost in a flurry of social and economic generalizations'. After roundly criticizing the curriculum extremists and those who over-reacted to them he goes on to consider the special values of geography in education. His concept of balance is two-pronged — there is balance within geography as a subject, and there is balance in the curriculum as a whole. Geography is justified for its methodology, with observation, recording, and interpretation the essential forerunners to the final stage of generalization. These he applies to regional geography, 'the very heart of geography'. In the 'new geography' the demand is for a reassessment of methodology in the study of geography in schools. Stereotyped regionalism has been rejected, to be replaced by 'a more scientific attitude towards both physical and human geography and a greater use of mathematics and statistics than would have been thought appropriate as recently as ten years ago' (Department of Education and Science 1972). For Honeybone, geography, if well taught, is seen to be superior to social studies. If geography were not well taught then who or what was to blame — teachers, pupils, the subject, teaching materials or the organization of schools?

The theme of this paper is not a new one, for the problem of internal balance in geography has been before us in this country, ever since Mackinder argued the case for a unified geography in his famous address to the Royal Geographical Society in 1887. The words that he spoke then have a curiously contemporary ring. 'One of the greatest of all gaps,' he said, 'lies between the natural sciences and the study of humanity. It is the duty of the geographer to build one bridge over an abyss which in the opinion of many is upsetting the equilibrium of our culture. Lop off either limb of geography and you maim it in its noblest part' (Mackinder 1887), and later, 'As a subject of education, however, and as a basis of all fruitful specialism within the subject, we insist on the teaching and the grasping of geography as a whole.'

Despite this insistence, however, it was still true in 1901, that 'for want of observance of this principle, there may still be seen on some timetables lessons quite disconnected under the heads, geography and physical geography' (Rooper 1901), and it was still necessary for Professor Wooldridge in his paper to the Geographical Association only five years ago, to emphasize the serious lack of attention in schools to the physical basis of our subject.

The question of internal balance in geography is, therefore, one which has been with us for a very long time; and indeed, is one which must, of necessity, be always with us. A discipline which recruits its students from the sciences and the humanities alike, has continually to keep its synthesis under review, as Mackinder insists, both 'as a subject of education . . . and as a basis of all fruitful specialism within the subject'. Every teacher of geography, whatever his approach to the subject, must not allow his particular interest or, possibly, lack of interest, to distort his teaching. If his pupils are not led to an understanding of the value of the geographical synthesis, then he is failing in his full task. His own lack of balance has been transmitted to his pupils.

The teacher's task is, however, made more complex by the fact that he must project his geographical synthesis into an educational synthesis; or in other words, that he must not only achieve a balance in his geographical thinking, but must also achieve a proper balance between his subject and the total educational needs of the children whom he teaches. There is nothing new in this statement, but nevertheless, many teachers have found it difficult to achieve this balanced outlook in geography in particular, and in education in general.

We stand now at the beginning of an era, potentially more fruitful for the teaching of geography in school than any that has gone before; and it is helpful to look back over some of the extremes to which geographers have strayed during the last twenty to thirty years, so that we may be better prepared to take advantage of the opportunities of the present day.

Many members of the Geographical Association will remember the accounts given last May of the conditions in the Department of Geography of University College, London, during the nineteen-twenties. Fieldwork was unknown, large scale maps practically non-existent, and the facilities for research severely limited. I am not suggesting that the calibre of the undergraduates was lower than it is now; far from it, for some of the early graduates of this department are now numbered among our leading geographers. But I do suggest that these earlier students went down from their universities with less experience of the philosophy of their subject, and with less practical knowledge of field work and map interpretation than their post-war successors.

These conditions were not, of course, confined to University College, London, and I venture to suggest that if pre-war graduates were to compare their own undergraduate training with that of their post-war successors, most of them would fully realize their own early inadequacies. Many, and I include myself among them, were woefully ignorant of the real meaning of the physical basis of geography. Those who became teachers not unaturally reflected this weakness in their teaching.

Ironically enough, they were to some extent fortified in their lack of geographical balance, by the widespread influence of the late James Fairgrieve. Those who worked under him, of course, were brought to a full understanding of the geographical synthesis; they knew of his approach to geography through his beloved Scottish hills; and they understood his oft repeated phrase that the best way to learn geography was 'through the soles of one's boots'. But those who merely read his famous dictum on the function of geography in school with superficial understanding, imagined that here was the educational justification of their lopsided teaching. Fairgrieve asserted that 'The function of geography in school is to train future citizens to imagine accurately the conditions of the great world stage and so help them to think sanely about political and social problems in the world around' (Fairgrieve 1926). Many teachers, however, forgot the 'great world stage', so that geography came more and more to be a 'world citizenship' subject, with the citizens detached from their physical environment.

During the thirties, too, partly under American influence, a methodology, proclaiming that all education must be related to the everday experience of children, recieved a tremendous impetus. Taken to extremes, as educational ideas so frequently are, adherents of this methodology wished to sweep away much that was traditional and useful in our education. In terms of geography, they insisted that the approach must always be through life and the work of men. This is a premise with which many teachers of geography will agree, but when put in the hands of people untrained in geography or trained without a proper sense of geographical synthesis, it frequently meant that geography in school started with the life and work of man, and made no real attempt to examine his physical environment. In other words by 1939 geography had become grievously out of balance; the geographical synthesis had been abandoned; and the unique educational value of the subject lost in a flurry of social and economic generalizations.

While this development was occurring in Britain, an opposite course was being pursued in Germany. There, the universities had always had a greater physical bias than in this country; and, due to the relatively recent unification of the country in 1871, considerable emphasis was laid on the development of a feeling for the Fatherland, while, at the same time, allowing a great deal of importance to local regional differences, which in Germany had always been of greater significance than in Britain. There thus developed in the schools an over-emphasis on the physical basis, on local geography and field-work, and on national geography with a corresponding under-emphasis on the geography of other lands; and it was usual, until very recently, for German children to go to school at the age of six and not to learn the geography of any area outside Germany and its immediate neighbours until they were thirteen. In the inter-war period, too, the teaching of geography in Germany was used as a means of keeping alive a hatred of the Treaty of Versailles; and references to 'our lost lands' and 'our lost colonies' were common in the school textbooks.

Thus while geography in England was assuming a more social, economic and international flavour, in Germany it had a strong physical and nationalistic character; so that we have the curious position that, in the lands which had given rise to Humboldt and Ritter, and to Mackinder and Herbertson, the geographical pendulum had swung to opposite extremes. It is possible for each country to learn from the other's experience; in Britain we need more fieldwork, physical basis and national geography, and in Germany the need is for greater emphasis on the geography of other lands. And it is no matter for surprise that in Germany, at the end of the war, geography was reduced to one teaching period a week, and that, in England, geography was assailed by a new 'activity' called Social Studies.

In Britain, some people suddenly discovered the virtues of local survey, long advocated, but not sufficiently practised by geographers. They also suddenly discovered the virtues of integration, again inherent in the geographical synthesis, but frequently overlooked in school.

If geography had been widely taught in such a way that its value, both as a subject in particular and as a medium for education in general, had been clearly apparent, it is possible that these people would have turned to the geographer for co-operation. Unfortunately, the extremists among them, flushed by their own enthusiasm, could see only the worst features of geography. They were willing to throw overboard the experience of years; they wanted to discard one synthesis in the search for another; geography and history were to be swept away as separate subjects; the specialist teacher was regarded as old-fashioned; projects and freer methods generally were to replace class teaching; and the emphasis was to be on method rather than on matter, so that, in the words of the cynic, 'It didn't matter if the children did nothing, as long as they were kept busy doing it'.

These extremists, usually very vocal, have done a great deal of harm to the prestige of more sober educational thinkers, and also to their own cause. There is, of course, a great deal of value in projects and freer methods generally; there is a great deal of value in integration at the proper time and place; but there is also a great deal of value in class teaching; and a great deal of value in subjects well taught by the appropriate specialists. If these extremists had been people of better balanced outlook and more experience of life, they would have been willing to try to use the good things of the present and past as an aid to improving the future. They would have realized, too, that their own extremism would inevitably produce a strong reaction; and this has, in fact, happened in two ways. In the first place, the teaching profession with its sober good sense, has been very slow to adopt these ideas completely. Most teachers have continued to lay a good deal of stress on the importance of the matter. It may be, as I shall suggest later, that their stress on matter at the expense of method, has been too strong; but at least they have not gone to extremes. Projects are beginning to take a more balanced place in the teaching programme, and my friends in the publishing world tell me that the interest in Social Studies has dropped very markedly.

The other type of reaction against the extremists is represented by the pamphlet on Social Studies issued in 1950 by the Royal Geographical Society (Reading 12). I know that I am on thin ice in such company as this in criticizing this document, but in some ways it has had a boomerang effect. It was a valiant document, and useful in proclaiming publicly that geographers were very critical of the new developments in Social Studies. Where it was not so useful was in its selection of the more extreme manifestations of Social Studies as objects of criticism. We may complain that the N.U.T. report on the curriculum mentions the advances of geography (N.U.T. 1952), and then proceeds to ignore them by basing its recommendations on the worst features of geography teaching; but have we not in this pamphlet exposed ourselves to a similar charge? I must add in passing, however, that I have every sympathy for the members of the committee which prepared the pamphlet, for it must have been one of the hardest tasks of post-war education to find out what is meant by Social Studies and what its content is.

Discussion of the Royal Geographical Society's pamphlet is, however, quite subsidiary to the central theme of this paper, but it does serve to emphasize my point that in education, as in the wider walks of life, the pendulum does swing from one extreme to the other. Social Studies, interpreted as a substitute for history and geography, represents one extreme; the R.G.S. pamphlet represents a violent reaction. My own feeling is that we ought to examine Social Studies carefully to see if, beneath many of the extravagant claims of its advocates, there is something of educational value. It is not my intention to do this today, except to suggest that there seems to be developing a more sober approach, which, for want of a better name, I will call 'a study of society'. It may well be that towards the end of a modern or grammar school course, such an introduction would be a useful adjunct to the separate study of geography and history; but this is a topic that I do not intend to pursue now.

I do, however, suggest that just as it is important to examine the implications of Social Studies, it is equally important to examine the implications of our own teaching of geography. I am convinced that geography and history, well taught, can achieve all that is claimed for Social Studies, and a great deal more. I am old fashioned enough to believe that, other things being equal, the geographer can teach geography better than the non-geographer; and the historian can teach history better than the non-historian. If the teacher is a good one, the children will in no way suffer from specialist teaching. But the important words are *well taught*.

If the Social Studies controversy has no other effect than that of making us put our own house in order, then it will have made a very important contribution to the development of geography teaching in school. It is a pity that by reason of its brevity, the Royal Geographical Society's pamphlet could not develop the case for geography at greater length. We have a very strong and positive case; and as I have already suggested, the present time is particularly hopeful for a widespread advance in the teaching of geography in school.

In the universities, there has been an unparalleled advance in the number of staff and scope of the work in the departments of geography. In the University of London alone, there are now six chairs, four of them of relatively recent creation. Students, both graduates and undergraduates, are greater in number than ever before. Many of the training colleges and university departments of education are taking a full part in this progress; employers are realizing the value of the breadth of a university training in geography; and the Civil Service has recently raised the status of geography in its higher examinations. In fact, on all sides, we can see signs that, at long last, geography is forcing its complete acceptance as a major discipline in the universities, and that geographers are welcomed into commerce, industry and the professions, because they are well educated men and women; and perhaps, most significant of all, a wider public is beginning to read books written by geographers.

But what of the schools? Are they in turn taking an active part in this great advance? Or are they standing by passively, waiting for the ferment in the universities to trickle slowly down to them, like the lukewarm drips of a leaking hot-water tap?

It is true that the statistics of the university examining bodies show that geography, both at Advanced and Ordinary levels in the General Certificate of Education, is relatively more popular than ever before. But can we face our critics and honestly say that the water-tight barriers between subjects, of which they complain, are not of our making? Can we with good faith, stoutly assert, that we do in fact, lead our pupils towards the geographical synthesis, of which we talk so much?

The N.U.T. report on the curriculum published last year, states 'the study of geography has often become overburdened with data meaningless to the pupil' (N.U.T. 1952). It is illuminating to compare this criticism with one taken from the first volume of the *Geographical Teacher* in 1901. 'In British schools, geography has ever been a dull and uninteresting subject. It has been a dreary recitation of names and statistics, of no interest to the learner, and of little use except, perhaps, in the sorting departments of the Post Office' (Rooper 1901); and to compare this with Mackinder's words in 1887: 'When, however, the method of description has been adopted, and still more that of enumeration, each additional fact adds an ever-increasing amount to the burden to be borne by the memory. It is like throwing another pebble on to a heap of gravel' (Mackinder 1887).

Are we to believe from these quotations that we have made no progress since the end of last century? That is far from the truth, and the important fact to note is that the quotations of 1887 and 1901 were apparently of general relevance, while the quotation of 1952 is not. Even the N.U.T. report recognizes that progress has been made, although it unfortunately ignores it in its recommendations.

General improvement has, however, been disappointingly slow in some respects, and I often wonder what the contributors to the first volume of the *Geographical Teacher* would think of the position today. There is a tremendous amount of geographical and educational wisdom in this and the other early volumes. There are articles on methods in general, on the use of pictures and Ordnance Survey maps, and the value of fieldwork (Geographical Association 1949). These are all equally topical at the present moment, and it is worth stressing that the present emphasis on these topics cannot, therefore, be dismissed as a mere passing fashion. It is true that the teaching of geography has been completely revolutionized in this century, but I suggest that much of the early advice was unheeded mainly because the writers were before their time. Just as the effect of the work of Humboldt and Ritter in regional geography in the mid-nineteenth century was limited by the lack of knowledge of the regions of the world, so the effect of these early suggestions on the teaching of geography was limited because most teachers had neither the knowledge nor the experience necessary to carry them out.

Now, however, we have far more teachers with the knowledge and experience to take advantage of this advice, and that is why I suggest that we are standing on the threshold of a great advance in the teaching of geography. But we cannot advance very far unless we rid ourselves of the one factor which has remained persistently with us in the centre of the field, regardless of the extremes to which the rest of geography and education have swung.

As is so frequently the case, Mackinder sums up this problem for us in the words 'Can geography be rendered a discipline instead of a mere body of information?' (Mackinder 1887); or, in other words, can we put more emphasis on understanding than on memory? If we analyze the trends of geography teaching during this century, it appears that, although the type of memorization has changed, yet memory has always been very markedly the senior partner in the uneasy alliance of memory and understanding. At one time, there existed the much derided 'capes and bays'; at another, what we might call 'economic capes and bays', lists of products related in the flimsiest way to their environments; at another, the 'pseudo scientific capes and bays', the era of the isobars and the planetary wind system; and at the present time, we seem to be over emphasizing the 'regional account capes and bays'. The last, of course, represents a great advance over the first, but do not let us delude ourselves that a regional account, under the headings of Position, Relief, Climate, Natural Vegetation, Occupations, etc., necessarily represents a true geographical synthesis. Frequently, such regional accounts in school are mere feats of memory, with little or no relationship between the various parts.

Regional geography, in my view, is the very heart of geography, the central core, which more than any other feature, gives the subject its unique character. I have noted, with some concern, that there has been a recent tendency to move away from the regional approach to teaching. Although the so-called concentric approach has certain obvious attractions, and can, to some extent, be wedded to the regional concept, I cannot help feeling that its development is unfortunate for geography, both as a discipline and as a medium for education; and there is no doubt that this recent movement has derived its impetus in part from dissatisfaction with the sterotyped and debased form of regional geography so often found in schools.

The clue to an improvement can be found, as so often it can be found, if we turn again with a critical eye, to the development and methods of our subject. At the turn of the century in France, there was working a group of geographers under the inspired leadership of Vidal de la Blache. They went out, notebook in hand, and observed carefully, and recorded by annotated sketch-map and diagram, the nature of the landscape both physical and cultural. Back in the map room and library, they endeavoured to interpret their observations, so that finally they were able to enter into the personality or character of the region. Many of you will be familiar with their masterly regional analyses. Not for them the barren headings of Position, Relief and Climate. They regarded their regional accounts as regional symphonies, in which all the facets of the landscape were blended as are the strings, brass and woodwind of a great orchestra, creating in harmony an effect much greater than the simple sum of the instruments.

This threefold process of observation, recording and interpretation is the basis of all geographical method, and the essential forerunner to the final, and necessary, stage of generalization. It has been the major curse of geography in school, that the stage of generalization has too frequently been placed first, and the preceding three stages omitted.

It may be helpful, therefore, if we consider the methods of the French geographers in terms of our teaching in school. Instead of adopting a stereotyped approach to every region, we might, for example, first select a personality or theme, and then weave our regional account round this central idea. Furthermore, we should remember that the French geographers began, where all geographical work must begin, in the field. Clearly, in school, we cannot study very much geography at first hand, and we have, therefore, to approximate our classroom conditions as closely as possible to those of the field. The chief problem before the geography teacher then is to select material which his pupils can study in order to discover, as the French geographers did, the personality of a region. This material may take the form of maps, pictures, vivid descriptions, statistics, models and so on, arranged around the central theme.

An example will help to make this approach clearer. Let us suppose that we have a lesson on the Pennines with fourteen-year-old children. If they are from a large town in the South of England, we may wish to convey to them a sense of the bareness, the loneliness and the beauty of these northern hills. We can present to them a one inch or a two and a half inch Ordnance Survey map, and two or three pictures, and we can guide them by question and answer, written and oral, to a discovery and understanding of the character of the Pennines.

This approach has many merits; for not only is the matter geographical, but the method is geographical. Matter and method are wedded, and not divorced, as is so often the case. The children are experiencing in the classroom some of the stimulus of fieldwork; they are being made to think for themselves; and any facts which need to be memorized emerge as facts that have relational significance and not as unconnected snippets of information. Moreover, this approach is one of infinite variety and is one that can be used with children of wide age and intelligence ranges in primary, modern and grammar schools. It will, I suggest, successfully withstand the closest critical review both on geographical and educational grounds.

Time precludes any further examples, but it is important to add that this method, which already is in use in some schools, is showing signs of considerable expansion. It is a perfectly practical classroom approach, maintaining a balance between the elements of geography in particular and of education in general; but it is, of course, much more demanding of the teacher than some more traditional methods.

Two points need to be noted briefly. The first concerns the supply of the data, such as maps and pictures, which are needed as geographical raw material. Ordnance Survey maps are expensive, but the sets published by the Geographical Association are cheap and of very great value; and the Ordnance Survey offers spare copies of examination map extracts at very low rates. Some schools were fortunate enough to secure copies of the G.S.G.S. foreign maps, but it would fill a very great need if the Geographical Association would publish a series of foreign map extracts on the lines of its Ordnance Survey sets. Good teaching pictures, too, are available in packets and in film strips as never before. In other words, on the material side, the opportunities exist, even in these days of financial stringency.

The second point concerns the time available for teaching. Many teachers may tend to dismiss this approach because they think that it takes longer than other methods; but I suggest that it is relevant to argue that time taken can only be judged against the results achieved, and I am convinced that children who cover less ground, but cover it more thoroughly and with more geographical understanding, are better educated persons than those who cover every region of the world more superficially, and frequently with a monotonously stereotyped approach.

I have long come to the conclusion that every teacher of geography must sit back and think carefully over his syllabus to decide what he can cut out in order to give more time to certain areas which seem to him to be particularly significant in his pupil's total geographical education. This throws a great responsibility on to the teacher, but in this country, he enjoys more freedom than in any other country. The priceless privilege of freedom entails responsibility, and it is in cases like this that the teacher must fall back on his own balanced judgment.

Many teachers whose pupils sit for external examinations, however, may well ask 'But how can I afford to leave out parts of the syllabus?' This is, of course, a very natural question, but I repeat that this 'field study' approach is applicable equally to grammar and modern schools; and I can assure grammar school teachers that the candidates who are able to apply their knowledge achieve better results than those who often have more knowledge but less understanding. Schools which train their candidates entirely on a 'spot the question' basis not infrequently crash badly. Sets of notes, learnt parrot-wise and reproduced in a fashion varying from good to bad, are frequently offered, even if they have very little connection with the question set. I well remember one of my assistant examiners, after marking one particularly exasperating set of scripts, asking me to include in the the the next rubric, the statement 'Candidates are advised to read the questions before answering them'.

Teachers, I am quite sure, would be well advised to cover less ground in a more thorough way, and to say plainly to their candidates 'Here is a list of topics that I shall not cover. You must prepare them yourselves'. This is not a lack of conscientiousness, but plain common sense, and in practice pays handsome dividends from all points of view.

Examiners, both internal and external, on the other hand, can themselves help by setting more imaginative papers. Many of the questions of today still have a rather too close resemblance to some of the examination papers contained in the appendices to Scott Keltie's famous report to the Royal Geographical Society in 1886 (Scott Keltie 1886). A typical example selected from Scott Keltie's collection runs as follows: 'Where are the following rivers? Into what sea do they flow? (Name) Any one town on any of them; any historical fact in connection with any of them; — Tarim, Lot, Wharfe, Lualaba, Pisuerga, Mekong, Armançon, Bagradas, Canadian River, etc., etc.' But my favourite is the one that begins 'Draw a Chinaman, the Great Bear, and a yak.'

It would be salutary for teachers and external examiners alike to read an article by F. J. Wilkinson in the *Geographical Teacher* for 1901. 'The examiner,' he writes, 'who fills his paper with "Memory" questions debases the subject, encourages cram and discourages thought. The examiner who relies on "Rational" questions treats the subject worthily . . .' Mr. Wilkinson then goes on to analyze several examination papers, and of the Oxford Senior in 1900, he complains that 'Amidst a dreary mass of "Memory" questions (73 per cent), we only find a faint glimmer of the "Rational" method (16 per cent), with one physical question (11 per cent)'. Apparently in those days 'physical' fell into neither of the groups 'Rational' or 'Memory'.

I do not propose to submit modern examination papers to such an analysis now, but I would suggest that examiners have in their power an instrument for good or ill. They, too, have their responsibilities, as well as the teachers. If they set more and more 'Rational' questions, teachers and pupils alike will naturally adjust the emphasis of their work to meet the need for greater understanding, and thereby achieve a better balance.

In this paper, it has been suggested that geography in schools has not always maintained a balanced outlook; that some educational theories have been taken to extremes; and that the teacher, in order to restore the balance, must re-examine both the nature of geography and the nature of his job as an educator. I have suggested an approach in which method and matter are welded in a way that should satisfy geographer and educator alike; and I have suggested that, by reason of the improved status of geography in the universities, training colleges and the country in general, and the greater number of students and teachers well acquainted with the philosophy of their subject, we are now in a position to make a balanced and general progress in a way that was impossible for our predecessors. This progress can best be achieved if we refuse to go to extremes in either matter or method, and in either subject or child. We are fortunate that both the matter of our subject and its methods are completely in line with modern educational requirements; much of our work comes within the direct experience of our pupils, and most of it is closely relevant to their development both as individuals and as members of society; our approach is integrated and our methods are 'active', in that they throw the responsibility for learning on the children. So let us, in our teaching, emphasize the things that are geographical; and, of the things that are geographical, I would rate very highly for greater emphasis in schools: fieldwork for all age groups, including some local survey every year (Honeybone 1953); the 'fieldwork' approach in the classroom; a regional 'grammar', with a proper synthesis of physical and cultural elements; a physical basis that means the understanding of scenery and simple meteorology, and not a string of unconnected and generalized abstractions; the geography of Britain, including some Ordnance Survey map and picture interpretation every year; the sketch map as the geographer's 'shorthand', and not as a reproduction of the atlas or textbook map, thrown into an examination script as a supposed sop to the examiner; and, above all, understanding as well as memory. If we emphasize these things, we shall achieve a better geographical balance by insisting as Mackinder said, on 'the teaching and grasping of geography as a whole'.

But let us not, in our enthusiasm for our subject, forget that there are other fields of knowledge and other methods; or that, where geography abuts on to other subjects, we should take every opportunity to ensure that there is active collaboration by the other members of the school staff. This 'middle of the road' course that I have advocated is not a spectacular one; it will not satisfy those who seem to chase educational ideas to extremes; but if it assists us to maintain a proper sense of balance in geography and education, then it may well be that this Diamond Jubilee year of the Geographical Association will mark the beginning of a new era in the teaching of geography in school.

II

THE SEARCH FOR PRINCIPLES OF INTEGRATION

We have had virtually no theoretical perspectives or research to suggest explanations of how curricula, which are no less social inventions than political parties or new towns, arise, persist and change, and what the social interests and values involved might be (Young 1971).

The Proper Study of Mankind

MINISTRY OF EDUCATION (NEWSOM REPORT), 1963

The Newsom Report had relatively little to say about geography as such but it is of considerable significance not only for its frank appraisal of the teaching considered appropriate for the average and below-average pupils but also because, in making the case for the raising of the school-leaving age, it unleashed a vigorous movement for curriculum development which drew its strength from a series of projects mounted by development teams supported by the Schools Council and in scattered experiments in course organization in numerous individual schools. That there should be different curricular arrangements for pupils of different ability levels was a commonly accepted principle within the British educational system. Already we have seen the distinction made by Mackinder between the 'ordinary pupil' and the pupil who will go on to higher education and become the teacher of geography in the future. This distinction between the university-bound grammar school pupil, for whom academic subjects are a must, and the rest, for whom integrated courses or diluted subject studies may be appropriate, is a basic ingredient of the secondary school tradition inherited by post-war teachers from the pre-war period. Shipman described the suggestions embodied in the Newson Report and the experimentation which followed as a 'curriculum for inequality' commenting: 'the concentration of resources on developing relevant courses within new subject boundaries has contrasted too sharply with the parallel development of the above average pupils, where the priority has left the traditional subject framework intact (Shipman 1971).'

499. The importance of history and geography, or the social studies in which they are sometimes merged, seems obvious. A man who is ignorant of the society in which he lives, who knows nothing of its place in the world and who has not thought about his place in it, is not a free man even though he has a vote. He is easy game for 'the hidden persuaders'. A society in which he and his like predominate is at their mercy. We may turn Abraham Lincoln's saying to our situation: 'this nation cannot survive half slave and half free'.

Too often, however, the boys and girls with whom we are concerned do not see this. Geography and perhaps even more frequently history lessons are expendable as far as boys, and to a less extent girls are concerned. They cannot buy anything with this kind of knowledge as they can with physics and shorthand; they are not always willing to pay for it with hard work as they will for the skills of handicraft or dressmaking. Henry Ford's 'history is bunk', did they but know it, expresses exactly what they feel; but, of course, Henry Ford is as dead to them as Queen Anne — or history.

500. This is a grimly pessimistic view. In so far as it is true it represents a grave danger. But, while it holds good of many pupils in many schools, we see no reason why this should go on. If other schools can tell a different story, and they can, we are not confronted with a psychological barrier which prevents people of below average intelligence, that is to say about half the nation, forming a responsible and reasoned opinion about public affairs. Optimism is possible. The important thing is to discover and apply the means by which it can be justified.

501. They will be found in classrooms. A 16 mm film about an Indian village has just been shown. Here are to be seen temple and mosque, dung cakes and wooden plough, the monsoon bank of earth and nearby the building of a large concrete dam soon to result in a permanent water supply and the gift of electricity. Here in a Birmingham classroom in 1963 is present at one time a recapitulation of many thousands of years of human history. Maps, statistics, first-hand descriptions may lead on to questions of climate, food, birth-rate, clothing, caste, nationalism, religion, and governmental planning.

502. The film has raised questions. The answers call for contributions of many kinds from many groups of pupils. Discussion alone is not enough. Its purpose is to decide on a programme of work and to evaluate work done. In between comes the work. This requires the provision of much source material. Standard reference books will be needed; good maps; an indexed collection of pictures and diagrams. Some will be to hand in the geography room; some in the school library; the public library system will be involved. Eventually, when some final worrying area of ignorance remains to be explored — but, if the teacher is wise, only then — reference may be made to the Commonwealth Institute or to the Indian or Pakistan High Commission. The pupils will have been investigating real problems, using adult sources of information and becoming involved in a world situation in which they may have a part to play.

503. In another school boys and girls of the same age are engaged in what one might call a series of confrontations. Here, magnified, is a rubbing of a George VI half-crown with its superscription 'Ind. Imp.' and the date. Next to it on the display board, is a similar rubbing of a Victorian half-crown — how by the way was this obtained? The dates are compared and the heyday of the British raj is fixed. The class are debating what shall be put opposite the

half-crowns. The Indian flag? Mahatma Ghandi's spinning wheel? Is the latter already as dated as the George VI half-crown? Why? We are back to the population problem. Then, pictures. 'Forty years on', a line of melody from the school song, a silhouette of Harrow Hill and the pictures of Jawaharlal Nehru and Winston Churchill. Questions again: What brought Nehru to Harrow? Will other Indian boys in the future do the same sort of thing? Would they understand the language if they did? We are back before we know it to Lord Macaulay and on to this year's debates in the Indian parliament on English as an official language. Another confrontation: Mr. Ghandi again, but this time gathering salt, not spinning kadar. Side by side with this picture there is a recent photograph of English demonstrators sitting down in Trafalgar Square. What is the connection? And, incidentally, had Mr. Ghandi any connection with South Africa? Why did he choose salt? What has this to tell us about poverty; and, if the class is up to it, about elastic and inelastic demand?

504. Once again a full programme of work is mapped out; once again adult sources will be used; once again the boys and girls will become involved in a situation which calls, first, for understanding and then for commitment. Who was right and who was wrong? This is the first question they ask. What was right and what wrong in each side's action and why? That is the second question. The second question leads on to the third, which is very like the first but with a subtle difference. Who was right on balance?

505. These two lessons, or series of lessons, on India may stand as tokens to represent a whole programme of work designed to set ordinary minds working on world problems. Some parts of the programme, however, would be set much nearer home — almost on the doorstep or no further away than a school journey's distance. The identification of land forms, the influence of geology on landscape, the principles involved in national parks and nature reserves, the rights of different kinds of country users — young and old, walkers, motorists, naturalists and farmers, this is a totally different sequence from the Indian ones. It starts with the immediate experience of the perceptive eye and the field-sketching hand, but it too may lead on to the making of social judgements. Another home-based sequence, using immediate experience but this time of human relations, might study the ebb and flow of East and West as seen in the pupils' family history — uncles and aunts settled or working overseas, new neighbours from abroad; the epitome of world history in one of its main transformations as crystallized in grandfather's war and father's war — here the school in the slums is at no disadvantage and possibly somewhat better off than others. There is plenty of material which a good teacher can use to secure an intellectual and emotional break-through from the classroom with its text book and its lessons to the real world of human problems. To secure this break-through is more important than to explain the mechanics of the ballot — more difficult, no doubt, but more likely to hold the pupils' attention.

506. But the teacher needs space and time if he is to succeed. He needs space because his room will have to serve as a base, a workshop and a store. He needs good facilities for mechanical aids — projector, record player, tape-recorder, radio and TV receiver. He needs these to give the actuality of quasi-immediate experience to studies which time or space put at a distance. He needs a working surface where models can be made, a tracing table, perhaps a photo-copier (certainly ready access to one), map chests, filing cabinets, book-shelves. He needs time. The total time allowed by the school for English subjects is often adequate, sometimes generous. But when it is dispersed between three and four teachers with three or four different 'subjects' — social studies, current affairs, history, civics, geography — none has enough elbow room to undertake a programme of work such as we have suggested. The time needs concentrating, and the values specially associated with the various subject names secured by ringing the changes among them.

507. Something in depth for a short time rather than a little of everything all the time is probably the right approach anyhow for the boys and girls with whom we are concerned. A relatively short spell of work at a given theme — a term at the most — culminating in some definite evidence of achievement is a good formula. The evidence of achievement may take the form of an exhibition, the production of a class book, the making of a film strip, perhaps with a commentary recorded on tape — there are many possibilities. Different themes lend themselves to different methods; the important thing is that all pupils should be able to take part. Such a wide range of expression is possible that this general participation can usually be secured — but it does not happen without careful planning in advance. It is indeed often possible to get senior boys and girls so interested in what they are doing that homework does not so much have to be set as suggest itself. Some of it may even take the agreeable form of an evening's viewing — but with a constructive and critical purpose.

508. A programme of this kind will have failed if it does not lead to knowing what evidence is and what it will prove. At one time a class will be interpreting for themselves physical evidence: they will be learning, for instance, how to read landscape and how to interpret a map. A short time at a Field Studies Centre will make both map and science come alive for them. At another time they will be setting social facts against social facts. They will come to see that in any economic problem some facts will tell in one direction and some in another; that some groups of people will naturally pay more attention to one set than the other; and that this personal bias is something that they must guard against in themselves. The personal and social advantages of different forms of space heating is an obvious example. They may, and should, go on to problems where only some of the facts are known, but a decision has to be made. There is much argument, for instance, about streaming in schools. It will take a long time to find out what its true consequences are, but meanwhile schools have to be carried on. This is the sort of situation that could profitably be examined. It is possible to move

from co-operative situations like this, where everybody is trying to find out the truth or the best course to take, to situations in which there is no longer this common purpose. In war, for instance, the enemy's position has to be inferred in face of appearances designed to mislead. Boys and girls of quite poor academic ability are often well aware that a good deal of propaganda falls into this last category. They feel that they are being got at, that they are not being told the truth, or at least only carefully doctored truth. They develop a protective cynicism which leads them to believe everything; a more hopeful defence would be provided by an elementary training in evidence and how to handle it.

509. Even more important, perhaps, than this scientific approach to factual evidence is an ability to enter imaginatively into other men's minds. What is to be cultivated here is psychological sensitivity and intuitive awareness rather than rational fact-finding. It is important to keep good company and great company. People count. They count not only in their private lives but publicly. People make history. It is an enlarging of the spirit for our boys and girls to meet great men and to respond to them as men did and still do. The racy but rich speech of Abraham Lincoln can still hold fifteen year-olds in twentieth century England and show them as it showed men a hundred years ago what things are worth more than living. It is important, too, to know bad company and to avoid it. Evil men also have power. Were those who followed Hitler necessarily worse men than those who rallied to Churchill? Why did they do it? Might we not have done the same? How did some of his own people stand out against him? These are sobering questions which ordinary young people ought to face.

510. Need a teacher select his programme with an eye to more than its momentary acceptability to his pupils and its effectiveness in getting his pupils to pause long enough to think? If he remembers that there is nothing quite so dead as last year's sensation, he will probably conclude that he ought to have some better principle of selection than topicality.

511. Probably in history he will decide that in the last years at school he must choose contemporary themes which will help his pupils to understand the world in which they live, not only the world into which their fathers were born. History in schools now often, but by no means always, reaches 1939 and edges towards 1945. But in 1945 the Indian peninsula was still politically united and part of a British Empire; China was not yet Communist; and Africa was still a network of colonies and mandated territories with only a distant prospect of becoming anything else. The first atomic bomb had only just been exploded; Everest and not the moon was still the summit to be reached. History which does not take account of these and similar revolutionary changes will not seem to the limited minds of our boys and girls to be the history of their world. This does not mean that the cavemen and the open fields of their earlier years were just childish stories. They will find them still existing: no longer in our past but in other peoples' present. English boys

and girls need to get some idea of this compression of millenia of human development into one African generation and of the economic and psychological problems that go with it. They need, too, to understand the problems of India and China which are economically similar to Africa's but psychologically different because Asia is a continent of old and proud cultures. Some of our very modern history will take us back to very ancient times.

512. What is living and important in the world in 1963 cannot be explained only by what has happened since 1945. This is certainly true even when the topic is the U.S.A. and the U.S.S.R. in the world today. In British history perhaps the most important thing to do with the pupils before they finally leave school will be an assessment of Britain's true position in the world of today, an assessment which must be based on knowledge of the past as well as the present. Here is material for a life study, not for a year's work however generous the time allowance. The teacher will have to choose between the barest outline of events and the selection of limited topics which can be studied in sufficient detail to bring them to life. If he chooses the latter course, and this seems more likely to give his pupils understanding, he will want to select his topics carefully to give as representative coverage as he can to four or five themes of history today.

513. The same principles apply in geography. The list of possible topics is far too long for any school to exhaust. Once again the choice must lie between large tracts of barren outline and a few typical problems studied in depth. Once again the latter is the promising solution. A clear break in the syllabus is useful at the end of the third year, involving a change from a systematic course to selected case studies. It should not mean losing intellectual coherence. A wise teacher will probably distribute his fields of study as widely as possible so that examples are given of differences of climate and relief, different stages of economic development and differences in race and culture. The progressive nature of the work will not be determined by the sequence of examples, but by the depth at which they are tackled. Thus a detailed study of an Indian village if taken in the third year might stop short at vivid description. If taken in the fifth year it might initiate a discussion on the precise meaning of 'low standard of living' illustrated by comparative figures for Malaya, Britain and the U.S.A., leading to a consideration of how the standard could be raised.

514. Most of the illustrations in this chapter have been drawn from history or geography. Often very much the same ground was being covered, though in one case the approach was that of a historian, in another that of a geographer. No attempt has been made to set out all that history or geography can do for the education of the average and below-average boys and girls during their schooldays. We have concentrated on certain things and certain lessons which they need especially to learn during their last year or two at school and which we think history and geography can usefully teach them. We do not really

mind which does it. There are more than a sufficient number of teachers of both to meet the needs of the schools. It is only fair, however, to add that many of them would feel themselves singularly ill-equipped to undertake the kind of work which is suggested in this chapter. There is need for a review of what history and, to a rather less extent, of what geography is taught in higher education. There is quite certainly need for a large programme of in-service training.

515. Can historians and geographers do all that boys and girls need in this sphere? It seems to us that the answer must be 'no'. Most of the illustrations we used lead on into he field of moral judgements. No review of the world situation can fail to show boys and girls how strong and how various are the faiths by which men live. They are bound to encounter and admire the conviction and self-sacrifice which many Communists display. They will discover how Protestant pastor, Roman Catholic priest and Communist cell-leader alike were tried in the ordeal of Buchenwald and not found wanting. They will find, too, how men of all faiths can be cruel and evil, often with the highest possible motives. Both discoveries need thinking about. Turning back to one of our original illustrations, they will grossly misunderstand Mr Ghandi, if they fail to realize something of the subtlety of his relation to Christianity.

516. This involves among other things knowing what Christianity is. There is a straightforward teaching job to be done here. Just what do Christians believe about God and man, life and death? Many fourteen-year-old boys and girls will not know unless they are taught — but it is often assumed that they know this already. An information service is important, and they ask for it. In their last years at school there is need also to help them to see the difference that being a Christian makes, or should make, to the answers that have to be given to problems of living. Some of these problems are personal and immediate; some are collective and social — relations with parents and with friends of the opposite sex; problems of conflicting loyalties to friends and to moral standards; nuclear weapons and the colour bar; the care of the old and thalidomide babies. Problems such as these, and others mentioned in Chapter 7, come up clearly in any discussion about human beings which is more than skin deep. They lend themselves to treatment in the same kind of way as many of the themes already discussed in this chapter. Good teaching may often involve contact with those working outside the school. These contacts should be welcomed; they are part of the process of relating the school to the world. But this kind of contact is not the whole of the answer. Christianity is not to be defined as the religion of Englishmen. It is sometimes difficult for boys and girls to realize this and what it implies. They can be helped to do this if, for instance, they are brought into contact with the problems of Christians who lapsed under Mau Mau persecution and have since wished to come back to their faith. What line should the Church take? This was a burning question in the first Christian centuries; it still is. It cannot be solved

without probing deeply into the heart of man and the heart of the Christian religion; to observe Africans answering it is sometimes to shame ourselves.

517. In some schools it may be possible to bring the school's religious instruction into close association with the social studies with which this chapter has been mainly concerned. It should gain. But there is always need to remember the double conscience clause — the right of the pupil to be excused, the right of the teacher not to suffer professionally because he does not choose to give religious instruction. There is also a right of pupils to be taught. Until there is a much better supply of skilled and knowledgeable teachers the right to religious education at a true secondary level is bound in some schools to be little more than nominal.

Social Studies in Secondary Schools

CHARMIAN CANNON, 1964

For geography teachers anxious to preserve the identity of their subject in secondary schools this article by Cannon must have come as welcome relief. Her review of the rise and fall of the social studies movement is followed by a consideration of the causes for the failure of Social Studies which concludes with the statement 'a subject thus identified with the "non-academic" child has little chance of success in the English education system'. But this review is only a prelude to a plea for a new curricular innovation – a comprehensive course in the social sciences. This course would need well-defined content, academic rigour and clearly thought-out aims. It would also need specialist teachers with proper training in the social sciences. This in no way could be conceived as a take-over bid for the subject geography. Geographers could interpret it as a competitive subject competing for timetable space and thus comparable with economics and geology.

The recruitment of social scientists into secondary schools provided the academic expertise necessary for the development of new courses. This development has been traced by Rogers (1968) and Lawton and Dufour (1973). The publication of Cannon's article was soon followed by the setting up of the Association of Teachers of Social Science, one of a number of such associations which sought to promote new courses in secondary schools; others include the Politics Association, the Modern Studies Association and the General Studies Association.

Historical Survey

Ever since the Hadow Report's tentative statement 'The general character of the teaching should take account of the pupil's natural and social environment' (1927), successive reports on the secondary school curriculum have recommended that the education of adolescents should be more directly related to the realities of modern industrial society. In the post-war period such pleas have become more forceful and specific as in the N.U.T.'s proposal in 1952, that children should study 'life in the community, the growth and establishment of customs, of the material factors on which it depends for its existence, of the relationship between the individual and the community, and of the economic, social and cultural relationships of national and international communities' (N.U.T. 1952); a task which calls for a comprehensive course in the social sciences.

There seem to have been two main motivations behind this desire for more social relevance in the curriculum; the desire to educate citizens for democracy, and the sometimes dimly felt urge to equip young people to cope with the complex environment in which they will find themselves on leaving school. One or other of these is dominant in the literature at different periods. Starting during the 1930s, increasing during the crisis of war, and reaching its peak in the immediate post-war period, public discussion was preoccupied with the challenge to democracy. As is usual in such circumstances, education was expected to save the nation by producing the right values and attitudes; thus in 1945, 'totalitarianism has convinced of the need to make future citizens love democracy, the need for faith in the democratic ideals of freedom, justice, kindness, self-sacrifice and truth must be brought out over and over again' (The Council for Curriculum Reform 1945). Young citizens must not only be loyal to democracy, but must be educated for world citizenship by the cultivation of an international outlook; for 'we have reached a crisis that may bring civilization down' (Ministry of Education 1949).

The second view, that young people need to be more adequately equipped for modern life, has been part of the general post-war preoccupation with the problems of adolescence which has accompanied the growth of youth culture in the affluent society. There are several levels of argument here; first, the practical one, that school-leavers should be aware of the facilities and opportunities of their local community; second, there is the stress on the inculcation of fixed standards in a world of shifting moral values (Ministry of Education 1947); and third, the belief that it is possible to educate for social change in a more direct sense by encouraging the flexibility necessary to profit from and guide new social movements (Mannheim 1943).

In the immediate post-war period, many of these suggestions were based on a somewhat superficial analysis of the social situation of youth, but they were lent increasing urgency by the establishment of 'secondary education for all' in 1944, the raising of the school-leaving age, and the increasing focus on further education, all of which presented educationists with the problem of retaining the involvement in their schooling of non-academic adolescents looking forward to the adult world.

There has thus been some broad agreement about the ends to be sought by the new approach to education, but the means were not so clear. Some writers did not presume to make practical suggestions but left the approach to the imagination of the teachers. There was a solid body of opinion, dominant in the pre-war period, but not restricted to it, who took the 'traditional' view; that preparation for life would be best achieved through the conventional subjects wisely taught, and citizenship developed through its practice in the microcosm of the school community. The Norwood Report (1943) was perhaps the supreme example of this approach; the claims of new subjects to equip pupils for modern life, were rejected in the report on the ground that children could not be forced into experience beyond them, and were not ready to think as citizens: 'the most valuable influence for developing that sense of responsibility without which any amount of sheer information is of little benefit is the general spirit and outlook of the school — what is sometimes called the "tone" of the school'.

In the post-war period the traditional approach still had its advocates, but there was an increasing expression of the opinion, only tentatively expressed earlier, that the content of traditional subjects should be selected with a greater eye to its relevance, and that subject-barriers should be broken down to produce a new synthesis. The Ministry of Education pamphlet *Citizens Growing Up* (1949) saw history and geography 'as the answer to the how and why of the local corporate life and of the national corporate life which is the subject matter of citizenship', but it carried further the tentative suggestions of Hadow, that these should be made relevant through local studies and practical work (Ministry of Education, 1949) and carried this approach into its discussion of other parts of the curriculum.

This synthetic idea reflected, besides the motivation to introduce social relevance into the curriculum, the 'progressive movement' arising from the pragmatic influence in the 1930s; this was concerned to introduce a method more suited to the finding that children learn through experience rather than by the passive reception of facts. Subject barriers were looked on as artificial and the attempt was made to replace them by a series of 'topics' arising from the children's interests and drawing on material from all subject areas.

The third approach to the problem came from those who advocated the addition of new subjects to the curriculum, specifically selected for their social relevance: the Association for Education in Citizenship as early as the 1930s advocated the addition of economics and politics to the curriculum and rejected the assumption that one could expect an automatic 'transfer of training' from the traditional subjects (Association for Education in Citizenship 1935). In an interesting post-war investigation the Association surveyed experiments in the inclusion of psychology, politics, philosophy and logic in the sixth forms of grammar schools, and their relevance for the General papers of 'A' level (Association for Education in Citizenship 1949). The weakness of this approach lay in its practical application to the already overcrowded timetable of examination dominated secondary schools.

Social Studies
The culmination of the 'synthetic' and the 'additional subjects' schools of thought was to be found in the social studies movement of the immediate post-war years. It was reflected in official publications, textbooks for teachers, and articles in journals; and in the curricular experiments of the secondary modern schools which were supposed to be providing the 'New Secondary Education' untrammelled by examination requirements.

The tone was set by the post-war Ministry of Education pamphlets (1947 and 1949) which advocated a freer approach to the subjects of the curriculum with citizenship in mind; and a new approach to method through the project, which involved 'the collection and collation of facts, the consultation of sources of knowledge, the interpretation of evidence, the establishment of principles from particular examples, the analysis and synthesis involved, the realization that the requirements of an investigation demand at some stage the mastery of a technique before further progress can be made': a method which has come to be identified with social studies.

The synthetic approach was reflected in texts such as Nicholson (1949): 'What we now call Social Studies . . . is a synthesis: a broad highway to a working knowledge of Life in its widest sense. The quality of Social Studies differs from the isolated subject teaching . . . in being Discovery . . . of those aspects of life related to the experience of children.' But perhaps the most extreme exposition was to be found in Hemming's *The Teaching of Social Studies in Secondary Schools* (1949). His social studies 'combine the material of history, geography and civics together with relevant material from other subject fields, into a single integrated background course'.

The most disciplined statement of the need for Social Studies was however to be found in the Council for Curriculum Reform's answer (1945) to 'the well-meaning platitudes' of the Norwood Report (1943). The whole aim of their report was 'to make the content of our education more relevant to the present age'. The criterion for the inclusion of any subject matter in the curriculum was to be its relevance to meet modern social conditions and probable future trends. On this basis the social sciences were assured of a prominent place; they were to be based on general social studies taught by topics in the lower part of the school, giving way later to history taught for its relevance to modern life, economics, politics and social ethics.

The concern of practising teachers over these new approaches was reflected in articles on their difficulties and experiences in teaching social studies, and in books about the work of specific secondary schools (Happold 1935, Greenough and Crofts 1949, Mander 1948).

The Failure of Social Studies

This period of post-war enthusiasm and experiment had faded by the mid-1950s, by which time many schools appear to have returned to a traditional curriculum. The reports of several overseas teachers who came to this country to observe the teaching of social studies, were unanimous that there was a general air of disillusion and discontinuation of such teaching (Moore 1957 and Oliver 1954). One of these reports that replies he received from 30 Education Officers reflected the opinion that Social Studies was losing ground (Oliver 1954), and many teachers are reported to have returned to the more traditional approach after only brief experiment. 'A good many alternatives to "straight" history have made their appearance in the last decade or two, though not so many have survived' (Bramwell 1962).

What were the reasons for this failure of the new courses to become an established part of the curriculum? Most important probably were the social and economic pressures which led to an increasing concern for standards, and in particular to their expression in examination qualifications. Since 1947 there has been a steady increase in candidates for external examinations coupled with the growth of specialized and extended courses. These may be seen partly as an attempt by the secondary modern schools to close the 'status' gap dividing them from grammar schools, and partly as a response to the occupational demands of society (Taylor 1963). The trend culminates in the recent acceptance of the Certificate of Secondary Education at a level lower than GCE which is a reversal of the ideals expressed in the immediate postwar period.

Further reasons lay in the amorphous nature of 'Social Studies' itself. We have already seen how it had taken the form of a synthesis of existing subjects, a new approach to method, or the addition of one or more of the social sciences to the curriculum. Any teacher might be excused if he felt overwhelmed by the prospect of giving a child 'a complete and rounded understanding of his environment, how it came into being, and how he may establish relations with it'. This aim, put forward in a contemporary text, was seen to involve a content of twenty topics, ranging from 'The Pattern of the Universe' ... to 'the way forward from mankind', by way of 'the development ... of human society from prehistoric times ... the rise and fall of civilizations and struggle between powers, growth towards unity, man as an individual and social being' (Point 4) (Hemming 1949).

The content of Social Studies was thus variously defined, and sometimes included 'social education', sex education, and religious education (Brimble and May 1943). It was all things to all men, and its supporters claimed that this was its virtue, because its lack of definition made it suited to a changing world (Wright 1950), and anyway it was a 'technique of teaching an attitude of mind' not a body of knowledge.

The subject was as all-embracing in its aims as in its content. Hemming drew up a list of 10 objectives, of which No. 6 was: 'to foster the development of spontaneity, self-reliance, flexibility of mind, clear thinking, tolerance, initiative, articulateness, adventurousness of outlook, courage in the face of new problems, enjoyment of creative activity, sound standards of action and appreciation, world-mindedness, a sense of purpose, and a philosophy of life' (Hemming 1949). Most advocates are less ambitious, but put foremost among their aims the need to educate for citizenship, and to integrate young people into the community. The Council for Curriculum Reform (1945) draws a parallel with the primitive rites of initiation, in seeing the purpose of social studies as 'social initiation' into the community and the democratic way of life.

The teacher faced with such aims and subject-matter was in a worse predicament as he was rarely trained for the task. He was likely to be a conventionally trained historian or geographer, very rarely a sociologist or social anthropologist, and often a general subjects teacher in a secondary modern school. But the enthusiasts for social studies told him not to despair:

'the qualities required in a teacher of Social Studies are personal rather than academic. The chief requirement is a fervent belief and interest in life and man, and in youth as the growing point of civilization' (Hemming 1949).

While these reactions against over-specialization and the often arid method and content of traditional teaching deserve some sympathy, it is not surprising that teachers found the new ideals hard to follow. There was plenty of criticism of the social studies to be found in the writings of historians and geographers of the post-war period, who saw the new proposals as a threat to the integrity and status of their own subjects; and some (but surprisingly little) disquiet from sociologists who deplored the lack of that discipline which their own subject could have lent to the new approach. One can only conclude with one writer in 1950 that 'Perhaps Social Studies has raised its voice too loudly before it was confident that it knew what to say' (Stewart).

A final reason for the failure of Social Studies; because of the vagueness of its content, and its crossing of traditional barriers, combined with the increasingly rigid examination structure, the new experiments were mostly confined to the younger and less academic pupils; for them the new method if not the content, sometimes provided a more positive motivation towards school; but a subject thus identified with the 'non-academic' child has little chance of success in the English education system.

The Present Position in Social Studies Teaching

In recent years there have been many restatements of the need to relate the curriculum to modern society; perhaps the most sophisticated example is to be found in the Crowther Report's analysis of the social situation and needs of the post-war adolescent.

The modern justification has changed its emphasis; there is no longer the feeling of post-war urgency which led to insufficiently thought out pleas for citizenship education; rather the problem is seen in terms of helping adolescents to deal with the complexities of their social situation, and in particular to withstand the pressures of the mass media. Thus, the evidence to the Newsom Committee though very varied in practical suggestions, is almost unanimous in this: '... young people ... can hardly be aware of all the pressures that are brought to bear on them through the media of mass advertising and mass entertainment. It is the clear and urgent duty of social education to develop their critical faculties and exercise their powers of discrimination' (Hemming 1949, McNichol 1946).

In spite of these advocates, it is clear that at the moment little is being done to implement the need for a contemporary approach. There are some interesting experiments in comprehensive schools, but these tend to lack guidance and unity, and are too often confined, as previously, to the less able children in the middle school; for the examination pressures which helped to bring the downfall of the earlier movement towards social studies, are no less evident to-day. A survey of the curriculum of non-selective secondary schools in south-east England, after a fervent plea for relevance, and a recognition of the possibilities for building a curriculum around 'the rich complexities of modern life', still concludes that, 'Content and method ... remains largely traditional, with the assumption of transfer to the contemporary scene'.

The Teaching of the Social Sciences in Secondary Schools
So the field is wide open; but if the gap between school and life is to be bridged, and the pitfalls of earlier attempts avoided, the following conditions must be fulfilled:

(1) The work must have a well-defined content which can be adapted for pupils of a wide range of ages in a variety of educational situations.

(2) It must possess enough academic rigour to avoid Riesman's cogent criticism of American courses, that they are 'sheer piety or ... social slops' (Reisman 1958); an accusation which is unfortunately also relevant in England.

(3) The aims must be clearly thought out and conceived in less manipulative terms than good citizenship, or 'education for identification' (Council for Curriculum Reform 1945).

It is suggested that these requirements can be fulfilled by the introduction of the social sciences into the schools, the content being selected from whatever is applicable at the school level, of the social sciences as taught in the universities. Although the boundaries of such content are not clear (any more than the boundaries of older established subjects) they would include social psychology, social history, social and political philosophy and social economics. The core lies however in sociology and social anthropology, and the method followed would be essentially the same as at university level, that is, it would not allow the pupil to escape from the difficulties of trying to apply a scientific rigour to the study of societies.

Some of the subject matter of such a course has been included in earlier 'Social Studies' syllabuses, but it has been blurred by the inclusion of so much else, and rarely approached in a disciplined way; in fact one has the impression from studying the literature, that many of the advocates of a more relevant curriculum have been groping towards the content and methods of sociology, but have stopped short of it because they were not aware that a disciplined approach to such content existed. This is hardly surprising when sociology has only so recently established itself even at university level, and the supply of sociologists in the schools is still negligible.

It may be complained that the range of material is still vast; but it should not be difficult to derive from it more limited syllabuses, suited to the interests of children of different ages and abilities, which would avoid on the one hand the narrow dreariness of many 'local studies', and on the other the nebulous vastness of the world and the universe; for example a valuable introduction to contemporary society would be afforded by the study of comparative social institutions, social stratification, and the social structure of contemporary Britain. It would thus introduce subject matter which is of immediate relevance; but would make extensive use of comparative material, both historical and from different societies.

The teachers would attempt to fulfil specific aims, more modest than those of Social Studies and thus more capable of attainment. It would of course be an admirable vehicle for practical and group methods, but these are not to be equated with social science, which can in fact be taught in a highly academic and individualistic manner. It would also satisfy the need, now firmly established, to replace a vague 'hope of transfer' by a direct study of contemporary society; it would, moreover, not only bridge the gap between school and society, but between the arts and the sciences; and is therefore an essential '3rd-voice' to add to the controversy over the 'two cultures'.

'Clearly schools must do everything in their power to help these young people to become literate and numerate ... where the Crowther Committee added *numerate* to *literate*, we would add *sociate* to both ...' (L.C.C. evidence to the Newsom Committee).

As far as relating young people to society is concerned, the emphasis on 'integration' and 'identification' must be changed to what Mannheim called 'social awareness'. This by no means implies acceptance of society as it is, but seeks to establish the ability 'to see the whole situation in which one finds oneself, and not only to orientate one's actions on immediate tasks and purposes, but to base them on a more comprehensive vision. One of the ways in which awareness expresses itself is in the correct diagnosis of a situation ...' (Mannheim 1943).

The task of the teacher therefore, is to present, or show children how to discover, a wide range of facts about society and their own position in it; the teaching would help them to distinguish between facts and opinions, and reveal the gaps in our knowledge which have yet to be filled. The values the pupil forms are finally his own concern, but the teacher must try to see that he has the facts upon which to base them, and can distinguish which are most relevant to the decisions he must make. This aim is difficult enough to achieve in a highly stratified society in which the children arrive at school 'crammed full of values ... but very shy on facts' (Reisman 1958). But they will only be at all possible, if throughout the work, stress is laid upon the methods of the social sciences. As long ago as the Spens Report, a plea was being made for 'stress on logical thought and scientific method', but this was in mathematics and science; the social sciences apply such rigour to society itself, and it is in this field that pupils must appreciate it. This does not mean that the subject will be reduced to statistical tables, for it would be an arid approach to society which ignored historical and literary sources, and the use of the 'sociological imagination'; but the pupils must be made aware of the limitations, as well as the insights to be gained from such material, and constantly brought face to face with the complexity of the evidence needed to come to any conclusions about the functioning of societies.

A knowledge of the techniques of the social sciences becomes of increasing importance in a complex society which constantly employs them in its practical affairs. The Crowther Report reiterates that 'knowledge and discrimination are necessary pre-requisites of a democratic community'. This must also involve the ability to analyze the term 'democracy', question its assumptions, and recognize areas of society in which it fails to operate. In this sense only social science teaching can claim to be education for citizenship.

These aims can only be achieved if the subject is taught, at least to older pupils, by specialists; that is by teachers trained at university level (and later by the provision of good training college courses) in the social sciences. This is not to say that an able historian, economist or English specialist would not have much to contribute (indeed it is through history and English that progressive teachers are already beginning to introduce a sociological perspective); nor is it to decry the tendency to break down narrow specialist boundaries which is becoming the hall-mark of the new universities; but only to claim, as do other academic subjects, that the work must be guided by those who have become aware in sufficient depth, not only of the content of social science, but of its philosophical background and distinctive method.

Finally, the justification of teaching any subject at the school level, must lie in its value as a liberal education. Social science has all the necessary elements: a subject matter which is not only increasingly relevant, but intrinsically fascinating; a tradition of classical works as worth studying for their contribution to man's thoughts on the human conditions as are the classics of literature; and a disciplined approach which is the essence of liberalism. For the extent to which a field of study contributes to a liberal education depends finally on the way it is taught.

'To the extent that a student becomes aware of the methods he is using, and critically conscious of his presuppositions, he learns to transcend his speciality and generates a liberal outlook in himself.'

Curriculum Integration

RICHARD PRING, 1970

It is clear that discussion about the integration of subjects can proceed without reference to schools or children. The discussion can be kept on a strictly substantive plane and a variety of new subject structures can be produced by such discussion. In school terms however the discussion must acknowledge the problems besetting the teacher who seeks to motivate the pupil towards particular subjects and modes of learning associated with those subjects. Pring argues in this article that 'any particular recommendation for curriculum integration implies some underlying theory of knowledge or of value or of learning, and that to explain what one means by integration necessarily involves one in such theoretical considerations'. He goes on to identify reasons which might underly proposals for curriculum integration and in the readings in the third section of this book we find these reasons appearing as teachers and others describe courses in schools. Few teachers will consciously analyse the theoretical bases for the integrated courses they design and teach, and Pring's reasoning should serve to draw attention to matters of principle which are of considerable importance. The philosopher's approach is obviously different from that of the sociologist, as the article by Musgrove (Reading 18) demonstrates. Pring's apparent objectivity is supplemented by Skilbeck's article (Reading 17).

There is no doubt that integration is an 'in' word. Plowden and Newsom recommended it; junior schools have their 'integrated day'; 'interdisciplinary enquiry' features in many secondary schools; colleges prepare junior/secondary students for interdisciplinary learning situations; the Schools Council publishes examples of good 'integrated approaches'; and there is talk of the 'seamless cloak of knowledge', the 'unity of learning', or 'a single view of the world and of life', all of which, so we are told, can be reflected adequately only in an integrated curriculum.

Integration is also a 'pro'-word. It is contrasted with the *fragmentation* of the curriculum which typifies the *traditional* school, with subject *barriers*, the *compartmentalization* or *pigeon-holing* of knowledge, with specialization and *irrelevance* to life as a whole. Rather is it connected with the *natural* enquiry of children which does not respect subject divisions.

To be both an 'in' word and a 'pro' word has its dangers. Educational theory is rife with such words: 'growth', 'needs of the child', 'creativity', and so on. They play a significant part in much educational argument, are often accepted uncritically, and have an emotive meaning that dares anyone to challenge the educational aims which they embody. (Who for example would be against children growing, developing their personalities, fulfilling their needs, or even creating?) 'Integration' is quickly becoming such a word. Who would object to knowledge or personality or life being 'integrated'? Unity, integration, wholeness seem to have a fascination and value of their own. But what do they mean? 'Integration' as such is an empty word. There must be integration of something and one cannot really understand or appreciate what is meant by curriculum integration until one has clarified what it is that is being integrated. Yet to clarify this is by no means easy. It raises important questions in epistemology and ethics. Failure to see these questions, let alone to attempt an answer to them, renders a lot of writing on curriculum integration superficial in its agrument and confusing in its practical recommendations. What I would wish to argue at much greater length is that any particular recommendation for curriculum integration implies some underlying theory of knowledge or of value or of learning, and that to explain what one means by integration necessarily involves one in such theoretical considerations. Because of the failure of so many educationists to understand this, the word integration is bandied about as though its meaning were clear, and recommendations for curriculum integration are made as though its value were self-evident. Here however I can only indicate why its meaning is not clear, why its value is not self-evident, and why therefore there is a need for a much closer analytic and critical examination of 'integrated' programmes if education is not to be sacrificed to yet more conceptual muddle and practical confusion.

Curriculum integration is frequently contrasted with the 'compartment-alization' of knowledge which, apparently, is characteristic of the 'traditional' syllabus. A subject-based curriculum is said to limit enquiry, set up barriers, and confine study to a limited range of information. Often these barriers are seen to be arbitrary or simply conventional, and the integration of subjects is seen as a necessity if there is to be a 'truer', more comprehensive picture of reality. For, so it is argued, the division of knowledge into distinct subject division is artificial and does not reflect correctly the essential unity of reality and of our ordinary way of understanding and judging. It is foreign to the natural and spontaneous (words that frequently crop up in this context) method of enquiry. What is important for the school to do is to encourage 'enquiry' (and enquiry knows no limits) and for this purpose to provide a 'rich' and 'stimulating' environment.

At this stage however it is necessary for the 'integrationalist' to pause awhile and to examine a little more closely the case put forward by those who wish to retain a curriculum that is largely subject based, for the 'specialists' would argue that the distinctions between subjects are not arbitrary at all and that to blur or ignore these distinctions is to debase any claim to knowledge. To pursue this argument further would raise questions in.

the theory of knowledge that can be dealt with, in the limits of this paper, only in the most superficial way. But some attempt must be made to pinpoint where the issues lie.

Understanding (and education would seem to be about the development of the understanding) lies in the formation of conceptual schemes that consist in the organization, discrimination, and interpretation of experience so that it can be expressed and communicated symbolically. The development of meaning is the development of this symbolic organization characterized by certain general concepts and modes of inference and by certain accepted canons of verification and enquiry. Outside these unifying principles of experience there can be no meaning. No enquiry can take place except within a particular system of thought, and this involves recognizing the implicit rules of procedure built into the acceptance of *this* system rather than another. In a way it does not make sense to talk of children simply making an enquiry. It must be an enquiry of a certain sort. As soon as one 'enquires', one is involved in the use of symbols which already dictate, as it were, what moves are correct or at least permissible. Any enquiry must involve the meanings revealed at different levels within one or other of the disciplines. This is a logical point — it follows from what one *means* by mind, rational behaviour, and hence enquiry. The subjects on the curriculum, so this argument goes, are there because among other things they initiate the pupil into the different modes of understanding that are characterized by distinct organizing concepts, principles of verification, and logical connexions. Far from being merely conventional or arbitrary, they represent in their distinct disciplines of thought what it is to think, to know and to enquire (Hirst 1965, Phenix 1964).

I am not wanting to defend this thesis against the advocates of curriculum integration. I wish merely to say that it is with such a thesis they must deal if they are to suggest that subject divisions are merely conventional or arbitrary. They must argue either that such is a false theory of knowledge or that it is not a complete account of knowledge and that the recognition of autonomous disciplines needs to be supplemented by some form of integration within the curriculum.

Where the second line of argument is adopted, there can be distinguished quite different theoretical reasons for proposing curriculum integration, although in practice the reasons are rarely made clear. Firstly, integration might be argued for as follows. No proposition or argument of any enquiry is, admittedly, without a logical structure which can be identified as such and which determines to some extent the role it can play in the enquiry. One knows that a given proposition is, say, an empirical claim to truth within a certain conceptual structure and that the test of truth or falsity of this kind of proposition is such and such. One knows that a particular argument implies certain criteria of validity and one can compare this argument with the norms assumed by it. Nonetheless many problems including those of considerable personal importance cannot be raised, let alone answered, within any one cognitive structure. Different sorts of enquiry have to be brought to bear upon a particular problem. Sex education, or giving adequate answers to practical questions raised about sexual behaviour, is an obvious example. No one discipline can claim a monopoly of the sorts of consideration relevant to the determination of practical principles. In many areas of understanding, especially where practical decisions have to be made, the integration of distinct disciplines of thought is essential yet cannot logically be given within any one discipline. The putting together of the distinctive enquiries represented by the disciplines is itself an educational task that should have a place within the curriculum. In other words, one might recognize the autonomy of different bodies of knowledge while at the same time recognizing the problems inherent in their synthesis. And one might make provision in the curriculum for this synthesizing element by concentrating, for at least part of the time, on areas of thought and decision-making where such an integration is indispensable. One would, as it were, learn to integrate by integrating (just as one learns to teach by teaching (Pring 1970b)).

A second line of reasoning for some degree of curriculum integration might be summarized as follows. The disciplines represent the worked out structures of knowledge, the systematic organization of experience, the particular conceptual schemes which determine how one classifies, individuates, and proceeds with yet further enquiry. The disciplines therefore constitute in the most complete and developed form the logical structure of knowledge. They do not however reflect the pupil's level and mode of understanding, nor do they indicate the process whereby the pupil might attain these structures of knowledge. For, on this line of argument, the finished product, tidied up into the logical neatness of distinct disciplines, does not contain within it the way in which it should be presented. All too often, we are told, the subject matter is presented in its completed and worked out form, and not in the manner through which it was worked out (Dewey 1946). On the other hand, if the student were allowed to pursue his own interests and to satisfy his own curiosity, he would raise questions which would gradually be refined into the precise systematization characteristic of the different disciplines of thought. The 'natural' curiosity of the pupil, his 'spontaneous' enquiry, would lead to the gradual differentiation of a conceptual structure that typified the worked out modes of understanding. Although the end product might be the different forms of knowledge, the educational process towards this goal would be an integrated activity, focused upon or united in the current interest or enquiry of the pupil.

Of course it may be argued that there are not distinct disciplines of thought, characterized by different modes of enquiry. Rather is all enquiry a matter of solving problems — one is in a sort of forked-road situation. First, one is puzzled how one might proceed. Secondly, as much relevant data as possible is gathered. Thirdly, a principle of procedure is tentatively formulated in the light of this data. Finally, this is put to the test and applied in practice. Either one's problem is solved or the principle is rejected, or at least reformulated. In any case there is always the same pattern to any enquiry and the resulting knowledge is essentially that of tentative hypothesis constantly tested and reformulated. The differentiation of knowledge into distinct modes characterized by different processes of enquiry and verification is dismissed. Enquiry is basically of the same pattern, though the resulting structures of understanding might be distinguished by their respective organizing concepts (as physics is distinguished from chemistry). But the method is the same, and if encouraged and pursued will provide the integrating factor in all the classroom activities.

Sometimes of course the pupil does not appear to be 'spontaneously' or 'naturally' curious. In such cases the pupil needs to be 'stimulated'. Interdisciplinary enquiry sometimes begins with a key lesson in which the pupil is given a battery of 'stimuli' in order to 'spark him off'. Ideas are scattered freely, possible lines of enquiry suggested, problems presented, questions asked. Themes or topics might be provided and these, if suggestive enough, will make good 'starters'. Having started, the pupil is free to travel in whatever direction he likes provided that in travelling he is raising questions that open his enquiring mind to yet new experiences and fresh connexions of ideas. Themes or starters in this sense are not intended to control or set limits to the enquiry, only to trigger it off.

A further sort of reason underlying some proposals for curriculum integration rises more from ethical than from epistemological or learning theory. To the question 'What is the aim of education?' an answer might be given in terms of the needs of the child or those of society. Such an answer does not raise the epistemological issues that I have been considering. Whatever its nature, knowledge is said to be of value in so far as it meets the needs of the pupil or is of social utility. The 'needs' of the pupils are listed (different books give different lists) and these become the unifying factors in determining the balance of the curriculum. Themes like 'Man and his environment' are subdivided into smaller themes such as 'Family', 'Home', 'Leisure', 'Work'. To study material within the ambit of such themes will, it is claimed, enlighten the pupil in matters relevant to his immediate needs. Often such a programme of enquiry will be called social studies in which history, geography, literature, religious knowledge, and other subjects are integrated within the particular theme and are thereby directed to shed light on the needs of the pupil (Rogers 1968).

It has beeen the purpose of this brief article not so much to justify or to criticize the different proposals for curriculum integration, but rather to indicate some of the different theoretical considerations which at different times underlie them. Curriculum integration is frequently pursued without any analysis of the nature of knowledge and therefore without any clear cognitive objectives. However, where there is such an analysis and where areas of autonomous studies are respected, integration may still remain an objective for curriculum planners for the quite different reasons that I have given and that I summarize here. Firstly, it is claimed, a mastery of the different disciplines is not all there is to knowledge; there is a further educative task of integrating the disciplines in so far as these are brought to bear upon a problem which cannot be fitted into the limits of any one discipline. Secondly, the curiosity and free enquiry of the pupil might be seen as the integrating factor and the final systematization of knowledge, manifest in the different disciplines, would be said to develop from such an enquiry. Thirdly it is held by some that the method of enquiry itself is unitary and that there is no theoretical justification for the proliferation of modes of understanding upon which the fragmentation of the syllabus is based. Fourthly, it is argued that the value of knowledge depends on the degree to which it satisfied the 'needs' of the individual or of society; 'needs' give direction and purpose, and thereby an integrating thread to the educational process. Fifthly, certain concepts such as 'power' and 'communications' are complex in meaning, are central to our thinking in the different disciplines of thought, need close scrutiny in themselves, and thereby offer fresh ways of entering into different areas of knowledge.

I have sought briefly to identify quite different reasons which might underlie proposals for curriculum integration. Not to recognize these distinctions which raise fundamental questions of epistemology and value is a source of confusion in practice. Let me in conclusion show how this can occur. It is a frequent practice in interdisciplinary enquiry to suggest (or impose) a theme which, instead of the traditional subject, will be the focus of study. But in the light of the distinctions that I have made in this article the theme might function in quite different ways. Firstly, it might in some way delineate an area in which practical decisions have to be made and which must therefore be a focal point of interdisciplinary thinking (e.g. sex, war, authority, etc.). Secondly, it might be the name for a complex of information which is thought relevant to the needs of the pupil or of society. Thirdly, it might through an association of ideas be a starting off point for enquiry. Fourthly, it might itself suggest a certain structured body of knowledge that needs to be mastered but which transcends the subject boundaries, and here one often hears talk of 'exploring a concept' (e.g. 'power'). Not to have clarified beforehand the function of the theme or concept may lead to a very confusing situation. It may be used simultaneously both to trigger off a line of enquiry and to set limits to the enquiry — and these are quite different functions, often in practice incompatible with each other.

Depending, too, on the particular conception of curriculum integration that one has, are such matters as the role of the teacher, the pattern of the school timetable, the use of resources, and so on. Current writing on the 'integrated day' suggests the need for a 'rich and stimulating environment'. Resources are rather like pep pills — stimulating, maintaining, and extending the pupil's interest. On the other hand where the centre of integration is an area which *ought* to be explored by the pupil or which is judged relevant to his human needs and concerns, the 'bank' of resources should be developed with these quite different reasons in mind. Items are chosen because of the lead they give along a pre-conceived line of enquiry rather than for the interest they arouse.

Curriculum integration is a much more complex notion than is often realized, not only in its conception but also in its effect upon teaching roles, use of time, organization of the school and the class-room, and so on. There is not opportunity here to enter into this in detail. Suffice to give some indication of this complexity and of the need to look much more closely at the deeper issues that lie beneath it.

Forms of Curriculum Integration

M. SKILBECK, 1972

In this article Skilbeck succinctly outlines a hierarchical structure of subject integration. The simplest level is defined as the retention of the subject-based curriculum in which teachers adopt the perspective of the integrationist. He asserts that some of the objectives of the curriculum integrationist 'may be achieved by sensitive subject teaching'. This is the belief of those teachers, and others, who insist that good teachers have always gone beyond the limits of their subjects and have engaged in forms of teaching which are superior to anything that can be achieved in formally integrated courses. The second level involves the creation of cross-subject structures in which the identity of the separate subjects survives. It is only in the third level that subjects are abandoned to be replaced by 'themes, ideas and world views'. Bernstein has characterized the movement through these levels as a change from education in depth to an education in breadth and he goes on to examine the implications of this for teachers. He writes: 'There has been a shift from a teaching role which is so to speak, "given" (in the sense that one steps into assigned duties), to a role which has to be *achieved* in relation with other teachers. It is a role which is no longer made but *has to be made.* The teacher is no longer isolated from other teachers, as where the principle of integration is the relation of his subject to a public examination. The teacher is now in a complementary relation with other teachers at the level of this day-by-day teaching' (Bernstein 1967). Skilbeck hints at these implications towards the end of this article and the theme is taken up again by Musgrove in Reading 18.

The progressive education movement of the inter-war years drew attention to pupil choice, the claims of children's expressed interests as a criterion for selecting curriculum content, and the educational value of a texture of interpersonal relationships in groups and small-scale communities (Stewart 1968). In recent years the collective movements which came to incorporate these and related aspirations have been criticised not only by Black Paper pamphleteers but also by philosophers of an analytic bent who have exposed the conceptual inadequacies of many of the progressive proposals and slogans. Criticisms have been directed at the related notions of the whole child, all-round growth, and the experience — or activity — centred curriculum. Philosophers and cognitive psychologists have offered us, instead of 'growth' and 'experience', a model of human action of which rationality in the form of reflective, intentional behaviour is the central feature. They have provided along with this model a programme for the cultivation of rationality through systematic study of discrete intellectual disciplines — history, mathematics and the like, a disciplines of knowledge curriculum. The new slogans are 'the structure of knowledge', 'disciplined inquiry', 'initiation into rationality in the form of the distinct domains of knowledge and experience' (Bruner 1966, Hirst and Peters 1970). The tradition deriving from Platonic and Aristotelian philosophy, has been revived by powerful groups of thinkers advocating strenuous study of the major domains of knowledge however they may be broken down for purposes of teaching and learning. Anything less is held to sell our pupils short even though it may have a superficial attraction resulting from its appeal to vocational, leisure and fun motivations (Tibble 1970).

Yet we have also witnessed during these years of enhanced intellectual rigor when traditional cognitive perspectives have been reaffirmed, a rapid growth in schools and colleges of a great variety of schemes of work which attempt to explore themes and issues across the disciplines. These schemes are often not simply inter-disciplinary investigations which preserve the integrity of the disciplines: conventional knowledge structures are often submerged in syllabuses which have no recognizable affinities with any particular set of subjects. Thus, we are presented in the arena of school practice with a wide array of approaches which, whatever their differences, have in common a dissatisfaction with the separateness of subject structures and discrete time blocks; hence the integrated day, or blocked timetabling, team teaching, mixed ability grouping, topic-based teaching, humanities and social studies programmes and, of course, general studies. Furthermore, despite the critical onslaughts of analytical philosophy, there continues to be amongst a handful of theorists an interest in the cultural ideal of the unity of knowledge — for example, the supposed methodological unity of the cultural and natural sciences, or the metaphysical doctrine of the ultimate oneness of nature and the potential harmony of all elements within nature. At a more familiar level, the educational slogan of the seamless coat of learning is intended to refer not only to the pupil's organization of his learning experience into some coherent repertoire of skills or unified perspective on life, but also, and critically, to the arbitrary and, in terms of cultural order, the disintegrating division of the curriculum itself into separate subjects. Proposals for the unity of knowledge and of culture are often vague and even mystical where they are not impossibly complex, but the aspiration to produce overarching principles of order in knowledge and experience is an enduring aspiration which every so often expresses itself in moves for curriculum reform.

Undoubtedly the analytic and what might be termed the synthetic approach to the problem of defining divisions within the curriculum are profoundly different in their assumptions and prescriptions. Yet for all their differences they do share an interest in wholeness. After all, the disciplines or domains of knowledge may be thought of as an all-embracing classification or a comprehensive overview. Again, the different disciplines are commonly differentiated according to common criteria such as the organization of central concepts, the different uses of the common concepts of evidence and validation of truth claims, and so forth. Similarly, supporters of more synthetic approaches either implicitly advance a comprehensive chart of knowledge and experience, but they are commonly more interested than are the disciplines' advocates in the use of this chart to promote awareness of relationships and some more or less mystical unity which it is important to grasp or apprehend as a whole. I should add, although it opens up issues which cannot be explored in a short paper, that exponents of the unity of knowledge frequently relate their criticisms of the splintering of the intellectual realm to a critique of socio-cultural disunity, or the breakdown of traditional order. The achievement of a unified understanding or cognitive perspective thus becomes part of a wider programme of cultural reintegration (Mannheim 1951).

However, this latter point has taken us some way from the commoner forms of curriculum integration. We may note several distinct positions any one of which supporters of curriculum integration are likely to adopt. Their positions range from some modest pedagogical propositions about the organization of learning experiences to the full-blown holistic theories.

In one very obvious sense, all teachers have an interest in promoting a more integrated view of the world in their pupils. This interest is expressed by any subject teacher who in innumerable teaching episodes relates one item in a learning sequence to another, e.g. as an illustration of an argument, in the development of a generalization or a norm, as a reinforcement of learning, or as a stimulus to further enquiry. It is of course common in such episodes to employ the method of contrast, making distinctions, pointing up differences as well as similarities. By each of the common teaching strategies of assimilation and differentiation, subject teachers who are promoting effective learning produce in their pupils understanding of wider and more coherent sets of relationships. In this manner, otherwise miscellaneous and unintelligible phenomena are organized as data in emerging systems of thought and action. To this extent, in acting as organizers of learning within clearly defined traditions of enquiry, subject teachers are practical advocates of one form of curriculum integration.

Much progress might be made if a policy could be pursued which set out to minimize impediments to integration in the sense I have been outlining. These impediments are real enough in the secondary school, in the form of rigid timetabling, the arbitrary alternation of one activity with another, lack of interchange in depth of ideas across subject departments, examination syllabuses built up in piecemeal fashion, lack of imaginativeness in teaching, and a heavy weight of unexamined assumptions about the purposes and directions of schooling. Work is of course proceeding in all of these areas but it is extremely uneven. Systematic reformism in an essentially subject-centred curriculum could produce many worthwhile results. From long experience we know that imaginative and resourceful teaching of any subject can facilitate in pupils powers of wide generalization, can stimulate them to seek for conceptual links and metaphorical resonances within their growing store of ideas, can promote the inter-penetration of theoretical and practical knowledge, can be the basis of wide-ranging and coherent maps of knowledge and experience. These are objectives of the curriculum integrationist which, it should not be forgotten, may be achieved by sensitive subject teaching. Because these objectives may be attained within a conventionally organized curriculum, I shall call this a first level of integration.

Enthusiasm for curriculum integration usually takes its adherents beyond this first level, of perspectivist teaching of separately timetabled subjects. More visible cross-subject structures are erected, for example combinations and concentrations of scientific and humanistic studies, yielding humanities or perhaps environmental studies, or social studies, or maybe technology. It is important to note that the logical coherence of the separate disciplines which are drawn upon in constructing these programmes may either be maintained (the historian has his say, then the biologist, and so on in an interdisciplinary course) or dissolved in topic- or problem-centred courses taught by polymaths or teams whose members abandon their particular subject identity. The step from the one to the other form of organization may appear not to signify very much, in the short run, in terms of school administration, but it is an important one all the same. It signifies the need for role changes, shifts in subject identities and in relationships with professional associations, and the possible breakdown of departmental structures. For theorists, the abandonment of a disciplinary form marks a shift from one conceptual system or enquiry model to another, from a curriculum intellectually grounded in the formal properties of the discrete disciplines to the much less clearly articulated realms of themes, problems, and unified world views. These world views consist essentially of some set of principles for determining content (e.g. that of voluntary engagement in learning through expressed pupil interest; fulfilling functional or normative social expectations; problem-solving approaches to social issues; building up a cultural map). But not only does this third level of curriculum organization call for the formulation of some clear principles for content selection and articulation; equally important for pedagogical discussion is a theory of enquiry comparable to that which the disciplines embody. The most fruitful for purposes of curriculum integration is Dewey's analysis of reflective thinking. This was designed as a general model of enquiry through which a practical integration of scientific problem-solving might be made available across the whole spectrum of curriculum activities (Dewey 1910 and 1938).

What I have suggested, then, is that in thinking about and planning for curriculum integration we might conceive a first level of the analysis of learning in which separately taught subjects are organized for transfer. Main purposes at this level include teaching pupils to relate phenomena, to generalize, and to rationalize their experience. At the second level, subject matter is visibly combined in curriculum programmes, for example in grouped or interdisciplinary courses often taught by teams. The disciplines of knowledge, at this level, provide subject matter, methods of enquiry, patterns of organization and a community of understanding which serve as recognizable data for interdisciplinary programmes. At the third level, a new kind of community of understanding replaces the separate communities of the disciplines of knowledge. Various new principles of organization emerge, e.g. the replacement of the logical categories of history, science and so on by schematizations of pupil characteristics and needs, and socio-cultural categories comparable to those used by historians of culture, anthropologists and sociologists (Smith, *et al.* 1957).

Obviously, the third level of integration opens up a very wide and complex range of issues, including the validity of the distinctions between psychological and logical principles of organization of subject matter (McCellan 1951). These I cannot explore here, but it should be noticed that in curriculum literature and practice it has become common to find a central, organizing principle for the third level integrated curriculum in one of three ways: arguments are adduced for the over-riding importance of (1) the culture sciences especially history, literature and cultural anthropology; (2) the natural sciences and their applications; (3) social functionalism, including life adjustment and vocational courses. There is nothing new about the search for a single central core of studies: for centuries the classical theory of grammar yielded a core of linguistic study about which other subjects, including mathematics and the sciences, could be grouped in a hierarchy of diminishing importance. Reference to this theory is a reminder that the reduction of a variety of modes of discourse to handmaidens to some central intellectual-political principle has at times seriously hampered the progress of thought and of political emancipation. Monolithic intellectual systems frequently degenerate into dogmas whose guardians serve as a clerisy of conservative socio-intellectual agents. There is a close parallel between this situation in education and religion and that other well-known form of integration, viz. ideology. All run the risk of achieving unity of outlook and action at the expense of diversity of behaviour and critical appraisal (Corbett 1965).

A further problem to bear in mind when operating at the third level of integration has to do with the social organization of knowledge in our society. Knowledge is typically organized into institutions and communities of scholars who share a common language of problem analysis and whose thinking informs teaching at all levels. Subject teaching in secondary schools is obviously nourished by this pattern of organization; for example teachers are able to identify, both in training and in their professional relationships, with active professional associations. Just as the intellectual structures at the third level of integration are novel and usually unclear except in very general outline, so is the supporting institutional and communitarian structure relatively underdeveloped.

These are difficulties but they are of no particular consequence unless determined efforts are being made to build up curricula at this third level of integration. The question that must be answered is, integration for what? Are the arguments primarily pedagogical in the more limited sense of devising efficient strategies of learning? Is it the intention that teachers should work more cooperatively and make more efficient use of their particular expertise? Are pupils to be taught to appreciate the similarities and overlappings of different areas of discourse? These kinds of questions can be tackled quite adequately at the first and second levels of integration that I have designated. But if it is the more shadowy ideals of the unity and order of culture and the inter-relationships of elements within the socio-cultural system that are being pursued, then it would be more appropriate to explore a core curriculum built around the major categories of cultural action. These categories include language, myth and belief systems, patterns of political institutions, work cultures, child-rearing and education, the maintenance of social order, the arts and scientific culture (Bruner 1966, Skilbeck 1970 and Broudy *et al.* 1964).

Despite the difficulties, there are arguments in favour of a core curriculum centred in the analysis of these and similar categories of action as they are experienced in the problem situations and patterned activities of contemporary life. In seeking to redress shortcomings, for the curriculum of the common secondary school, of the conventional array of academic disciplines and practical arts, we have two alternative strategies: to reform and adapt the existing model, or to develop a major alternative. A five-year cultural core, with options (which include the academic disciplines) is an alternative to reformism which could be fruitfully explored. In view of what I have said about the importance of the communitarian and institutional aspects of knowledge systems, such explorations would profit from the support of associations like the Association for Liberal Education and the General Studies Association.

Power and the Integrated Curriculum

FRANK MUSGROVE, 1973

In an earlier article Musgrove wrote perceptively: 'A subject is a social institution with its sense of identity and loyalty exacted from its members. In conflict with other subjects it defines its boundaries and its sphere of influence. Subjects are highly organized, hierarchic, bureaucratic. They are busy discovering reasons for their existence and importance. They develop their own defensive systems against encroachment' (Musgrove 1968). Having expressed this specialist position it is a short step to a more thorough exploration of the implications of curriculum integration for institutions and teachers. In this article he expresses in a scholarly and provocative style a sociological argument for a vigorous pluralism in the curriculum. This argument is likely to prove convincing for geography teachers in schools where geography is a respected established subject, and especially for the heads of geography departments in such schools; but Musgrove's approach will be viewed cynically by geography specialists in those schools where authoritarian heads are keen to introduce integrated courses, or where assistant teachers are working under heads of departments whose interpretation of school geography is either out-dated or ultra-progressive.

The odd fact about modern mass society is that it is ever less 'massified'. It is ever more pluralistic, decentralized, differentiated, heterogeneous — fragmented, if you will: varied, contrastive, and infinitely interesting. Its solidarity is not, in Durkheim's terms, mechanical, segmentary, based on sameness and linearity; it is organic, multidimensional, based on specialization and the division of labour. We need to look carefully and critically at all countervailing proposals for unification, homogeneity, synthesis and integration: whether political, ideological, organizational, cultural or intellectual. It is not simply that they tend to be boring: they are also dangerous. They are the foundation of monopolies and of undue concentrations of power. I am doubtful of unified and integrated curricula and corresponding organizational structures. I believe that they are as dangerous as they are finally inefficient. My plea is for pluralism in the world of organization and in the province of the mind.

The Roots of Specialization

The argument for subject specialization in the first half of this century was powerful, and it prevailed. It was not an argument about status and power — although we can see that these were involved; it was not even an argument about effective intellectual functioning. At root the argument was aesthetic: it was an argument about good taste. And good taste is a matter of selection, exclusion, constraint, discrimination. In 1946 Sir Richard Livingstone wrote: 'Any good education must be narrow . . . Education prospers by economy, by exclusion.' Anything less restricted would be offensive to finer sensibilities. 'Overcrowding, in education as in housing,' wrote Livingstone, 'means ill-health, and turns the school into an intellectual slum.' The good teacher is known by the number of subjects he refuses to teach. A. N. Whitehead had said much the same and for similar reasons. In his famous and influential *Aims of Education* (1932) he maintained: 'Mankind is naturally specialist . . . I am certain that in education, wherever you exclude specialism you destroy life.' Of course he made a famous attack on 'inert ideas', and this involved seeing ideas in different contexts, throwing them into new combinations. But his first educational commandment was this: 'Do not teach too many subjects'. And the final aim was aesthetic — it was an intellectual *style*, defined in terms of economy and restraint. Style, maintained Whitehead, is the 'peculiar contribution of specialism to culture'. And, indeed, more than that: 'Style is the ultimate morality of the mind'.

Neither the Spens *Report on Secondary Education* nor the Norwood *Report on Curriculum and Examinations* diverged significantly from these views. (The former was published in 1939, the latter in 1943.) The Spens Report maintained that each subject had its distinctive individuality and represented a unique intellectual tradition: they should not be 'unified' or otherwise 'fused'. The Norwood Report examined the concepts of an 'integrated' and a 'balanced' curriculum but found them largely meaningless. But both Reports were really counter-attacks: they were answering a case. The case had been presented by Dewey and largely accepted in the Hadow *Report on the Primary School* in 1931. It was in this Report, of course, that we have the famous pronouncement: 'The curriculum is to be thought of in terms of activity and experience rather than of knowledge to be acquired and facts to be stored'. At least with children of primary school age, traditional subjects had no place. I would not dissent from this view. But I believe it is closely connected with the remarkable power that a number of studies have shown primary school heads to wield over their staff. It is the head who makes the decisions and staff meetings are virtually unknown (Sharma 1963, Brown 1971). In the absence of an intellectual and organizational pluralism, I would expect no less.

Specialization and the division of labour were of interest to 17th and 18th century jurists and political theorists; they were of interest to 18th and 19th century economists, and to 19th and 20th century sociologists. Eighteenth-century political theorists were concerned to separate the judiciary, the executive and the legislature in the interest of efficiency and justice; 19th-century economists were concerned with the division of labour and productivity and profits; 20th-century sociologists have been concerned with problems of social cohesion and divisiveness. (Psychiatrists have been interested, too, seeing fragmented, repetitive work as a source of 'alienation' and mental ill-health (Fromm 1956).) But the philosophers of Fourth Century Athens and contemporary Britain were also interested in specialization in a way which has some relevance to my theme. Their interests have been in labelling and the classification of phenomena as an aid — indeed a prerequisite — of efficient and systematic thought.

It is often said that life and its problems are not neatly divided into nicely bounded subjects: they are multidisciplinary, even interdisciplinary. The curriculum should reflect this reality. But life is a bad teacher, for the simple reason that it *is* interdisciplinary and confusing. It needs sorting out. Of course, the language we learn in infancy helps us to do a lot of preliminary sorting out; and when a language is adjectivally rich a great deal of subtle sorting and re-sorting is possible. We do not need to regard black cows as a wholly different category from white cows. But language is not enough. In spite of Illich and the de-schoolers, we also need schools. Their job, essentially, is to bring some sort of order out of the bombardment of impression and experience to which real life exposes us.

The Sumerians erected one of the earliest civilizations on lists. In a rather crude way they wrote down on their tablets lists of things that seemed to belong together (Childe 1942). The Greeks made better lists, based on more subtle and rational criteria. Both the natural and the social sciences have important, even fundamental, classifactory functions. The first social science was law, and it was quite properly a matter of codes. Efficient codification lies at the heart of efficient intellectual activity; and I would not think it demeaning to speak of teaching and learning as 'decoding'.

Our contemporary philosophers have also been busy sorting out, putting together things that belong together. Paul Hirst distinguishes between 'forms' and 'fields' of knowledge. 'Forms' — like mathematics, science and history — have unique conceptual schemes and tests of truth and falsehood: they can be discovered and isolated by logical analysis; 'fields' — like geography and engineering — are in some sense 'artificial', drawing on different forms of knowledge to illuminate a particular class of phenomena. The boundaries of fields and forms are differently drawn, but they are boundaries nonetheless. And Hirst is very cautious about lowering, removing or re-drawing these boundaries in the interest of some greater synthesis. Forms of knowledge have boundaries and are autonomous. Hirst (1966) concludes, 'It is not at all clear what is meant by synthesizing knowledge achieved through the use of logically quite different conceptual schemes.'

Our contemporary zeal for synthesis and curriculum integration has many sources: Bloom's famous taxonomy of educational objectives (Bloom 1956) is now perhaps more influential than Dewey's pragmatism. Objectives rise hierarchically, as you know, from a humble 'knowledge of facts' to the pinnacle of 'synthesis'. I would not regard really knowing a fact as a humble accomplishment; but Bloom's allegedly ascending order of intellectual operations suggests that all our endeavours should aspire to the condition of synthesis. This famous taxonomy has been used to legitimize the most unlikely hybrid degree courses in our newer universities. It is assumed that Bloom's taxonomy applies universally to all subjects of study. I have doubts about the ordering of Bloom's objectives; I have graver doubts about their general applicability.

Boundaries and the Division of Labour

Formerly a hybrid was something of a bastard; today it is received in the most polite circles. I have phrased this in socio-moral terms, because at bottom the issue we are dealing with is moral. It is about the immorality of boundaries. The concept of a boundary is one of the most discreditable in contemporary consciousness. The immorality of boundaries is central to the complex of values which we call the counter-culture. It finds its supreme expression in encounter groups, and similar social exercises in boundary removal. The counter-culture is essentially tactile: touch has replaced death as the Great Leveller and academic hierarchies are stroked to extinction. Drugs remove the boundaries of normal experience. The first injunction of the counter-culture is to 'blow your mind'.

Now in a general way I strongly support the counter-culture and the complex of values which it promotes. This is the curriculum of the future: essentially expressive rather than rational-instrumental, tactile rather than verbal, contemplative rather than active, sensationalist and psychedelic rather than cerebral and devoted to restrained good taste. But this is for the future: appropriate to the social order we may have by the end of the century. In 1972 it is an exploratory curriculum for a highly gifted minority. At this point in time we must have some concern for system-maintenance. It is, regrettably, as a system-maintenance man that I talk today. I am talking about schools and academic systems as we know them; but by the end of the decade this may be a complete irrelevance.

Boundaries are of interest not only to philosophers and moralists but also to sociologists. Indeed, fashionable role theory is essentially about boundaries (and in the counter-culture the notion of a defined social or occupational role is as discreditable as the notion of a boundary (Reich 1971) — for the same reason). But boundaries have interested sociologists as sources of social solidarity or division. And this is precisely the issue in discussion of the curriculum: the alleged 'fragmentation of knowledge'. I shall argue that respect for the autonomy of subjects is neither intellectually nor socially divisive; and that it is a vital defence against centralized autocracy. The division of labour does not divide; it cements.

Subject specialization is simply one instance of the division of labour.

Emile Durkheim wrote about the general problem and the specific instance in 1893 (Durkheim, in translation, 1933). He was discussing the question of social solidarity — the basic problem of sociology, the nature of the social bond. He distinguished between mechanical solidarity based on sameness, 'a system of segments homogeneous and similar to each other'; and organic solidarity based on differentiation and the division of labour. There was no doubt in Durkheim's mind that organic solidarity was superior: the more developed, advanced, even the more moral, form of social bonding. Mechanical solidarity was like an earthworm: its rings, all alike, juxtaposed in simple, linear array. By contrast, organic societies, 'are constituted, not by a repetition of similar, homogeneous segments, but by a system of different organs each of which has a special role, and which are themselves formed of differentiated parts.'

Durkheim's prime example of the efficacy of organic solidarity was modern marriage: conjugal solidarity based on the sexual division of labour. Here was no advocacy of unisex or even Women's Lib. (as I understand it). Marriage is strong and stable when there is a marked division of labour between men and women: 'Permit the sexual division of labour to recede below a certain level and conjugal society would eventually subsist in sexual relations pre-eminently ephemeral'. (Of course this begs the question whether we actually want strong and stable marriage: the counter-culture would deny this. But one thing that will be extremely problematical when the counter-culture generally prevails is the nature of the social bond.)

More than a century before Durkheim, Rousseau had attacked (in the *Social Contract*) the division of labour and the money economy that made it possible. It was the certain way to servitude in the sense of the dependence of everyman upon everyman. Durkheim also noted the interdependence, and applauded it. The division of labour, he maintained, 'passes far beyond purely economic interests, for it consists in the establishment of a social and moral order *sui generis*. Through it, individuals are linked to one another. ... Instead of developing independently they pool their efforts'. Rousseau's prescription was for individual self-sufficiency and social anarchy. So too, in the last resort, is the integrated curriculum.

Durkheim recognized that the division of labour had certain pathological forms — in the world of industrial production, and in the world of learning. Extreme forms of academic specialization led to an 'anomic' condition of the division of labour. Different specialists, said Durkheim in 1890, 'proceed with their investigations as if the different orders of fact they study constituted so many independent worlds. In reality, however, they penetrate one another from all sides. ...' I am sure Durkheim was correct to call this condition 'anomic' and to deplore it as a pathological state. The division of labour normally has a contrary effect: it pulls people together. What I think we need to know much more about are the stages and levels of an academic subject at which interpenetration with others naturally occurs. Interpenetration is probably maximal at the very early advanced stages of study: in the primary school and the postgraduate department. We see the relevance of other subjects when we have reached the boundaries of our own and push through them. It is true that the most exciting and creative work is occurring today on the boundaries between subject areas; but this is very advanced work that we are talking about. At lower levels, interdisciplinary work is more likely to lead to naïve and inappropriate transfer of concepts. Terms like 'feedback' and 'programming' are today ubiquitous. When we transfer concepts we are usually inventing metaphors. Metaphors have their uses; but we delude ourselves and our students if we think they correspond precisely with reality. (Sociology is largely a gigantic metaphor; but I am sure Durkheim knew — and I hope we do, too — that society, however 'solidaire', is neither a machine nor an organism.)

Durkheim certainly knew the difficulty of curing the pathological condition he had diagnosed. He had no faith in adding liberal to specialist studies; and he did not see intellectual unity and synthesis as an individual achievement, something occurring in any one mind. The answer lay in sensitizing students and scholars to what was being done by others and their dependence on others' work. I will quote him on this crucial matter: 'For science to be unitary, it is not necessary for it to be contained within the field of one and the same conscience — an impossible feat anyhow — but it is sufficient for all those who cultivate it to feel they are collaborating in the same work.'

Social solidarity does not mean the disappearance of specialists and the rise of the generalists (as championed by the Swann Report): it means interaction among specialists. Durkheim said, 'The division of labour presumes that the worker, far from being hemmed in by his task, does not lose sight of his collaborators, that he acts upon them, and reacts to them.'

The Power Base of the Curriculum

Specialization means neither intellectual fragmentation nor organizational anarchy. In other words, teachers can cooperate without losing their subject identities and without being denied a strong departmental base. Whenever subjects are to be integrated, the departmental base is threatened. I am a very strong Department man both through intellectual conviction and bitter experience. Only one man wins when you integrate subjects and dissolve departments — the man at the top. Everyone else — pupils and students as well as staff — is exposed, vulnerable. I would not willingly work for the headmaster or vice-chancellor who thought that 'subjects' were dead.

We see the close connection between organizational power and subject boundaries in Sloman's Reith Lectures. Subjects are not only intellectual systems; they are social systems: they confer not only a sense of identity on their members, they confer authority and they confer power. Sloman's strategy as the new Vice-Chancellor of Essex was to promote more integrated courses and reduce the power of departments. These are really two sides of the same coin. He said: 'Students ... will be admitted to schools, not to departments and they will follow in their first year a scheme of study common to the school. Staff will collaborate with other members of the same school in providing integrated courses. . . .' (Sloman 1964). Throughout the lectures we have approval of integrated courses and a corresponding attack on departments and the power of professors at their head. Academic subjects, departments and departmental heads have become wholly immoral in the last decade.

I have dealt elsewhere with the interplay between subject specialization and organizational power (Musgrove 1971). Within the loose boundaries of pre-bureaucratic schools and universities, academic entrepreneurs were often remarkable for their vigour, dash and enterprise — one thinks of Hawtrey at Eton and Hope at the University of Edinburgh in the early decades of the 19th century. It was possible for virtually autonomous, private enterprise departments to be established within the framework of a school's general organization. Stephen Hawtrey established a private enterprise mathematics department at Eton in 1837. He obtained a 40-year lease on a site in the college, built his own mathematical school in the form of a rotunda, a lecture-theatre which would accommodate 350 pupils, and recruited his own assistant mathematical masters. In 1851, after 14 years in this endeavour, he pursuaded the college authorities to make mathematics a compulsory subject (three hours a week). But he had been at Eton for 19 years before he was officially recognized as a member of staff. His assistant mathematical masters never were.

I have no particular nostalgia for pre-bureaucratic forms of educational organization: they could spell servility at one extreme, or deadlock at the other (as commonly occurred in conflicts between the headmaster and the usher). Bureaucracy has provided the mechanisms for co-ordinating the work of different centres of power. But these power centres are essential to educational vitality. It is nowadays customary to attack departmental heads as 'robber barons'. Those who make the attack in these terms have profoundly misconceived the character of the medieval world. But much nearer to our own day, I think we can see in the intellectual history of 19th- and 20th-century Europe that great universities have arisen when professors have been given their head: when departments have been strong and unassailed by centralizing influences. Centralization commonly entails standardization and servility. Vitality lies in a vigorous, even defiant, pluralism.

Models for the Future
Open-plan architecture and integrated curricula are part of the process of homogenization which social analysts see as the dominant trend of our times. I believe that the opposite is the case: that post-industrial societies are not characteristically homogenized and 'massified'; they are ever more segmented, differentiated, diversified. Differences are not removed but accentuated. And the trend is *not* toward more bureaucracy, if by bureaucracy we mean highly centralized forms of organizational control. Contemporary curriculum development and its organizational corollaries are a curious throwback: a retrogression which has no enduring place in post-industrial societies. In more homely terms, they take us back to all-age classes with class teachers all

working in an unpartitioned hall. Both teachers and pupils work under conditions of maximum visibility. No-one is more vulnerable. We are back to headmasters who enjoy undisputed sway partly because they can see everything, but chiefly because there are no firm centres of subject power and authority.

I believe that our schools, colleges and universities must be very loose confederations of diverse centres of academic power. This is the organizational style of the future: fluid, flexible, improvisational, with the centre de-emphasized and power on the periphery. The French sociologist, Crozier (1964), has given us a sketch of this process of debureaucratization. He maintains that the broad historical trend is for large-scale bureaucracies to become less bureaucratic in the severity of their control over members. But in schools we still demand loyalty (and conformity) of the order required by the great bureaucracies of history: the banking houses of Augsburg and Florence, the Jesuits, the Janissaries of the Ottoman Empire, the Prussian Grenadiers. Leaving was equivalent to treason — as it was at Oundle when the headmaster, Atkinson, was asked, not so very long ago, to resign because it became known that he was looking for another job.

Schon, in his recent Reith lectures (1971), gave us a still more kaleidoscopic picture when he talked of 'the loss of the stable state'. One of his major themes was the irrelevance and decline of the centre-to-periphery organizational model under conditions of rapid communication and widespread innovation. (Toffler (1970) similarly talks of the rise of 'ad-hocracy' in which managers lose their monopoly of decision-making.) The classical centre-to-periphery model is unable in times of rapid change to handle information centrally and provide the feedback that is essential. A network is now the appropriate model, rather than the wheel. Centres on the perimeter must assume responsibility and autonomy and make their own decisions. This is a far cry indeed from the contemporary school where effective innovation occurs only if the head says so.

I would support, then, unabated subject pluralism and a corresponding network or loose confederation of subject departments: not in order to prevent change, but to promote it. And I would accentuate distinctions and diversity in the curriculum, because the world is ever more differentiated and diverse. We have ever more structural differentiation in society, based upon age-grading and job specialization; it would be remarkable if this led to a 'mass society' of cultural standardization. And it does not, except to a very superficial view (cf Wilensky 1964). Social structure and culture do not vary so independently. What we have, in fact, is a surfeit of subcults, a bewildering diversity of life-styles available to us (Toffler 1970). And future generations will have genuine choices available to them. This fact should be central to all thinking about the curriculum. As Toffler says: 'How we choose a life style, and what it means to us . . . looms as one of the central issues of the psychology of tomorrow (1970).'

In conclusion I will come back to the argument of Durkheim: that the division of labour does not divide or fragment society, but holds it together.

It promotes interdependence and strengthens the bonds which unite men in societies. But the division of labour may become anomic or pathological; and in these circumstances it has the opposite effect. There have certainly been signs of 'anomie' in the academic division of labour. What is necessary is that all subject specialists should come together to decide on their common objectives and how each will make his distinctive contribution. 'Output goals' should be constantly under review and the interlocking contributions of different subject areas evaluated. But a centrally-directed master-plan is inadequate in a situation of rapid change and adaptation. Co-ordination will occur through the interaction of relatively autonomous subject specialists in more diffuse networks.

It has been feared that the headmaster may have no place in the operation of an integrated curriculum (Hubbard and Salt 1969). I have argued, on the contrary, that he is likely to have unprecedented primacy, as he busies himself more directly and personally in everyone's affairs and encounters none of the traditional centres of academic power. It is in the network that he will finally be lost, an archaic irrelevance, and subject teachers actually take the important decisions that are properly theirs.

Geography, Social Science and Inter-disciplinary Enquiry

N. J. GRAVES, 1968

By 1968 the raising of the school-leaving age, which had been a major proposal of the Newsom Report, was in the forefront of secondary school teachers' attention. It was a time to take stock of the curriculum and to examine the possible lines of advance for particular subjects. 'Newsom pupils' became the 'ROSLA pupils' and schools were to respond to the additional year of schooling by providing, in some cases, new buildings, new staff members and new courses. The Schools Council, which came into existence in 1965, supported projects some of which sought to develop new approaches to the teaching of ROSLA pupils. Graves, in this article, reviews post-war changes in geographic education and pays particular attention to new course arrangements in which geography as a subject may be involved. Like Mackinder in 1913 he acknowledges that for some pupils – 'less able pupils or those from culturally deprived homes' – the 'quasi-logical structure of the traditional subjects' may not be appropriate. What is implicit in Graves' discussion is that a distinction can be drawn between the furtherance of geographical education and the furtherance of the education of the pupil. It raises a fundamental question concerning the contribution which geography as a 'pure' subject makes to the education of the less able pupil, the pupil who is subjected most to curricular experimentation. This Reading serves as a valuable backcloth to the readings in the final section.

The writer was asked to prepare this paper by the Education Committee of the Royal Geographical Society in order to clarify the position of geography within current experiments with the curriculum, in the schools in England and Wales. The Society had originally published a pamphlet in 1950 entitled *Geography and 'Social Studies' in Schools*, the aim of which was to defend the position of geography against a possible 'take-over' by a new subject then labelled 'Social Studies'. This pamphlet was revised in 1954. In 1955 the Education Committee of the R.G.S. provided a further report on the situation of geography in schools under the heading 'Geography in Education' in Vol. 121 (pp. 190—6) of the *Geographical Journal*. This report was essentially a reaffirmation of the value of geography as a 'discipline' in the education of pupils and students. The nature of this 'discipline' was stated to be that of the accurate observation and recording of information and its subsequent analysis and interpretations.

The present paper was submitted to the Education Committee of the Society at its meeting on 26 January 1968. The writer assumes that, though the Society is interested in the position of geography in schools, it accepts that schools must be free to experiment with their curricula, with the consequence that, in the case of geography, not only may the factual content of courses change, but the concepts or principles taught will evolve and the curricular contexts in which such subject matter is taught may alter with time. This paper will therefore concentrate on: (*a*) stating the various ways in which curriculum planning may involve geography either as a separate subject or as part of a broader teaching scheme; (*b*) assessing the advantages and disadvantages of teaching geography as part of a 'combined subject field'. Throughout this paper the word 'subject' is used in preference to 'discipline', since the latter word often has connotations implying status in relation to other subjects, which are irrelevant to the purpose of the paper.

Historical perspective. — When the original R.G.S. pamphlet on *Geography and 'Social Studies' in Schools* was written (Reading 12), education in the U.K. was recovering from war time austerity and was in the process of being transformed by the 1944 Education Act. In the 'Brave New World' atmosphere which then prevailed and in the excitement which attended the formation of the new secondary modern schools, there was a feeling that the curriculum of these schools should be different and challenging. It was recognized that in the humanities, if the teacher was to make education child-centred rather than subject-centred, then a start could be made by finding out what interested pupils and to develop these particular interests no matter in what subject fields these lay. However, such procedures, whilst they might be easy to implement in the primary school where teachers stayed with one class for long periods, might well run into difficulties in secondary schools where subject specialists operated and where a greater depth of understanding was required. Consequently, there was a tendency to compromise and to argue that such new ways of treating the curriculum might be achieved on a more limited basis by joining history, geography and civics together into 'Social Studies' and thereby enabling the teacher to develop such themes as appeared appropriate to him in the light of his knowledge of the class he was teaching.

Though there is little quantitative evidence available, this type of combined subject never achieved a wide measure of popularity in our secondary schools, no matter how taught, except in certain areas where groups of 'progressive' teachers experimented with a social studies syllabus. The increased output of geography and history graduates from the universities and the development of geography in the Colleges of Education led to a teaching force which had, to some extent, invested its intellectual capital in one or other of the subjects and naturally preferred to teach either history or geography. Further, the subject associations were generally hostile to such developments and continued to foster the development of their individual subjects in schools. Only in the primary school, where systematic study of the individual humanities subjects had never been felt to be desirable, did the study of the environment, especially the local environment, develop on a 'centre of interest' basis regardless of the subjects involved. Recently, however, stimulated partly by the growth of the team teaching technique in America, and partly by the need to plan for the time when all pupils would stay at school until 16, the question of including geography as part of a broader integrated unit of teaching has been raised again. Thus today we are witnessing another attempt to modify the curriculum of our secondary schools at a time when geography as a subject is undergoing some radical changes in orientation at university level.

Present proposals, — In the first place it is essential to realize that the present trends are not absolutely clear, that various proposals in the field of 'social studies' are nebulous, and that those experiments which have got going have not been operating for very long, so that the evaluation of these is unlikely to be authoritative. In the second place it is necessary to understand that there has been some change in terminology. Thus those who advocate that the curriculum need not be cut up into a series of subjects tend now to label the study of a topic from various points of view as '*Inter-Disciplinary Enquiry*' (I.D.E.). This is very similar to the 'project method' which was popular in the immediate post-war years. I.D.E. often involves team teaching techniques in the secondary school, since various aspects of a topic may best be studied under the guidance of a specialist in a particular field. Those, on the other hand, who are after a greater development of the study of society than has been current in our schools tend now to write about 'social science' in schools rather than 'social studies', partly because 'social studies' have been discredited as a hotch-potch of various subjects and partly because 'social science' is a more accurate description of the sort of courses which they have in mind. These have a much greater affinity with sociology as an academic subject than with history, geography or civics. Team teaching need not be used to teach such courses, but a social science aspect might be included in I.D.E. Sometimes the term 'integrated teaching' is used. This indicates a scheme similar to I.D.E. It follows from the above that whilst geography may feature as an aspect of I.D.E. it seldom if ever appears in courses labelled 'Social Science'.

To sum up, the curriculum on the Humanities' side may include today:

1. *Social Studies:* the remnant of the combined history—geography—civics amalgam which was launched in the post war period.

2. *Social Science:* the teaching of various aspects of society, particularly

war, social relations, race relations, sex relations, elementary legal aspects of society, the family in society, etc.; all this may be taught at an elementary or more advanced level, and may be taught in the traditional classroom manner. Geography is seldom involved, since the teaching of such a subject would be in addition to geography rather than in lieu of geography.

3. A combination of 1 and 2 whereby 'social studies' are widened to include topics from sociology and economics. Geography is usually involved.

4. *Integrated teaching schemes* which may be (*a*) taught by one teacher; (*b*) taught by a team of teachers. The main distinction of these integrated teaching schemes is that the content to be taught involves some sort of interdisciplinary enquiry. Consequently geography may be involved in certain topics.

As far as may be judged, comparatively few schools operate any of these schemes. Some examples are Kidbrooke School which teaches 'humanities' in the 1st and 2nd year; Walworth School where 'social studies' are taught from the 1st to the 3rd year; Norwood Girls' School which operate an 'integrated teaching' scheme using team teaching techniques with first year children; Durrants School, Rickmansworth, which integrates the teaching of English, history, geography and social science. In the case of Walworth School, complete integration of teaching has not proved possible and, in practice, periods of 'social studies' may be allocated in some terms to geography topics and in others to history topics.

Assessment. — Most of the schemes postulated are aimed at groups of adolescents for whom the traditional curriculum seems to have had little attraction. On the other hand, for pupils of *average* or *above average* ability, curriculum development seems to be occurring within the bounds of the traditional subjects; for example, new type mathematics, 'Nuffield' science, new aspects of geography. Integration with other subjects may occur quite naturally in so far as, for example, in geography one may teach a relationship which may be expressed mathematically or one may have to resort to elementary chemistry when discussing the weathering of limestone. But for less able pupils or those from culturally deprived homes, it was felt that the quasi-logical structure of the traditional subjects was not the right basis for learning and teaching, that by exploring topics in which the pupils became emotionally involved, they would be willing to learn and profit from their school experience. It was felt, therefore, that such topics as pertained to the immediate environment of these pupils, to their personal and family problems, to their vocational aspirations, would be more likely to involve them than subject matter which might be intellectually stimulating but remote from their experience. Further, such topics as were tackled by team teaching or individual (pupil's) work methods, would be more appropriate than class-teaching methods, given the wide range of interests, needs and abilities of these pupils. It would be fair to sum up these curriculum experiments in integrated teaching as attempts at making the fare that schools can offer palatable to those whose tastes are not academic. They are not fundamental attempts to reshape the whole content of education for all school pupils. Over and above this, there are, in some school sixth-forms, some attempts to use minority time by setting students work involving 'interdisciplinary enquiry'. In such cases the main aim is to counterbalance the specialization which may go on in the sixth-form. Thus a 'project' in the humanities may be embarked upon by students whose majority time is in mathematics and the sciences. In such cases goegraphical aspects of the 'enquiry' may be taught to students who would otherwise be getting no teaching in geography. In the case of the weaker pupils who are subjected to curriculum experiments, the total time devoted to geography within I.D.E. or any other scheme may well be less than that which would have been allocated to geography under traditional teaching methods. The only point at issue is whether geographical education will have been better furthered by I.D.E. or by teaching 'pure' geography. This is a question that no one can answer in general terms, since so much depends upon the conditions in the schools concerned. Depending on the team operating the I.D.E. scheme, the nature of the enquiries proposed, the facilities available, the schemes may be a success or a failure. Similarly the traditional class teaching method, as is well known, may succeed or fail according to who is teaching. Thus if a new curriculum development scheme succeeds in interesting pupils who were unmotivated towards learning by class teaching, then clearly it has achieved something worth while. But if it fails, then there is nothing to commend it over class teaching.

If, however, one considers those pupils who are less of a problem from the motivation point of view, then the issue is a little clearer. Here the relevant questions seem to be: (1) Are the contents of courses conceived within an I.D.E. scheme as worthwhile educationally as the contents of the separate courses which might otherwise be taught? (2) Is the method of exploring a topic in its various aspects better than that which explores the principles, skills and concepts of the individual subject? The first question is very difficult to answer in the affirmative because so few I.D.E. schemes are available for inspection. It is clear, however, that developing a worth while course on I.D.E. lines must be an extraordinarily difficult task, since the topics chosen must not only enable the dovetailing of various disciplines in some coherent pattern, but each succeeding topic chosen must build upon the previous topic in such a way that principles and concepts learnt are gradually enriched and developed. This is no mean task within one subject; designing a scheme to cover many subjects centred around a topic is a job of enormous complexity. It is not yet clear that 'integrated teaching' has solved this problem. It is perhaps symptomatic that many such schemes which begin in the lower school do not proceed to the upper school. It is certainly doubtful whether a class of pupils which was submitted to a regime of integrated teaching for five years from 11 to 16 years, would in fact have covered in that time the content which might have been taught in the ordinary class teaching of geography. In answering the second question, it might be argued, however, that if through I.D.E. the students acquired a better understanding of the way subjects of various types were related to one another, then the gain might be worth the loss of some individual subject content. There is something to be said for this point of view, if it is impossible to show, through individual subjects, how these relate to one another. However, it is not an impossible or very difficult task to show such relationships, particularly in geography. Thus though the inter-disciplinary exploration of a given topic may be a useful and valid procedure from time to time, partly to change teaching methods and partly to highlight subject relationships, these are probably insufficient reasons for basing the whole curriculum on such procedures. It could further be argued that as one proceeds to acquire understanding in depth, then the acquistion of the concepts, skills and language of a particular subject are all important.

This latter point is worth developing briefly. One of the characteristics of a maturing mind is the ability to distinguish clearly between various aspects of knowledge. In other words as a student matures in understanding it should become possible for him to assess whether a particular problem or question rightly belongs to the natural sciences, whether it is amenable to mathematical treatment, whether it has an economic aspect, whether it involves spatial considerations, whether an important element of value judgment is involved, and so on. The ability to differentiate the various 'forms of knowledge' is important because any problem has to be analysed before a solution to it can be found. Success in finding the solution involves applying to the problem those concepts and skills which are appropriate to it. Failure to find a solution to a problem may often be attributed to the use of an inappropriate conceptual framework. Consequently it would seem important that students should be led to an understanding of the essential nature of the concepts and thinking which have been developed in particular subjects, to deal with particular aspects of problem situations. This is best done by study within particular subject frameworks under the guidance of subject specialists. Since students at school will be exposed to more than one subject, it is doubtful whether their thinking would ever be imprisoned within the conceptual framework of one subject. In any case most subjects overlap with others. A further but important practical consideration is that once an aspect of a problem has been isolated and accepted as being within the field of a special subject, then the particular concepts and skills needed to solve it must have been mastered by the person dealing with the problem. Once again, therefore, such mastery of knowledge and techniques may best be taught by the specialist within the subject field. Teaching a subject involves not only a disciplining of the mind, but also some training in skills, neither of which might be well done if all teaching were to be based on schemes of interdisciplinary enquiry.

Conclusion

Curriculum experiments must proceed. In so far as they succeed in modernizing subject matter and motivating pupils to learn, they make a valuable contribution to education. The specific curriculum experiment involving 'integrated teaching' might succeed with weaker pupils where traditional class teaching has failed — if it does then it should be welcomed. As applied to average or more able pupils; it is best looked upon, for the present, as an occasional alternative to subject teaching rather than a rival. There is, as yet, little evidence of a general move away from geography or other humanities subjects in favour of such integrated teaching, though various projects have been put to the Schools Council which might involve further experiments in 'integrated teaching'.

III

INTEGRATION: CONTEMPORARY PRACTICE

Cromwell described the laws of England as a 'tortuous and ungodly jumble'. That seems to me an excellent description of our education — at least of our secondary education. What an amazing and chaotic thing it is! One subject after another is pressed into this bursting portmanteau which ought to be confined to the necessary clothes for a journey through life, but becomes a wardrobe of bits of costumes for any emergency: and from time to time someone discovers a new need and points out how ignorant we are of the U.S.A. or of our Dominions, or of Latin America and urges the inclusion of Colonial or American history, or of Italian or Spanish or Russian. And so we move towards a curriculum which recalls Burke's description of the Duke of Grafton's government — 'a piece of joinery, crossly indented and whimsically dovetailed, a tesselated pavement without cement, here a bit of black stone, and there a bit of white' (Livingstone 1941).

Integrating the Curriculum — A Case Study in the Humanities

D. W. BOLAM, 1970/71

In the evolution of the secondary school curriculum the year 1965 is an important milestone. In that year the Schools Council was established and this brought together teachers, the local education authorities and the Department of Education and Science in an attempt to promote study and development of curricula and examinations in schools. The most publicised part of the work of this institution has been the support it has given, and continues to give, to curriculum development projects most of which have focused on single subjects or groups of subjects. For the geographer the first Schools Council publication of significance was Working Paper 11 (Schools Council 1967c) which quoted examples of courses in the broad field of the humanities which were in existence in British secondary schools. This publication was a warning that a massive project — massive in the size of the Schools Council—Nuffield Foundation grant — was soon to be under way, and in 1968 the Humanities Curriculum Project was announced. Since the setting up of the Humanities Curriculum Project a number of other projects have been initiated which have a direct bearing upon the organization of courses in which the subject geography may be involved. In addition to the two projects which look specifically at geography (Geography 14—18 and Geography for the Young School Leaver) the Environmental Studies Project 5—13, the Project in History, Geography and Social Sciences in the Middle Years of Schooling (8—13), the Social Studies (8—13) Project, the General Studies (15—18) Project and the Integrated Studies Project all have special relevance for secondary school geography teachers. Brief details of these projects with comprehensive bibliographies of their associated publications are provided in the annual Schools Council Project Profiles and Index. To provide a description of a project we have selected this article by Bolam, the director of the Integrated Studies Project. It is of particular interest for his analysis of modes of integration which provides a theoretical basis upon which to build the work of the project. The questions which Bolam poses at the end of the article are those which geographers may well apply to their specialist subject teaching in the first instance, and then again in deciding whether or not to engage in the integrated courses which could be designed in order to utilize some of the teaching resources supplied by the project team.

The project is examining the problems and possibilities of integrated humanities courses during the four years of secondary education (11—15) and across the whole ability range. The project is concerned centrally with the organization of learning most likely to lead to a relatedness of the disciplines and their distinct methods of enquiry and verification.

The Schools Council distinguishes between 'research projects' and 'curriculum development' projects (Banks 1969). The Keele project is one of the latter and shares their main features. The team is mainly composed of seconded teachers of proven competence in the classroom. The project aims to produce curriculum units for publication, but will first test them in a limited number of schools, who have agreed to co-operate in the experiment. The work of the project is continually scrutinised by a committee largely composed of representatives of the teachers; of the local colleges of education, and of the four local education authorities, who pay the salaries of four members of the team. At the same time, the project is based at a universtiy and one that has itself experimented in an integrated course (Iliffe 1968).

All this is apparent enough. What may be less so but of the greatest importance is that a curriculum development project, over and above its immediate concern, offers the interest of a process. In the long run, this process will need to be scrutinised for its effectiveness in achieving change in the educational system. Its immediate significance for those engaged on the project is the degree to which it determines their approach. The reason for any suggested area of enquiry or method must be understood. Every step requires consensus. The basic problem is communication.

I

The problem of communication was increased by the nature of the task undertaken. Integration could not be regarded as a proven method with an understood and widely accepted rationale. Far from integration being an established part of the school system, that system used the opposite structuring principle of single subjects. The very attempt to employ subject approaches in a thematic enquiry introduced a complex of questions — both academic and organizational — whose answers might be guessed at but were substantially unknown (Henry 1958). In these circumstances, the project accepted integration as an 'intuitive first solution', and decided that an operational model of curriculum development was inappropriate (Taba 1962). Instead, a more open-ended, trial and error exploration was more likely to throw up insights that would enable it to assess the validity and limits of integration. These insights might well then offer the starting point for a second stage of research.

Early Definitions

The first definition of terms was in the original application to the Schools Council, concerned to establish the need for an enquiry. The statement referred to alternative ways of looking on the 'humanities'. One was that of 'studies grouped around subject organizations like English, languages ancient and modern, history, philosophy, theology'. Another was that of the social sciences, and a third was 'the expressive arts'. 'Humanities' could even be thought of as 'all subjects except pure and applied science and mathematics'. In addition, it was stressed that 'the likelihood of building new relationships in knowledge is accepted without question'. For its own purpose, it decided to define 'humanities' as including 'English, languages ancient and modern, history, divinity, geography, art and craft, music, drama, movement and physical education'. Such a definition aimed to extend the enquiry beyond the range suggested in Working Paper No. 11 — English, history, geography, and religious knowledge — to give scope to 'expressive subjects'. As for 'integration', no definition was attempted, but its two dimensions — strategic and academic — are implied in the questions it suggested the project should study:

'I. How far does the organization of teaching in secondary schools lead to a division of labour which runs counter to the production of a common strategy by the teachers?' . . .

IV. Is it possible to regroup ideas and knowledge between subjects in the Humanities in the secondary schools so as to provide new and intellectually reputable curriculum?'

By the second definition in July 1968, the project had been working six months and had been looking at existing integrated courses in schools. Work of this kind could mainly be found at three points: in primary schools; in courses for fourth form leavers, and in sixth form general studies. In addition, the Goldsmiths Curriculum Laboratory was encouraging experiments in what it termed 'Inter-disciplinary enquiry' in the early years of secondary school (James 1968). The qualities and limitations of this work helped in definition. Much of the activity with juniors seemed valuable in establishing the idea of enquiry, but too unstructured, and sometimes focused on too narrow a theme, to provide a full answer for the secondary school. Work with fourth form leavers brought out the tactical need for topical, personal, and perhaps vocational relevance, but was often left to the ingenuity of one teacher, and sometimes stressed data rather than issues. Sixth form general studies excited by its innovatory content — anthropology and psychology, for instance — but was generally seen only as a complement to a student's main specialist studies (Schools Council 1969). In terms of the range of the humanities, these diverse approaches all showed the value of including elements of the natural sciences, expecially human biology; aspects of technology; and also of the social sciences, even though they were not yet established school subjects. In terms of approach, it was clear that subjects should be seen not as bodies of information, but as modes of enquiry.

Any definitions at this stage, however, needed to do more than summarize these considerations, they needed to be terse, easily understood and broadly acceptable. Such definitions were to serve as a focus in the negotiations with teachers, encouraging them to co-operate with the team in both preparing materials and trying out integrated approaches in their schools. 'Humanities' was defined as 'any subject or aspect of subject which contributes to the rational or imaginative understanding of the human situation'. 'Integration' as 'the exploration of any large area, theme, or problem which:

(a) requires the help of more than one subject or discipline for its full understanding, and

(b) is best taught by the concerted action of a group of teachers.'

Certain modifications were assumed, but not stated. It was, for example, understood that in any given school the range of a humanities course would partly be determined by the interests and specialisms of the teaching team, and it was accepted that a headmaster might select a team for the personal qualities of its members rather than to achieve a particular combination of subject expertise. Also, the idea of 'concerted action' was deliberately left vague, as each school was to be encouraged and left free to develop its own approach to team teaching. What is now explicit, however, in the definitions, even if unexplored are the two key aspects of integration: integration as the co-operative use of the forms of knowledge, and integration as the school organization needed to make this accessible to children.

There were to be eighteen months before the project next attempted to define its position, with both aspects explored and elaborated. The working need to look more closely at forms of knowledge arose from the practical problems of structuring themes and preparing curriculum material. The necessity to explain its position, and at some length, arose from the need of teachers in trial schools to have a basic understanding which offered guide-lines for their handling of the themes and materials in their schools. Before looking at this re-definition, however, a brief summary is necessary of the curriculum units:

Each unit contains an analysis of the area of enquiry; suggested activity patterns; teaching materials, and information on further sources.

THE FIRST STAGE PACKS — intended for juniors in forms 1 and 2 (11—13 years old)

I. *EXPLORATION MAN* — an introductory unit concerned to introduce pupils to the idea of integration and to the extent of the humanities field. The pack is focused around two themes: the complexity of the human being, and the range of ways of finding out about him.

II. *COMMUNICATING WITH OTHERS* — the ability to communicate is seen as an activity basic to man, and essential for his personal development and social competence. Among the aspects explored are: the range of 'languages' — verbal, visual, and musical; the origins of communication both in an infant and in human society; the inter-relation of cultural forms in a given historical period; oral tradition; and barriers to communication — physical and social.

III. *LIVING TOGETHER* — this unit explores the variety of human experience and standards of living throughout the world by using five comparative studies: the children's own community; Tristan da Cunha; Borneo, and China at two stages of development — imperial China and communist China. Certain themes are common to each study, e.g. home and family; education; law and order; work. The underlying issues are: the problems of group living; the effect of environment on the life of man; the implications of social and cultural change.

THE SECOND STAGE PACKS — intended for forms 3 and 4, and as a basis for later examination work (13—15 years old)

I. *DEVELOPMENT IN WEST AFRICA* — West Africa is first studied through three explaining frameworks: environmental, historical, and social. Case studies of individual poeples are used to appreciate art, religion, family patterns, social organization, and technology as facets of a total culture.

The second part concentrates on Ghana as a 'developing nation': the political sequence; technological change; social adaptation; human experience.

II. *MAN-MADE MAN* — this is concerned with a double enquiry: the image of man in the expressive arts, as well as the extension of man's capacities through technology. This double theme is elaborated through exploring man's use of materials (wood; clay; iron and steel, and plastics) both aesthetically and functionally. A study of man's attempt to gain understanding of himself and his social encounters through the arts is complemented by a scrutiny of man's relations with machines and the quality of living in a technological society.

III. *OUTGROUPS IN SOCIETY* — after asking the question 'What is society?', this unit looks at the issue of rules and rulebreaking, with illustrations from deviant groups in Great Britain. A study in depth is made of the gypsies, stressing their arts and way of life. Finally, comparative examples across time and from other countries are looked at, including the Levellers and Diggers in 17th century England; the opposition in Nazi Germany; the Jews across history; women; protest movements and skid-row in the U.S.A., and the communist seizure of power in contemporary China.

Clearly these do not represent a complete course, and this was another of the things the new statement had to explain. The following represents the basis of the argument, even if not the final formulation for teachers.

II

Integration is most readily thought of in curriculum terms as a way of organizing learning. The project's concern with themes, issues or problems of felt human importance is an expression of its desire to develop a central and centralizing humanistic study based on man himself.

Although the project is not producing a full course, it has had to strike a number of balances. On the one hand, any broad consideration of the 'problems and possibilities' of integrated studies must recognize that inter-disciplinary units are viable within a number of different patterns, but that this variety must not threaten the programme as a whole with anarchy. Again, such units, when established, can be justified within a number of frameworks. One possible cause of confusion is that the same categories (e.g. 'subjects') can offer both a basis for organizing learning and a checklist for balance. Thus the traditional subject-dominated curriculum is organized into subjects and offers, through its quantities timetable, a balance between them.

Any attempt to argue a balanced, integrated course based on the study of man raises a number of interlinking considerations. The most immediate of these concerns the nature of man himself — suggesting guidelines and principal themes to be explored, and offering a measure of their importance (see *Man: A Course for Study* in Bruner 1966); but the most fundamental in curriculum terms are those centring on the nature of knowledge and the modes of integration.

The Nature of Knowledge

The various 'forms' of knowledge, the 'disciplines' or school 'subjects' offer a consistent checklist for balance. Equally they suggest themselves as a possible basis for 'parcelling' knowledge for teaching and learning. A number of Keele units explore the growing edge of particular disciplines, interesting areas of overlap, and so forth. An underpinning conviction is that the disciplines, forms of knowledge, or school subjects are essentially instruments of enquiry, each offering distinctive skills, procedures, explaining concepts and methods of verification, however inter-related. This is a difficult area to deal with, because a number of useful ways of breaking down knowledge into categories suggest themselves. It is not the intention of the project to offer a philosophical treatise: rather to define its own position in relation to some of the more obvious distinctions that have been drawn.

A possible starting point is the difference between public and private knowledge (Berman 1968). This is not a clear-cut or easy distinction to make. Some knowledge is characterized by skill in manipulating a public system of symbols; other forms of knowledge are less accessible, more subjective, not entirely verifiable by reference to public principles. As the distinction appears to suggest two different modes of enquiry, it seems reasonable to suppose that a whole programme would offer some balance between them. The distinction has not been made the basis for any unit of study. All Keele packs take account of both.

Another fruitful approach has been the identification of four 'forms of knowledge'. In broad terms the four main areas have been seen as:

1. *The Arts.* Activities arising out of man's wish to understand and communicate his personal experience. Perhaps best seen as inner exploration,

'private knowledge', reaching out in an attempt to establish a public form, and criteria of taste by which the forms can be enjoyed. The arts would include a number of disciplines — the study of languages and literature, music, dance, and the fine arts.

2. *The Natural Sciences.* Originating in man's concern to control and explain the material world. Disciplines within this band would include mathematics, physics, chemistry and biology. In a 'humanities' course, selected elements would be particularly relevant, including some basic concepts (such as 'life'), the biology of man, and some aspects of technology.

3. *The Social Sciences.* Essentially concerned with understanding and ordering the society in which man lives. To the school, the most familiar disciplines within this band are history and geography, but some of comparatively recent development may be linked with the need to appreciate the rapid changes of the modern world, e.g. economics, sociology and psychology.

4. *Morals, Religion and Philosophy.* Man's quest for significance and meaning in life; his discovery of social and personal values and commitments. In one sense this is the most general of the forms of knowledge, distinct and yet best studied as a dimension of the others. In another sense it is the most personal of the forms.

Such a framework is offered as a broad starting point for discussion. It may be useful to stress again the potential double usefulness. The forms of knowledge offer an overall check for balance, but they may also suggest 'natural' groupings of disciplines, and therefore provide a possible basis for organizing interdisciplinary work. For example 'Outgroups in Society', a pack based around a social problem, may have a natural (although by no means exclusive) tendency to specialize towards the social sciences.

A number of further points need to be made about the forms of knowledge. Although they are groupings of disciplines or, more approximately, of school subjects, they inter-relate and overlap. Technology overlaps both the natural and the social sciences. Myth could very fruitfully be handled both under arts and under religion. Again, it has already been suggested that moral issues might be explored as a dimension of other areas. In terms of the school curriculum, this implies that moral education need not be separately timetabled or separately taught. A further qualification is that various cross dimensions of the forms of knowledge suggest themselves. One fundamental one is the symbolic skills involved in language. In school terms, the issue under discussion is the claim of English language to be separately taught. Lastly, alternative analyses are always possible. Philip Phenix in *Realms of Meaning* distinguishes a realm he calls 'symbolics', which comprises all means of communication between human beings, including languages, mathematics, and such discursive symbols as gestures, rituals, and rhythmic patterns (Phenix 1964).

However one analyses the forms of knowledge, the difficulty comes when one attempts to relate them to school subjects (White 1968, King and Brownell 1966). School subjects are in some ways the least satisfactory ways of approaching the nature of knowledge as they claim no more than practical validity. They are only imperfectly to be regarded as 'disciplines', and they include 'fields' of knowledge, such as geography (Hirst 1965). Further complications arise from current attitudes and the school situation. There is a tendency, for instance, to define qualities too narrowly: 'creativity', for example, is regarded as more appropriate to arts subjects than those of the natural or social sciences, instead of being seen, appropriately interpreted, as a dimension of all learning. Again, subjects will need to be seen as ways of finding out, and not as bodies of information. What are the key explaining concepts? What kinds of problems are identified? What counts as evidence? How does one move from raw data to conclusion? How is the claim to truth tested? If some subjects are based on fields of knowledge rather than on an individual discipline, they will characteristically employ several modes of enquiry. Lastly, any attempt to use school subjects as an index of 'balance' must meet the difficulty that arises because some important disciplines are not yet established as school subjects. The outstanding example is sociology. One recognizes real problems, but without it any enquiry about society will lack a cutting edge.

There is a final and fundamental consideration. The relevance of knowledge to any live society depends on the use to which the knowledge is put. Bruner suggests that for the human species, the typical way in which we increase our powers comes through 'converting external bodies of knowledge embodied in the culture into generative rules for thinking about the world and about ourselves (Bruner 1970). This involves problem-finding as well as problem-solving.

The fact that knowledge is 'put to use' suggests that it may be useful to look at the role played by different kinds of knowledge in the total culture. Broudy (Broudy *et al.* 1964) has developed novel groupings of knowledge from this standpoint. At least two of these offer themselves as a possible basis on which knowledge could be organized for instruction and learning:

1. Societies organize knowledge along routes of social, cultural and historical development.

2. Societies organize knowledge and identify problems in areas of social and moral uncertainty. The social problem based curriculum unit brings education under subjection to real issues that invoke a genuine passion. This is a clear 'growing edge' in man's quest to control his personal and social world. To discuss examples, however, of 'groupings of knowledge' is already to have begun considering modes of integration.

Modes of Integration

Curriculum units that cross discipline boundaries appear viable within a number of organizational frameworks. It would be absurd, for example, to assume that junior environmental studies offer the same 'problems and possibilities' as social problem based education for the school leaver. If the project's experience is to be usefully shared, it must identify with some care the various kinds of integrated units it is examining.

Before doing so, it may be fruitful to distinguish three 'levels' at which it seems appropriate to consider integration. First, integration at the 'macro' level argues the wholeness, balance and relatedness of the course as a whole. A number of ways in which this could be approached have been indicated above. Secondly, integration as a curriculum concept (to recapitulate briefly) is a way of organizing units to bring out the modes of enquiring of the different disciplines, and their relatedness. It implies inquiry into themes, topics, or problems of felt human importance, upon which the various skills and approaches can focus. Lastly, integration as a learning concept implies an ability to perceive relationships. At a 'micro' level this could be to understand a particular relationship inside a single discipline; at a more complex level an ability to perceive the relevance, structure and relatedness of the course as a whole, and its explaining value in the world at large. Out of these three, the curriculum argument must necessarily concentrate on the second, but this is not to say that the first and third are anything other than essential concomitants.

How then can the different modes of integration be conceptualized? The following are 'kinds', or 'theoretical models' which have interested the project.

1. *A unit organized around a single subject or area of study.* Perhaps classics as traditionally taught (literary-based, offering content, standards of taste and personal style). An area of study can develop, perhaps after the pattern of the Oxford 'Greats', offering an amalgamation of the language, literature, history and philosophy of the Greeks and Romans.

The Keele Foundation Year partly reflects this philosophy, developing a synoptic overview of western civilization.

In organizational terms, it is likely that this kind of integration could vary between a correlation of contributing disciplines, separately taught, and a breakdown into subthemes.

2. *A unit organized around an overarching concept distinctive of the humanities.* Such a theme would be an umbrella term like 'expressionism' or 'communication'. How it is subsequently developed would depend on the balance sought between private exploration and identified sub-issues or explaining concepts. A school approaching a theme like 'communication' has no obvious logic of enquiry to determine (for example) the range of activities or the degree of open-endedness.

3. *A unit organized around a focused human issue.* Under this broad heading it may be useful to distinguish three kinds:

(a) *A 'perspective' unit* that uses a broad explaining base like 'evolution' or centres itself on a very general question like: What is a Man? Perspective units are often either introductory or retrospective.

(b) *A social problem unit.* Addressing issues that have some bearing on the grievous problems facing the world, ourselves, social organization and human relationships. These issues are more specialized, and require study in depth.

(c) *Cognitive and evaluative Maps.* Theoretical and practical issues, with an emphasis on building up conceptual nets. This kind of study concerns itself with explanations and meanings, and aims to produce a synthesis of contributing insights. A map of inquiry would be more appropriate than a syllabus. The ideas emerge from relevant evidence, guided reflection, and related activities.

Here then are the main lines of the project's theoretical approach, which will serve as a basis for the next stages of its work.

III

The current trial of the curriculum units in schools raises two key questions: What is the most appropriate approach in the classroom to develop a child's own capacity to appreciate inter-relationships? What are the necessary changes in organization within the school? Both these problems can be illuminated by reference to some of the theoretical issues already raised.

Teaching and Learning Strategy

The main concern is that pupils have a sense of the direction in which the course is going, perceive its relatedness, and are themselves skilful in developing an 'integrated' inquiry (Lamm 1968). The test of this will be evidence of an underlying competence in handling the various aspects of each human issue encountered. This aspect of the project is as yet the least developed. It must depend particularly on the analysis and explanation of trial experience, but during the early months of trials teachers have generally been more preoccupied with problems of organization than of presentation. Some issues which they will be increasingly concerned with have been raised again by integration, but are by no means unfamiliar from other experiments: the making of a variety of resources available, including their own subject expertise; planning for flexible personal relationships, to allow for the full gain of pupil-pupil and pupil-teacher inter-action; the development of new forms of assessment, appropriate to the widened range of qualities they claim to be encouraging. One task, however, is crucial: the need for the teacher to provide an ideas framework. This is both resisted and misunderstood. Resistance may arise from teachers who continue to stress information rather than skills of enquiry. Even if they do not, the change-over from handling ideas within their own discipline to the continuous encounter with several other approaches creates a novel situation, which takes time for readjustment. Misunderstanding arises if the framework is thought of as rigid, as something decided and fixed before the enquiry begins. Instead, it puts a teacher in a position of continual alert to appreciate what significant issues are emerging, and to decide which new direction the enquiry should take.

One extremely valuable guide for a teacher in maintaining such an ideas framework is to relate the curriculum units to the modes of integration. As this will also help to clarify the intention of the units and the significance of the categories already discussed, as well as giving a sharper sense of the teacher's task, a quick analysis is given of four examples:

1. *Communicating with others.* Based on an overarching concept distinctive of the humanities, also corresponding to one of Bruner's great humanizing forces (language). A careful balance between open-ended creativity, and a more structured approach to the role of language and communication in the human situation. The concept is basic enough to suggest a number of complementary approaches and explorations, but relative to a focused issue, selection of content for this kind of unit has an element of arbitrariness, is less susceptible to a 'logic of enquiry'. There is an emphasis towards the arts, but overlap towards other areas.

2. *Living together.* A focal concern with man's social organization. The exploration is less of an overarching concept (although there is an element of this) than an attempt to relate an environmental study and a series of carefully selected cross cultural comparisons. Each community studied is viewed as an attempt to solve certain life problems arising out of man's attempt to organize a society in a particular environment at a particular time. There is an emphasis towards the social sciences, but a strong interest in values, beliefs, and world views. A number of the communities raise problems of evidence and judgement and are relevant to live social issues. It provides a bridge between a descriptive environmental study and social problem education.

3. *Africa: a developmental study.* Up to a point, this unit could be regarded as an area of study. It extends the view that geography is a field of knowledge, to include a whole range of cultural and social considerations (from art forms to African nationalism). Equally, it reflects an increasing tendency for societies to organize knowledge along routes of social, economic, and cultural development, particularly apt in the context of 'developing countries'. No less significantly does the continent of Africa raise vital contemporary issues. The unit inter-relates a full range of disciplines or forms of knowledge, with particular emphasis on the arts and social sciences.

4. *Outgroups in society.* 'Outgroups in Society' is organized and focused around a perplexing human issue; indeed one sufficiently sharp and baffling to be called a social problem. It extends the concern of *Living Together* for what Bruner calls man's 'social organization', exploring the fact that some groups in society are different, disturbing, exciting or threatening. The pack has a careful logic of enquiry which provides a framework for discussion and enquiry. Considerable use is made of explaining concepts, particularly from the social sciences, although there is an ultimate engagement with issues requiring judgement both of value and appropriateness.

This necessity of providing an ideas framework cannot be separated any more than any other teaching problems can — from a consideration of the organizational problems raised by integration.

The School and the Curriculum

It is in the area of organization — using this word in a broad and comprehensive sense — that integration presents the most disturbing threat to schools. This can be appreciated if development towards integration is compared to attempted changes within the teaching of a single subject. First, a single subject is well supported: textbooks, accepted syllabuses, public examinations, teachers trained to teach the subject. One might add that single subjects have the backing that is implicit in the salary structure, and even in school buildings. Admittedly, a reformer may well find some of these supports extremely restricting, but he has the advantage of attempting change from an established base. Integration is innovatory and has no such base. Secondly, a move towards integration cannot be contained, as it were, within a single subject room and remain unnoticed by the rest of the school. The most basic intrusions arising out of integration will be into time-tabling, with the need for 'inter-disciplinary blocks', and into the pattern of decision-making, through the planning responsibilities of the humanities team. There may also be a substantially modified use of school resources, including a more flexible use of premises to facilitate variety of groupings. For many teachers one of the most disturbing signs will be the greater mobility of children, on and off the premises, with its threat of disorder.

Faced with a sense of insecurity, schools may well make undue demands on a project for reassurance. What schools can fairly ask, however, is that the project offers not answers, but some broad lines of approach as guidelines to their attempts to answer a difficulty. Any comments made may in themselves represent a crystallization of the experiences of a number of other trial schools. One example may be taken from the vital area of curriculum decision making. More specifically: 'How can one assess the potential worth of an integrated course?' The difficulty arises from the fact that if a school takes out a group of single subjects, with their established content, acceptability, and methods of examining, then it has to satisfy itself that the replacement is educationally valid, though not necessarily that it is defensible on the same grounds as the single subjects. As a possible approach, a number of test questions have been drawn up: 'All these questions need to be asked at the planning stage, and some will need to be referred to continually. All need to be applied to the Keele packs, and could equally well be asked of integrated courses being developed in schools. For the present purpose, references to the Keele packs are largely limited to aspects not discussed in the individual statements.

A. *For all integrated courses:*
　(a) Is the theme important and on what grounds? (As an aspect of man? As a contemporary social problem? As an introduction to an area of knowledge? Out of the psychological need of adolescents?)
　(b) *Has it been structured to increase understanding of the disciplines?*

B. *For courses offered to a particular age group:*
　(a) Are they appropriate? e.g. Level of difficulty? Accessibility to children? Felt relevance?
　(b) *Are they balanced?* Particularly are they balanced between the aspects of man and between the forms of knowledge. For example, among the first

stage packs, *Exploration Man* offers range; then *Living Together* and *Communications* complement each other by studying the two key areas of the arts and the social sciences.

(c) *Do they inter-link?* As well as the basic focus on man, the second-stage packs have two important cross-links: the concept of change, and an interest in the nature of modern technological society, e.g. *Africa* looks at a developing society, facing the problems of rapid modernization; *Outgroups in Society* includes groups who are in a sense the victims of modern society; and *Man-Made Man* explores the quality of living made possible by technological advance.

C. *For courses across a range of age groups:*

(a) Are they graded in difficulty? Difficulty may depend on language as well as concepts. A desirable increase in complexity may arise from a narrowing of range of interest and a closer scrutiny in depth, e.g. compare *Living Together* (First Stage Pack) with *Outgroups in Society* (Second Stage).

(b) *Do courses build on skills and concepts learned earlier?* This will be an important issue to look at in the second year of trial.

(c) *Is there a logical development between stages?* The first stage packs are based on over-arching concepts, the second stage packs on focused issues. As well as being more difficult, as suggested above, this is also the sequence likely to be most helpful to a child's understanding. The over-arching concepts explore a basic idea which is common to a range of disciplines. By doing so, they introduce the children to the significance of these different approaches and some of their techniques. Only then will they be in a position to consciously use these approaches to scrutinize a more limited issue.

(d) *Are there any thematic or content links between stages?* One very important framework that runs through all the Keele packs is the human life cycle: birth, childhood, initiation, marriage, old age and death. A resources bank is also being built up around this theme. The local environment also is used as a continuous reference point and source of examples. Again, the technical skill of man, used both to express himself and to control his environment, is an aspect of most packs'.

It is in a continuous working interchange of ideas and experience such as this, between the project team and the schools, throughout the trial that some appreciation of the organizational issues will be arrived at.

If this account sometimes suggests a certain sense of stops and starts, then it fairly reflects the conditions of curriculum development. Just as an integrated enquiry in schools requires an ideas framework, so too does a project, and that is why it has been stressed in this description. But one must not leave out of account its slowness to evolve; the interaction of hunch, practice and theory; the continuous influence of working problems and teachers' opinions; the need to think again. The process of curriculum change has much in common with Dewey's wish for education that it should be a continuous re-examination of experience and re-stating of how best to explain it.

Integrated Studies — Some Problems and Possibilities for the Geographer

G. G. ELLIOTT, 1974

In this article Elliott expresses his concern over the theoretical models for subject integration which are currently being employed in secondary schools. His viewpoint is that of a geographer working in a curriculum development project which was set up to produce teaching materials for use in schools in the age range 8–13. The Liverpool Project — History, Geography and Social Science 8–13 — asserts the uniqueness of school situations and identifies four basic variables which must be considered when materials are designed. These variables are children, teachers, schools and environments. Elliott reviews the Keele Integrated Studies Project (Readings 20 and 22) and the Humanities Curriculum Project from the point of view of the geographer and then he examines types of integration which have been encountered by the Liverpool Project team. He classifies the courses into three types, all of which he finds unsatisfactory. He concludes that it is the absence of an adequate curriculum theory which is most striking. In studying the readings which follow the reader will be struck by the variety of assumptions which are made, the objectives which are suggested and the organizational arrangements which are made in various schools, and it is worth considering these in terms of their theoretical underpinnings.

Introduction

Integrated Studies forms the framework of the curriculum in many schools and geography teachers are currently working within a wide variety of humanities and environmental schemes. Now it is *not* easy to find a satisfactory working definition of integration which accurately conveys the sense in which many schools use it. Integration is an 'in' word, and, as Pring has remarked, it is a 'pro' word which is too readily associated with the 'better' ways of organizing subjects, syllabuses and timetables (Pring 1973). However persuasively the argument for some form of Integrated Studies has been put, an examination of their context and content reveals that many have all the mystical qualities of a siren's song. In fact if we turn to Homer's *Odyssey* we can find the outline of a model for Integrated Studies in the honeyed words which lured many unsuspecting sailors on to the rocks:

Turn that black prow towards the shore
Taste the sweet delights
Waiting here for heroes dear
Through magic days and nights.

We know the noble past,
Know the future's plan,
Pause with us and go thy way
A happy wiser man.

If for 'noble past' we read *History* and for 'know the future's plan' we read modern *Geography* (after all have not Haggett and others reminded us of the ability of theory-laden geography to predict future spatial patterns) we can see the particular lure of this mythical model of integration! (Chorley and Haggett 1965). It also contains those other elements essential to the advocates of integration in the form of a more motivated and therefore happier means of learning. In fact who would want to identify himself as an 'anti-integrationist' when by inference subject teaching is seen as being synonymous with the fragmentation of knowledge, its pigeon-holing into water-tight compartments and the creation of artificial barriers in what some would say ought to be a seamless cloak of learning. Of course one's immediate reaction is — can this be a legitimate presentation of the case? Is the pursuit of knowledge, the broadening and deepening of experience through a study of academic disciplines, as arid and artificial as some would suggest? Where is the evidence? The simple answer is that there is little empirical evidence for or against. As both Miel and Kricher have said, this is a classic case of oversimplification and a presentation of the polarization of views in an either-or context (Miel 1971). It is through such gross oversimplification that the main problems of Integrated Studies have been neatly sidestepped. Much of the debate has fed on the emotional rather than stressed the intellectual as the titles of recent works seem to indicate (James 1968, Hunt 1969).

This is not to deny that the disciplines of knowledge as represented by school subjects have their problems. But are we to accept the system as it is, or do we work for it as it could be? In examining the implications of such a proposal we are working towards the articulation of a curriculum theory which is adaptable to change and from which the right sort of teaching schemes, whether single subject or integrated, can be derived. As yet no such coherent body or curriculum theory exists but because two Schools Council Projects have worked in this field their rationales are worth examining in more detail.

Two Case Studies

(a) *The Keele Integrated Studies Project* has tried to justify its approach both philosophically and pragmatically (Bolam 1972). The rationale involves focusing attention on a 'theme, area or problem' whose study requires 'the help of more than one school subject for its understanding and the interest of more than one teacher in achieving this'. It is, of course, a recognition of the self-imposed limitations of school subjects and of ourselves as individual teachers. For example, English is not likely to concern itself with the development of arable farming in Lancashire or the location of steelworks in Wales. Nor do we all as teachers possess the complete range of skills and familiarity with subject content that the 'ideal' teacher should have. While the Keele approach recognizes the fact that the curriculum in a typical English primary or secondary school cannot avoid being broken down into some form of organizational categories, they emphasize that subjects, themes and problems each represent a *different* kind of internal coherence and the Keele Project's choice of organizing part of the curriculum through a grouping of subjects rather than as an amalgam of single subjects is an attempt to tackle the complex issues of content, skills and attitudes which many themes embrace. It is the very complexity of what they call 'the key issues and problems of the modern world' which demand that they be looked at from many different perspectives. They can only begin to be understood by 'using the insights and enquiry methods of a number of different subjects'.

Such a structure or framework is one in which the geographer could work. The difficulty arises when we begin to think how these objectives can be translated into the bricks and mortar of curriculum materials and methods. For example, what skills are important and how are they to be used? While limiting their references to cognitive skills the Keele Project goes no further than to say 'Specific subject skills are taught when a child comes up against the need in his own researches'. This seems to evade a central issue. It is the need to identify such skills and their relationship to content objectives that is a major task requiring some understanding of both the discipline from which the skills are derived and the insights of child psychology which will help to translate them into language and experience appropriate to age and ability levels. For example recent research on the use of map skills in the classroom stresses the need to link Piagetian psychology to children's understanding of relationships and symbolism, to their perceived needs and interests, and to the potential of hardware models in relating three- and two-dimensional space (Dale 1971, Bartz 1970, Towler 1970).

In looking at this and related problems it is evident that schools are faced with a facet of the 'knowledge explosion'. Teachers find it difficult to monitor relevant research findings and it is in this context that most Schools Council Projects have prepared their pupil material or packs. The Keele and other Projects can be compared to the American High School Geography Project which spent over 7 million dollars to bring Geography teaching in line with recent advances in the subject at University level (Ball *et al.* 1971). But if this is seen as characteristic of the relationship between schools and development projects we seem to have all the characteristics of what can be described as the *Atavistic Curriculum*, in which atavism is defined as 'the return of a disease after the intermission of some generations'. It may be that we are in danger of fixing an ailing car with a new silencer when what is really needed is a new model.

(b) *The Humanities Curriculum Project* also has integration as an aim (Stenhouse 1968). The use of the label Humanities in the title indicates this. While once more stressing the need for selecting themes about which there is public concern, Stenhouse and his team have also stressed the need for an 'internal logical coherence' in their study. They advocate associations of content which seem 'inevitable rather than clever' and are concerned with the need to link the themes to a 'core curriculum'. As the humanities concern themselves with both human experience and human behaviour there appears to be a role for human geography in its teaching, but one is struck by the marked absence of a geographical perspective in the materials the Project has published to date. In this case it is evident that the composition of a team, whether in a Project or a school, gives a particular direction or slant to each integrated syllabus.

But if, as suggested, a geographer could be involved in this type of integration how would that role be defined, written and interpreted? There are at least two aspects of this problem which deserve comment. In recent years there has been a growth in geographical research relating to issues of direct human concern, from studies of black ghettoes in American cities to the implications of changes in government power structure on regional development programmes. The role of personal values has become more explicit in this work and as new content for school courses is derived from these and similar research programmes there will emerge a type of 'radical geography' to replace some elements of current school syllabuses. Secondly, it seems evident that a historical perspective on spatial aspects of world problems has an important place in the explanatory framework which can help put sources of human conflict in focus (Smith 1971).

In both these case studies the Project rationale has stressed that, while academic disciplines can contribute to an integrated approach, much of the success in such a venture rests with the teacher being 'prepared to cross subject boundaries'. But whereas both Projects have supplied a signpost clearly pointing the direction, there is an omission of the detailed route to be followed. As Stenhouse says, 'the logic relating the different fields has to be explored' and it is left to the individual school or teacher to do the exploration.

The School Context

This seems an appropriate point to shift the focus and look briefly at what has emerged under the heading of Integrated Studies in a sample of schools with which the Liverpool Project (Schools Council Project: History, Geography and Social Science 8—13) have had contact. In analysing various integrated syllabuses we have been able to identify a number of types.

(1) There are some schools in which integration has begun in name only and is at the level of aims. A typical case is the linkage of history, geography and R.E. to 'understand the natural and social environment' and one wonders why the obvious potential of the contribution of the natural sciences to such a scheme has been omitted. This is particularly so where the syllabus includes topics such as 'the origins of the earth and theories related to it'. There are many cases where the role of geography is the provision of 'geographical background', and the subject is still regarded as a gazetteer of capes and bays. Such schemes result in a formless, irrelevant hotch-potch. In one syllabus the role of geography in year one of a comprehensive school was 'to introduce the Solar System, the structure of the earth, seasons and tides, fossil evidence, concept of time, an introduction to the physical geography of Asia, Africa and Europe, soils and climate of the Mediterranean, the use of maps and map reading'. It is obvious that this is some crude attempt to use geography as a stagehand creating a physical platform across which history and R.E. teachers paraded early man and stories from the Bible. One can only hope that such syllabuses are critically reviewed whenever they appear and that someone can show where for example geomorphology and climatology link to other social sciences to provide a more meaningful form of integration.

(2) In what can be called the 'skills-based' setting many schools have adopted the I.D.E./M model. The problem here is that a critical consideration of content is sacrificed for emphasis on skills, and there appears to be little regard for progression in learning. Theme follows theme in a cavalcade of topics through which the pupils are asked to 'look at the collection and use of relevant source material, the ability to select the right line of enquiry, and the ability to deal with unfamiliar words'. One wonders what these 'unfamiliar words' are and how they are to be dealt with. Is it imagined as an exercise in the use of a dictionary? If so, it seems to ignore the development and use of the concepts which these words describe. And why limit it to words? In *Explanation in Geography*, Harvey has included a chapter on 'Mathematics — the language of science'. Is there not a need in some topics or problems to quantify the data children collect, whether it be traffic flows, distribution of land use types, population distribution or rainfall amounts? As Harvey and others have indicated, such an attempt to quantify data in the social sciences is useful not as an end in itself but because it demands prior classification of concepts and propositions for empirical study (Harvey 1969).

We would also see one of the roles of language as an aid to understanding the emergence of regional differences. In this context the regional dialects of the British Isles can often be used as a key to the past. Take for example the English Lake District. Children in a Lakeland valley learn dialect words such as 'dale, fell and mere' as part of their everyday speech to express the concepts of valleys, hill and lake. These words are part of the region's folk culture going back to the Norse settlements and some understanding of them and their derivation contribute to a fuller understanding of the area's history and geography. Even a description of a Lakeland dale farm would benefit from a recording of some of this speech and we cannot begin to understand the Lake District sheet of the Ordnance Survey Map without some knowledge of it.

But equally, it is evident that it is the way concepts are learned which is as important as the language we use to describe them. For example the purpose of using the recording of the Lakeland farmer might have had the objective 'to encourage empathy and to correct the straw in the mouth image of farmers which our urban-based children have gleaned from grossly inaccurate infant readers'. In this sense language is being used not only as a skill but as a resource and it is the learnings of this and associated concepts which is the primary objective.

(3) A third type of integrated syllabus is heavily biased towards content. It is most common in the primary school and has appeared in many recently compiled middle school syllabuses. It frequently represents a teacher's dominant interest and may suffer many of the faults of the previous two. A topic is chosen, for example, Water, and a string of associations follow: rivers, ancient Egypt, oceans, Sir Francis Drake, pollution, icebergs, the Titanic disaster and so on. To the initiated these are linked by a web or flow-line graph, and if there is a geographical bias it frequently emerges as the 'local', 'national' and 'other lands' trilogy being superimposed on the web as a crude sampling technique. The false assumption is that the lines on the web represent meaningful connections and these give the topic coherence. It is evident, however, from recent work on network analysis in geography, that a network is only a ground plan and flow can only be created when a dynamic element is placed in the network. What this type of approach has not yet revealed is the real nature of this dynamic element (Abler *et al.* 1972). Similar schemes for example on Oil could be quoted, leading to the inclusion of Halibut oil, development of oil painting, Brylcreem, oil of Ulay, poetry of oil (Black, sticky, smelly, pungent) as topics for study.

Each of these three types of integrated syllabus poses a similar set of problems and indicates how existing curriculum models are being adapted for use in schools. Their inclusion is yet another timely reminder of the need for a curriculum theory that will restore the balance between content and skills, translate the tensions between rival claims of subjects for inclusion on the crowded school timetable either as single subjects or part of Integrated Studies and once again emphasize the need to look at curriculum as a process (Wheeler 1967).

Integrated Studies Project

ARFON WILLIAMS, 1973

It is appropriate to follow two readings concerned with Schools Council curriculum development projects with a description by a schoolteacher of the ways in which a particular project influences course arrangements in a school. Each curriculum development project has a number of trial schools associated with it and these schools experiment with proposals for course organization and strategies of teaching originating from the project team. An essential element in these arrangements is the freedom of the school or the individual teacher to modify proposals and resources in the light of the conditions pertaining in particular schools. In this article Williams indicates some of the distinctive features of this school and describes the ways in which a new course was initiated, suggests some of the difficulties the teachers encountered, and outlines some of the achievements. Two particularly interesting features of this article are firstly, the references to the need for team teaching in integrated courses and the way in which a team was organized, and secondly, the tensions which were created among the staff both at the point of initiation and during the teaching of the course.

The aims of the project were outlined at a meeting to which all members of staff were invited. We agreed to participate as a trial school and undertook to run *Living Together* with the 2nd year and *West Africa* with the 3rd year. Teams were formed initially from the Art and Craft and Handicraft Departments, as well as English, History, Geography, R.I. and Drama, under the leadership of the Deputy Head.

A good deal of hard work was put in during the preliminary planning stage — meetings were held during lunch hours, after school and holiday times, discussing the outline material, amending it, suggesting new material, methods of approach and adapting material to the school's needs.

In the early stages there was a fair amount of inter-subject bickering, a lot of heart searching and head shaking and prejudice. Complaints of time being wasted, the whole thing should be scrapped, loss of privilege, etc, constantly rang out; but eventually a team with a common purpose emerged.

With the help of an American exchange teacher, who was used to team teaching and integration, we made a start in September 1969. Planning meetings were reduced to one or two a week per team, apart from the agitated panic meetings during lunch hours. Our American colleague constantly complained that shortage of money would severely limit our scheme, despite a small launching grant from the county.

The Project produced some friction in the staff room. The group in the corner, talking and arguing, tended to irritate the others. However, as time passed, the staff room began to accept the talk philosophically and, with the expansion of Integrated Studies and team teaching, more are becoming involved, either as members of teams or as specialist advisors or speakers.

The time allocated was 2 x 40 minute periods and 3 x 40 minutes for 2nd year, and 3 x 40 minute periods for 3rd year. The timetable was blocked and the time taken from the humanities subjects — with the proviso built in that the school could easily revert to separate subject disciplines.

The method of approach adopted was a lead lesson, usually factual with visiting speakers and films where possible, and follow-up work in groups sometimes working on the same topic sometimes on different topics. Sometimes the lead lesson was varied — when studying Tristan da Cunha we used improvised drama with a case of 120 boys plus staff in the darkened hall: we had a shipwreck and the stage acted as the island, volcano and all.

The follow-up groups were structured mixed ability — so many from each stream — selected by the team members. Their work included posters, drawing, paintings, graphs, models and written work.

Each time a section was concluded an exhibition was mounted in the school hall. Particularly 'good' pieces of work (the criterion being the amount of effect) were exhibited somewhere immediately. Continuous assessment on file and display work was implemented together with an end of year examination.

At first many of the more able boys disliked the Project — they thought it a waste of time, they were interested in passing as many exams as possible. The less able thought it was a 'skive' but became interested because of the variety of follow-up work, and they then made good progress. The remedial boys were occasionally out of their depth and at one stage were removed except for selected sessions.

The Keele material had already stimulated an approach to integrated studies and team teaching among an enthusiastic group of teachers when, in 1970, a Humanities Department was created and I became Head of the Department.

'What is Integration?' we asked, and looked at the following:

1. 'Nothing more really than an excuse for doing your own pet thing all day and every day.'
2. 'I've heard as many definitions as there are teachers who do it.'
3. 'Fashionable nonsense — those damned modern methods.'
4. 'It's too ephemeral. You can't test it, evaluate it — and if you can't plot it on a graph of distribution there is no point in considering it seriously.'

5. 'Have children to be bound in the straight-jacket of subject areas in order that they can be "taught"?'

6. 'Perhaps it is because we have far too long ignored the aesthetic content of education and concentrated upon narrow subject areas that our environment, natural and man-made, is becoming more and more painful to live in.'

7. 'Changing from formal to informal work is full of toil, tears, sweat and mistakes, but well worth the trouble in the end.'

Integrated Studies and team teaching are very much related — in fact we feel they cannot operate separately — because in an interest centred area of education we have to get away from the traditional classroom situation.

We had agreed to continue our trial period with Keele for another year. At times the Keele material was most unsuitable for use with all the children and we decided to scrap the West African Pack and design our own study unit on U.S.A. We now had the confidence to do this. One of the team had spent a year in U.S.A. on exchange, and several had built up useful contacts for resources on U.S.A. We had taken the stand that we were going to use Keele and not Keele use us, and we had full co-operation from them in this.

Deciding on Aims
We discussed the aims of the course we were designing for our school and after much discussion we decided that the aims of our integrated studies course for our first three years should be: to provide the pupils with the skills to find out, reason and evaluate their findings, to communicate their ideas verbally and in writing to others and to be creative in their thinking and activities.

All the boys from the top set to the remedial set are now included in our courses. We have 120 boys per year group with six staff per year.

We use the Key Lesson — which is stimulating rather than factual. After the key lesson the boys split into either Friendship or Interest groups and then a team member conducts a mini key lesson with these groups. This is followed by discussion on the initial task sheet and suggestions for secondary task sheets. The task sheets operate with numbers of sheets, books, magazines, slides, tapes, etc., relating to a particular area of study — the tasks or questions are arranged so that the pupils follow a progression — discovery, reasoning, analyses, conclusions.

The topic dictates the type of pupil group — Friendship or Interest. We use Friendship Groups for all year topics (eg Civil Rights) and Interest Groups for particular topics (eg Transport — Rail Group, Road, Air, Sea, etc.).

The group work is brought together in a Teach-In when children report their findings through display, drama, discussion, verbal accounts, etc. During the Teach-In members of the team prepare questionnaires, based on information given in the Teach-In and group sessions, which are given to the children to test recall of knowledge. We have found — and are now happy after the initial shock — that the children retain more from their peers than staff. After all, that is something that integration brings about — it's a joint learning process with staff and pupils working together.

Assessment Dimensions

We assess progress with continuous assessment and questionnaires. We base our continuous assessment on social and work factors — whether a pupil usually/ sometimes/rarely perseveres, obtains materials and works, shows initiative, etc., shows concern for others, exercises self-control, abides by group decisions, etc. We assess basic skills, content of work, ability to express an opinion, social awareness, general attitude and involvement, personal and social confidence, imaginative and creative skills, the ability to pursue an enquiry. We use two grades (one for effort, one for attainment) and comments folders; group leaders keep record sheets, teams discuss assessment and standardize marking. The pupils are orally questioned and hold discussions, they have written tests — mainly questionnaires but also essay type, arrangements of given facts in graph form, logical arrangement, multiple choice, etc.

We are not timetabled as teams for planning and so we hold our meetings after 3.45 pm. As the scheme has progressed we have found the meetings have become slightly shorter. Planning meetings deal with material, children, organization problems, etc. We find we must plan in general at least 12 months in advance and in detail at least six months in advance. We have found that we must plan more than we need because if something is not going very well we must be prepared to scrap it. It is very hard to do this sometimes, but we try to put the children first. However, this does not mean we do not play it by ear

In a planning session we may have to decide whether to take a theme or study individual topics and develop from there. When we deal with *Living Together* we deal with a local study first — children come to understand their own society first and then move from the known into the unknown. The local study provides areas that can be studied in Tristan (simple society), Borneo (primitive society) and China (complex ancient society). The areas are family homes, law and order, customs and beliefs, work, transport, communications, leisure, education. We have found that the China material is sometimes rather difficult and so we concentrate on creating a dramatic display — Chinese Festival. The children write poems in the Chinese manner, experiment with music, attempt Chinese theatre portraying legends, paintings in the Chinese manner, etc. They look at the role of the storyteller and make dragons (life-size), lanterns, kites. The school hall is transformed into a Chinese village celebrating a spring festival with the children dressed in pyjamas and wearing Chinese hats. The celebrations are suddenly disrupted by a group of boys throwing off their tops to reveal battle-dress; revolutionary speeches are made and the school disturbed by 120 children chanting and waving red books. Discussion follows and an attempt to understand imperial and modern China. The team on the whole believe that it is all a very worth while exercise for both staff and children.

A Common Course

Now all pupils follow our integrated humanities scheme in their first three years. Old subject empires have vanished and we are moving towards a situation whereby team members are integrated. However, R.I. has departed from the integrated scene because the staff concerned felt that the subject was not having a fair crack of the whip. More departments have become interested and correlate at suitable times in our scheme. The Art Department in particular and the Science, Music and PE Departments all add considerable depth to our studies.

Integrated studies in the 1st, 2nd and 3rd years occupy 8 x 40 minute periods per week in blocked time, while 3 x 40 minute periods for sets 1 and 2 and 6 x 40 minute periods for sets 3 and 4 are devoted to 'basics' (mainly English). In the 4th and 5th year we have developed a number of Mode 3 CSE courses — English (English language and literature certification), history, geography, Social Studies. We hope this will develop into a multi-certificated Integrated Studies course, and we have had the confidence to operate these courses because of our work lower in the school.

Physically the school is not designed for integrated studies: our rooms are far flung in all corners of the school, but during our block sessions we have the use of the school hall, library, remedial room, art room and two classrooms. However, we are attempting to concentrate the humanities rooms in one area centred on the library and build up a central reference area. We have recently obtained the services of a typist/resources organizer so our tasks will become a little easier.

We feel that the children as well as the staff have benefited and are continuing to benefit from our new learning situations and that it is all really worthwhile. We no longer have complaints from the more able — they see how important the skills of discovery, reasoning, evaluation, reporting, communication are. The less able are far more confident, and the remedial boys respond to the stimuli and grasp concepts that previously seemed out of their reach. In fact, relationships between less able and more able have been helped all round — the children are far more confident, self-assured, able to deal with problems and *all* feel they have something to contribute.

Our start as a 'trial' school led to a good deal of curriculum development in the school itself. We are now beginning to hold planning sessions with the children in which they will participate fully in designing future schemes and topics of work. Parents, too, are becoming more interested and we are holding soon our first Integrated Studies evening in which they will participate.

We have found that the team situation has been beneficial to every member. Now we all have the confidence to plan our own 'schemes', use published materials to supplement our own and not rely on outside props too much. We certainly believe that published materials should suit the needs of the school and not the reverse.

Urban Environmental Studies

MARK HEWLETT, 1971

In mainstream geography courses the teaching of urbanism has become increasingly important. It is to be expected that when a geographer decides to contribute to a minority-time general studies programme in a sixth form he may wish to teach a course which is devoted entirely to a study of urban themes. Such themes would, in themselves, appear to be of interest and of relevance to contemporary adolescents and would also provide a suitable basis for a complete course to meet the more general criteria for minority time studies outlined by Hewlett in this article. Teachers with a strong interest in the urban environment will find encouragement and support from the Town and Country Planning Association which publishes the *Bulletin of Environmental Education*, a newsletter which provides accurate, up-to-date information on urban developments, and is active in promoting the establishment of urban study centres – the city equivalent of field study centres in rural areas. In addition, resource materials published by the Schools Council's curriculum development projects have relevance for such purposes, especially the 'Living in Cities' study kit produced by the Humanities Curriculum Project.

The Place of Urban Studies in the Curriculum

The scheme outlined here is in operation at Henley Grammar School where it forms part of the general studies programme. Though designed specifically for sixth-form General Studies, providing an inter-disciplinary element and reducing fragmentation, the scheme, either in whole or in part, could be readily adapted for use (a) in technical college liberal studies programmes, (b) in social studies or humanities courses for school leavers in the 14–16 age range (it may, for example, provide a framework for a CSE Mode 3 course), (c) in the context of specialist GCE courses in sociology, economics, and geography: for example the section on field work research method provides a model for A level geography fieldwork projects.

The Nature of Environmental Urban Studies

It is possible that the inclusion of this article in an issue devoted to environmental studies may lead the reader to look for a peculiar environmental studies methodology. Though environmental studies, as I understand them, are concerned essentially with the *range of diverse elements* in the *local* environment, it would be to the detriment of coherent study in depth to attempt to consider all the elements of the local environment, and at the same time, there is no merit in deliberately avoiding the study of places outside the local environment where one will find valid comparative illustration. In practice, of course, the nature of the study depends on the identification of certain fundamentally important considerations which determine the method of approach and the selection of subject matter. In this particular scheme these were:

1. Maximum relevance to problems which will directly affect the lives of the students involved.
2. The importance of inculcating an active sense of responsibility for their social and physical environment.
3. Emphasis on (a) rigorous methods of empirical enquiry; (b) conceptual structures covering the wide range of phenomena studied.

Relevance

Urban studies need little justification: (a) about 80 per cent of the inhabitants of this country live in urban areas and very few, if any, live beyond an urban sphere of influence; (b) we live at a time when people are increasingly concerned about the quality of the environment, whose problems, essentially the product of the growth of urban industrial functions, are concentrated in towns and cities which are foci of human activity where physical, economic and social pressures are greatest.

These problems demand urgent attention and it is increasingly recognized that far more needs to be known about our environment, in order that better decisions may be made not only on particular problems such as noise, pollution and congestion, but 'in shaping the distribution of employment, housing, education and the social and commercial services, the distribution of income and the network of communications which give access to these things; the social composition of urban neighbourhoods and the opportunities available within them; and the political, administrative and professional procedures which govern the development of urban society' (D. Donnison, Centre for Environmental Studies).

Active Involvement

It is not enough to point out that problems exist: even to describe in detail and attempt analyses of the problems may achieve very little, unless some sense of responsibility for the environment is inculcated. Assessment in the form of post-school follow-up studies to test levels of active involvement in the community may be difficult to administer; nevertheless if the work done is not to be fruitless, it is important that one thinks positively in terms of post-school assessment and does not lapse into thinking of aims and assessment in terms only of carefully compiled projects which represent the rather arbitrary and superficial goals that we as teachers are in the habit of satisfying ourselves with. The basic aim of practical problem solving must be explicitly emphasized and not left as vague ideals which one can never approach in practice.

It should be possible to show how problems concern all individuals in the community who, if sufficiently critical and well informed may be able to contribute directly or indirectly to their solutions. It will of course be clear that many problems are susceptible of solution only through the complex machinery of government and big organizations: here it may be possible only to go as far as (a) establishing what sorts of solutions may be reached, (b) who is responsible for making decisions, (c) the degree to which private citizens can bring any influence to bear on decision makers, (d) gaining some insight into the work of those professionally engaged with the problems being investigated and finding out about career opportunities for those who themselves may be interested to contribute professionally when they leave school.

But whatever the difficulties encountered and however limited the areas of action may be, it is of the essence of the project that the elements of the environment are not treated merely as phenomena to be observed, described and classified but as aspects of our society about which we should be concerned.

Methods of Enquiry

While the basic aim is concerned with encouraging social involvement, equal emphasis must be laid on rigorous methods of study. Commitment may be commendable but commitment without understanding may be worse than total apathy.

Here we are concerned with such concepts as intellectual honesty and objective method — which I hope will reassure those who may feel uneasy about 'commitment'. These concepts, implicitly accepted in academic work, are often unappreciated in the context of the formal regulated study of emotionally neutral material; but where the students are working with problems complicated by prejudice and genuine emotional involvement, they assume significance, and the methodology of scientific investigation becomes fundamentally important. This is not to suggest that the objective should eliminate the subjective. Through literature, art, film, etc., every effort should be made to sensitize the observer's faculties. This project is concerned in a preliminary way with the sort of social engineering which will become very much more widespread in the coming decades, and while our social engineers must be able to *use* the right machinery they must not *be* machines.

Structural Framework

A further point of academic technique lies in the establishment of a rational framework. Clear structural patterns are essential in order to make sense of such heterogeneous phenomena as are considered in urban study in particular facilitating understanding of the way different elements of the environment inter-relate, thus reducing any tendency to over-simplify particular problems.

The primary structure is that presented in tabular form below. It is derived from a geographical view of towns and cities as Central Places providing a wide range of social and economic functions for their own inhabitants and the inhabitants of their neighbouring regions which constitute their spheres of influence. The selection of a framework based on a geographical view does not pre-suppose emphasis on essentially geographical problems. It is, however, the case that geography's concern with the co-relation of diverse elements does enable it to produce a coherent structure for this particular purpose.

Within this framework, particular topics will inevitably raise and require explanation in terms of generalizations from different disciplines: indeed, urban studies may be seen as a means to introduce students to the elements of a variety of academic disciplines with which they may be unfamiliar, and this may constitute a subsidiary aim of the course.

Content Framework
Method of approach

General introductory course of approximately half a term, during which, through lectures, films, reading, resource banks if available, students recieve basic information and are introduced to general concepts. The content, given in incomplete and summarized form below is susceptible to considerable variation in emphasis. Certain themes will run through the work: 1. The evolutionary view: past, present and future. 2. The comparative view, with reference to towns and cities of contrasting character. 3. Actual and potential areas of conflict. 4. Planning.

Allocation of groups

The formulation of key questions. It is so crucial that these are relevant and specific, not general topics which will lead to the uncritical collection of copious information. Below are a few examples of appropriate subjects for examination.

The Urban Complex

Definitions of towns and cities, their growth, form and functions. Central Place, Concepts, Spheres of Influence, Classification. The essential nature of the town or city as a socio-economic focus, and its inevitable problems.

I. The commercial function

The growth of towns as centres of exchange. Concepts of specialization and division of labour: wholesaling; retailing; markets; supermarkets and small shops. Shopping centre hierarchies, threshhold concepts. Rent and site.

Changes in shopping habits. Price variations between shops. Quality and range of retail provision (comparative study). Accessibility by public and private transport.

II. The industrial function

Reasons for the nature and growth of industry in towns. Basic theory of industrial location. Trends in industrial employment. Declining vs growth industry. Problems of site. Social vs economic considerations.

Problems of labour recruitment. Unemployment figures; stability in short and long terms. Effects on traffic, noise, pollution. Journeys to work involved.

III. Administrative and public service functions

The structure of local government and the range of its functions, in particular for example health and social services, law, framework, courts, police, offenders. Range of private professional services.

Levels of public awareness of functions of Local Government and the qualifications of elected representatives. Adequacy of provision for those in need.

IV. Educational, social, cultural-recreational provision

The structure and organization of education; the nature and range of provision. Range of cultural, social and sporting facilities for all age groups. Open spaces.

Adequacy of provision for the pre-school child. Public attitudes to education. Adequacy/inadequacy of social, cultural provision.

V. Residential provision

Range and quality of residential provision. Classification of residence: Old vs new; flats and houses, public and private. Extension of residential areas, urban sprawl.

Quality of planning and design. Localization of residential types; special problems relating to new estates, slums, flats. Relationship of residential type to social characteristics.

VI. Communications

Communications as a key to the essential nature of the town as a focus of activity. The intra-urban network; links with the urban sphere of influence, inter-urban network. Modes of transport; road, rail, water. Private and public transport. Growing demands on transport systems.

Congestion — relating to economic efficiency. Road accidents, parking, pollution. Road vs rail. Traffic engineering in the local region.

VII. Physical and aesthetic aspects

The site and situation of the town; its extent and form. Problems imposed by the physical environment: relief, drainage, water supply, effluent disposal. Natural and planned growth. The appearance of the whole and its constituent parts. Architectural character.

How far has the town been a victim of the original choice of site? How could the appearance of the town be improved? Do people care about the appearance of their town or city?

VIII. Population

The synthesizing nature of demographic study. Growth and structure of population. Classification by age, sex, employment, social class. Localization of social and racial groups. Overcrowding. Concepts of optimum population.

Needs and problems of particular groups. Evidence of social friction.

Amplification of Enquiry Method

(This will be used as a framework for a written summary by each student.) Discursive introduction (a) summary of major elements and their interrelationships, (b) brief notes on related disciplines, (c) reading lists and other secondary sources. This will consist of duplicated information, notes (from books and lectures), etc., forming a written record of the first six or seven

weeks of the course during which the students are receiving prepared
introductory material (indicated in the content framework).

Each student, either individually or as a member of a group, will select one
of the key questions posed which will lead on to individual or group research
project work. Each project will be developed under the following headings:

1. Statement of hypothesis to be tested (or problem to be solved). Clearly
   defined and selected to produce meaningful results within the time
   available.
2. Detailed preliminary considerations: of the type of information required
   for the particular purpose: problems likely to be encountered in the
   collection of data, mainly practical, logistic problems, e.g. time availability, division of work among members of the group.
3. Collection and description of data. Examples of sources and methods:
   maps (e.g. blank outline base maps, street maps. Ordnance Survey maps of
   various scales and editions, land use maps — dependent on nature of the
   problem); statistical records, e.g. census figures; documents from National
   and Local Government sources (e.g. Health Department, Borough Engineers Departments); Police sources; private sources, e.g. Estate Agents,
   Solicitors, Architects; newspapers (qualified by reference to accuracy,
   objectivity); questionnaires (after preliminary work on formulation,
   sampling techniques, etc); tape-recorder interviews; photographs; physical
   measurement by precise survey interviews (e.g. road/pavement widths,
   shop frontages); traffic counts; case work (e.g. in hospitals, mental homes,
   children's homes).
4. Storage, presentation and classification of information: collation of data;
   presentation of statistics; histograms, graphs, etc.; maps: density, distribution flow maps, etc.; models (theoretical or material), film, photo display.
5. Testing and assessment of information: accurate and concise written
   conclusions: statistical tests of significance and correlation.
6. Acceptance or rejection of hypothesis, or statement regarding inconclusive
   nature of findings leading to (a) statement of further information required
   to give significant results, (b) possible action to be taken such as
   (i) presentation of findings to individuals or groups who may be able to
   take further action to remedy problems or deficiencies exposed, e.g.
   Council members, Local Government departments concerned, architects,
   trade-unionists, managing directors, preservation societies, local newspaper, M.P.s, etc. (ii) offers of assistance to charitable institutions
   (iii) establishing a local Civic Trust.

The Role of the Teacher

The word 'teacher' which may seem inappropriate (a) because an extensive
project of this sort (involving approximately sixty sixth-form students at
Henley for example) require three or four teachers, and (b) because the term
has the connotation of instructor. Although traditional didactic methods may
be employed in the general introductory stage, throughout most of the

course, the staff involved will be more in the roles of supervisors and co-ordinators; indeed the term co-operators might more accurately reflect the desired functions and attitudes of staff. They should:

1. Introduce the project, painting a broad general picture, summarizing and relating component elements.
2. Specify objectives.
3. Provide detailed information on sources.
4. Assist in the formation of hypotheses.
5. Act as general co-ordinators to avoid unnecessary duplication of effort.
6. Deal with practical problems such as size and membership of research groups.
7. Periodically review the work done by individual groups in order to maintain overall coherence.
8. Arrange links with other schools (perhaps with a twin school in another country).
9. Arrange lectures, visits, films, etc., in the most effective sequence.
10. Carry out assessment, checking the method of approach and quality of work done throughout the year, without, as far as possible, appearing to interfere with what should ideally be independent self-motivated enquiry.

Although it need hardly be said that the success of the project depends on the skill of the staff involved, the qualities most required are not necessarily those related to academic training (though other things being equal, geographers, economists and sociologists will be most familiar with the range of subject matter under consideration). As important as knowledge of subject matter is knowledge of technique, and it may be that neither is as important as the ability to convey enthusiasm and the excitement of original research.

The Humanities Programme in Thomas Bennett School

PETER MITCHELL, 1972

The relationship between a newly formed faculty of humanities, the raising of the school leaving age, and the Certificate of Secondary Education, is at the heart of this article by Mitchell which describes one aspect of curriculum innovation in a secondary school. The problems are quite different from those faced by Hewlett in a grammar school sixth-form context (Reading 23). As Mitchell suggests, the establishment of a faculty structure may improve communication between departments and between departments and headmaster in large schools, and it may promote curricular innovation. As Musgrove puts forward in Reading 18, such a structure also has implications for authority and power in schools. Certainly from reading Mitchell's account it is clear that the faculty structure has permitted the careful design and development of courses. The emphasis on planning in the design of integrated courses is an important element requiring heavy investment in time on the part of the participating teachers — a fact which also emerges in Williams' account (Reading 22) — and for teachers considering the mounting of integrated courses planning and organization time must be in the forefront of their deliberations. Mitchell goes on to point out the difficulties encountered in the utilization of study kits and work cards, two of the distinctive resources in integrated courses, and the importance of Mode 3 of the Certificate of Secondary Education for the examination of integrated courses also comes through clearly in this article.

The raising of the school leaving age has prompted much educational innovation for children of low achievement. Schools have been able to pursue educational change without the pressure of external Mode 1 examination and their emphasis on pupils acquiring bodies of factual knowledge. The benefit of this opportunity to experiment can be seen in such projects as team teaching and integrated studies where staff have begun to work outside their discipline with staff from other departments. These 'ROSLA' or 'Newsom' courses have been particularly popular in that area of the curriculum broadly described as 'Humanities'. The Newsom Report and Enquiry 1 confirmed, what many teachers knew to be the case, that history, religious education etc. were held in low esteem by pupils with low achievement. They were bored by subject matter and learning experiences which hardly seemed relevant to their perception of their particular needs. When it is appreciated that these pupils see vocational ends as the principal purpose of education the prestige of the humanities area of the curriculum is hardly surprising. In many ways these under-achieving pupils are displaying a realistic approach to what they consider to be of value in their education and their reluctance to automatically accept the teacher's assessment of the correct curriculum balance shows an appreciation of what society will demand from them in the future. The notion of the 'ideal' pupil, who achieves examination success, includes as one of its qualities the acceptance of the teacher's learning as enabling the teacher to prescribe courses which go unquestioned as to their content and the learning experiences they involve.

While ROSLA has been the subject of considerable publicity in the past year the subject has been with us for a number of years and many schools are now in the advanced stages of planning their curriculum changes to meet the new demands. Where a school is streamed or broadly banded, ROSLA is almost automatically perceived as a problem associated with the under-achieving child. In the summer term 1966 the headmaster of Thomas Bennett school created a faculty structure which was designed to group together related departments in a way which improved communication in the school and at the same time encouraged innovation between related departments. The publication of the Schools Council working Paper II (1967c), 'Society and the Young School Leaver', coincided with the establishment of the humanities faculty (history, geography, social science, religious education, classics and home economics), and the first task of the faculty was to create an integrated humanities course which was to be taught to the lower of two broad bands in the school. The regional CSE board has an integrated studies panel and we were able to create a Mode 3 examination based upon course work, project work and an oral examination.

Our early enthusiasm for innovation was in part sustained by the feeling that we couldn't possibly produce a course that was less motivating than the more traditional, single subject Mode 1 CSE examinations in the humanities. Our discussions centred around such questions as — how can we make the work relevant for these particular pupils? What information do these pupils need about their community? How can we break down the barriers between their experiences at school and their future work in the community? In common with many such 'ROSLA' courses we chose to develop the course around a framework provided by studies of the individual, the family, the neighbourhood community, the town, the nation etc. This concentric approach was designed to explore how individuals develop as personalities and then to proceed to consider various types of community at increasing levels of complexity and distance from the pupil's own experience. The course had the advantage of beginning with the familiar but was unsure of the balance of emphasis between information about 'practical' living and analytical studies about society. Marten Shipman (1971) and John White (1968) have both discussed the limitations of these types of courses, and, during the first year of running the course we became convinced of the need to consider the curriculum provision for all abilities of children made by the faculty.

Two positive gains came out of the 'ROSLA' or 'Newsom' course. We had established a pattern of working together as historians, geographers and social scientists (anthropology, sociology, psychology and economics all being represented in the department) and we had introduced social science into the curriculum. Our reasons for promoting a greater emphasis on social sciences centred on the belief that they provided concepts which would help children understand more fully the complexities of their own and other societies, and that the inductive mode of inquiry, associated with studies in social science, would provide a framework of guidelines for developing pupil inquiries.

One year was spent planning the change from a humanities integrated curriculum provision for under-achieving children to a common programme for all children, to be set alongside mathematics and English, as the compulsory part of the curriculum. We were now beginning to consider the curriculum of successful pupils who would normally take O level history and/or geography, and the level and quality of debate was of a different order than that we had engaged in when discussing a 'Newsom' course. An important concern was the assumption, by some historians, that social science, with its emphasis on the development of theories and generalizations, is in some sense incompatible with the work of the particularist historian whose concern is the study of unique events. This was a subject-centred debate which is fairly typical of the type engaged in when discussing the curriculum of successful pupils. In initiating innovation it is necessary to explore fully these types of issues when it is appreciated that staff identity and status is closely related to what they consider to be the importance of their subject to the child's education. This should not, however, detract from what was our central concern with helping pupils to gain confidence in their own ability to form judgments through analysis and reasoning. The complexity of modern society, and the demands it makes on the individual's powers of judgment, suggest that an emphasis on factual information is an anachronism and that the emphasis should switch to learning experiences which develop skills of inquiry and encourage individual and group participation in making judgments.

Planning the design and development of the course went beyond the consideration of content and syllabus production. Discussions helped to clarify that in general the disciplines represented in the programme should be used to study problems that are of concern to young people and adults alike. We were conscious of the difficulties of dealing with these problems in the classroom — particularly of the tendency for discussions to lead to pupils taking up a public stance based upon their knowledge of the problem gained from the mass media, peer groups etc.Humanities teachers must face the fact that many pupils will assume that they know all there is to know about problems such as race, war etc. under consideration. Evidence presented by the teacher can be of little value in the face of such firmly held convictions. The planning of the course has therefore been concerned with identifying the concepts and methods of working that would bring children to an understanding of what is meant by making an informed judgment. Implicit in this notion of the child making judgments is a reduction of the dominance of the child's learning by the teacher.

Clarifying ideas on what one hopes to achieve in initiating a major curriculum innovation can give an oversimplifed picture of the curriculum process. When the team began to plan learning experiences and to select subject matter the constraints of working on a two year programme for the pupils' fourth and fifth years became evident. In the first 3 years the pupils followed conventional subject teaching and had little experience of how to respond to the opportunity to plan inquiries which involved handling a wide variety of evidence. Not only were the skills of inquiry often new to the children but the concepts of social science such as role, socialization, peer group were also new. It was with these two points in mind that the planning of materials and learning experiences, for the first year of teaching the humanities programme in 1969–70, involved a high degree of pupil guidance, through work cards. Kits of materials were produced on twenty themes with the idea that pupils, where possible, would be handling raw data rather than the processed data of the text book. Kits were also favoured because they could be more easily subject to updating and improvement. An attempt was made to balance the control of pupil inquiries with opportunities for free inquiry which aimed to give pupils the opportunity to extend the range of their inquiries by including aspects of work in which they, as individuals, were particularly interested. Free inquiry also served as a means of evaluating the extent to which pupils were displaying a personal mastery over an inquiry process.

The pupils work in mixed ability groups for the first three years and, in the fourth and fifth year of the humanities programme, they are taught in one of three broad ability bands, into which the 14 forms are divided.

Examining work in the programme has been on the basis of Mode 3 O level and CSE examinations. Two grades were awarded in Geographical and Economic Studies and Historical and Social Studies. These titles describe the grouping of content for the purpose of assessment. The Mode 3 nature of the assessment allowed us to include course work as contributing 50 per cent of the marks towards the final grade, the other 50 per cent being based on an examination paper. Eight periods per week are devoted to the course and pupils may be entered for a minimum of one CSE and a maximum of two O levels, on completion of the course. This represents an attempt to devise a common examination at 16-plus within the framework of the existing examination system. Unlike the common examination at 16-plus, under consideration by the Schools Council, it caters for all but a very small minority of pupils at the end of their fifth year.

The first two years of teaching the course took place under difficult conditions with four of the eight periods being spent in huts away from the humanities area. This difficulty exacerbated the problems which related to the teaching of new subject matter by inquiry methods. If this article is to be of value to other secondary teachers it should be frank about problems that can be attributed to innovation. The planning discussions, already outlined, eliminated many initial difficulties but on reflection it is clear that we should have given more thought to (a) pupil expectations in the learning situation and (b) the changing pattern of pupil-teacher interaction brought about by emphasis on individual and group work. We predicted that pupils would find the move from a basically didactic learning situation to classroom inquiries a difficult one; our response to this, by providing support for the pupils through work cards, was miscalculated and allowed insufficient balance from other learning experience, particularly, for example, opportunity for discussion. As has been pointed out, in *The Language, the Learner and the School* by Douglas Barnes *et al.*, the work card can isolate a child from communicating with his peers and his teachers and inhibit the growth of language as an important precursor to the child understanding the subject he or she is studying. By seeing the pupil's inquiry skills developing over a five-year period it is possible to envisage pupils displaying an increasing mastery over them, throughout that period, with decreasing control by the ubiquitous work card.

The changing pattern of pupil-teacher interaction that is implicit in a move towards greater emphasis on pupil inquiries was the second subject on which we miscalculated. The kit of materials produced by the 'expert' can become a barrier between teacher and pupil — quite the opposite of what was intended by having pupils working as individuals and in groups. This is, in part, explained by the fact that much of the subject matter was new to staff and ourside their area of subject 'expertise'. It is also, however, true to say that the kit can be an effective form of classroom control. More awareness of the need for discussion and in-service training on this subject would have reduced its impact on the first two years of the course. With special reference to social science, it is also true to say that in studying subjects, such as education, the family and child development, we gave insufficient time and emphasis to the pupils' commonsense interpretations of the subjects.

The setting up of this programme was fortunate in the amount of outside help it received from financial support, research findings and examination moderators. Its eventual development, into an essential part of every child's curriculum, has rested, however, on the work of a group of staff who were able to translate their ideas into an ongoing programme of work and, through their willingness to evaluate and revise their materials, to ensure that the programme would continue to develop. All teaching is now housed in a humanities area centred on a resource centre. How to knit the resource centre into an extension of the child's classroom inquiries is a current subject for debate.

Interdisciplinary Studies

JOHN SEALEY, 1971

The title 'Inter-disciplinary Studies' is reminiscent of the courses labelled Inter-disciplinary Enquiry which originated in the Goldsmiths' College Curriculum Laboratory. The course described in this article may have been influenced by ideas from this source as well as from publications of the Schools Council. However, the author indicates in the first paragraphs that the course which he describes has its immediate origins in an enquiry mounted by a local curriculum development committee into the difficulties encountered by pupils in their first year of the secondary school. The interest in this article lies in the fact that the course described was for pupils in the first year of a secondary school. The courses described in the previous readings have been mainly in the upper parts of schools, for older pupils approaching school leaving. The clustering of the pupils into tutorial groups for administrative and pastoral purposes and the utilization of the same groups for teaching purposes highlights some of the difficulties encountered in large compre-hensive schools in the organization of the curriculum. Mixed ability groups are frequently presented with integrated courses in which geography is usually included. A geographer looking at the five topics listed by Sealey as the starting topics for the studies may express surprise that these should be seen in an inter-disciplinary context; it poses important questions about the distinctive contribution geography can make to the education of pupils in the early years of the secondary school and whether this contribution can best be made in inter-disciplinary courses such as the one described here.

In September 1968 a year's programme in inter-disciplinary studies in humanities was begun at Dunsmore School for Girls, Rugby, a bilateral school with about 700 pupils. Half of the first year intake of 128 pupils were selective; the remainder were non-selective. Thus a very wide range of abilities were included in the experiment outlined here.

Initial stimulus came from research carried out by the first to third year sub-committee of the Rugby area curriculum development committee. Answers to questionnaires sent to heads, teachers and children highlighted certain difficulties encountered by the pupils in the first year of the secondary school. These included problems arising from subject-teaching, changes in class lessons and teachers at frequent intervals, large numbers of books and new subjects. They showed the need for pupils to be firmly attached to a form or house; the need to consider the formation of friendship groups in the school; for the reduction of lesson changes and homework to a minimum. They also indicated that the best primary school 'topic methods' might be used to allow a degree of freedom in study.

If any realistic answer were to be given to these problems then a minor revolution would clearly have to take place. Moreover, the change would have to involve a radical reorganization of teaching methods rather than basic changes in the overall school staffing ratio, classroom space or book allowances.

The solution offered to the problems by Dunsmore Girls' School was a comprehensive one. A great deal of work was involved in preparing a syllabus for a five years' course using guided enquiry methods. This article briefly describes only the organization of the first year.

Organization
Subjects forming the basis of the scheme were geography, history, religious education and English, with some art and movement. When necessary other specialist subject teachers on the staff were available for peripheral information. Ten periods per week, each thirty to thirty-five minutes long, were utilized, blocked into two afternoons and half of a third afternoon.

The Dunsmore scheme did not allow for an entirely free choice of study. It was early decided that a limited choice and a more structured approach would be educationally desirable. But within this structure there was still much room for individual selection. At the start, five topics were chosen under the general title 'Beginnings'. These were:

1. The Land Begins. Origins of geophysical features.
2. Rivers begin.
3. Settlement begins. Prehistoric settlement. Roman settlements.
4. Village studies. Farming begins.
5. Modern farms.

Suggested lines of enquiry arising out of the main theme included: The origin of artefacts, e.g. clothing, the wheel, bicycles, etc., motor power and fuel. The origins of ethno-sociological groups, e.g. racial groups in early Britain, early Greek civilization. The origins of institutions, e.g. churches, schools, law-courts. The origin of methods of communication, e.g. speech (language), writing, drama. The origin of the fine arts, e.g. music, painting, sculpture. The origins of social habits, e.g. working a five- or six-day week, no sport on Sundays, the three-meal a day habit.

The 128 pupils in the year intake were divided into four tutorial groups. Each of these four groups contained a cross-section of abilities (as assessed in the 11 plus test). The tutorial group was the 'home base' or form, under the general guidance of a permanent tutor. Its major functions were to provide an administrative and pastoral care centre for the group. For example, registration, record-cards, inter-form sport and social activities were the responsibility of the 'home' form tutor. The first task of the group, before work could begin, was to organize itself into a number of sub-groups called 'clusters'. These were formed on the basis of academic interests and friendship patterns within the group. Thus, within a tutorial group of thirty pupils there might be formed five separate 'clusters' each consisting of six pupils. Then, a cluster of six in one group would join with clusters of six pupils in each of the three other groups making a total work-cluster of twenty-four pupils. This became the 'work-unit' within the organization. (In practice, there was no need for the numbers in the working clusters to be so symmetrical; it was possible for there to be either more or less than five clusters within a group since the choice was largely determined by the pupils' interests.)

Throughout the year considerable flexibility was allowed within the topic chosen by a particular cluster and the pupils followed many varied routes according to their interests and abilities. Sometimes two or more clusters would amalgamate for specialist teaching on a theme they had in common.

The four group tutors were only one part — though an extremely important part — of the teaching force involved with the first year experiment. The full group of teachers involved with the first year working clusters included specialists in history, geography, English, sociology, biology, art and craft, music, movement, religious education and remedial teaching.

The first task of all the teachers concerned with the first year experiment was to stimulate interest and imagination. Films on group work and on the chosen theme 'Beginnings' (Earth and History) were shown to the year as a whole. An exhibition of pictures, charts, geological samples and models illustrating 'Beginnings' was organized. Then, in the four 'home-base' tutorial groups, there was further stimulus through tutor-directed discussions on possible themes, group and individual work and diaries. The diaries included precise records and were brought up to date by the pupil at the end of each week. The tutors advised the groups on sources of information such as the fields of the specialist staff, film lists, and books for reference.

The group tutor kept a folder on each pupil containing detailed information on progress in both work and personality. At the end of each half-term the group tutor marked the pupil's topic with a grade and assessed such aspects as presentation, initiative, mental ability, motor skill, planning and the ability to link different aspects of her work into a cognitive whole. In assessing personality the tutor commented on such things as appearance, responsibility, concentration, relationships with adults and peers, adaptability and reaction to criticism.

Basic Knowledge and Skills
The inter-disciplinary study method used was not entirely open-ended. It was certainly seen to be important that the pupils should be allowed to choose friends with whom they felt they could work; it was also true that within the five main headings selected by the staff a wide choice of different aspects of the work was permitted. However, it was thought desirable at the outset that

certain basic knowledge and skills should be specifically taught. This specific content was 'injected' at points where the required knowledge or skill seemed appropriate to the particular study. For example, it was thought desirable to teach, in geography, the use of maps, physical concepts of the earth, weathering, rivers, man's relation to his physical environment, specific correlation of land, soil, climate, demands, labour and type of farming. In history: the idea of the past, beginnings of people, life in prehistoric Rome, and medieval Britain. In religious education: how writing began (pictographs, cuneiform and hieroglyphics), how stories began (myth, legend, fable, parable, allegory, fairy-tale, fiction and history), the origins of the Jewish religion, Christianity, other religions and Christian denominations.

About half the year's intake at Dunsmore is non-selective and this inevitably brings to the school its share of slow children. The enquiry method of study allowed remedial teaching to be carried on without the disruption of classes and staff which is sometimes necessary in the more formal situation.

Integration

One of the major objectives of the interdisciplinary method is to break down traditional subject barriers. The nine months or so of work put into their studies by this school's twelve-year-old girls has gone a long way towards doing this. For example, a group of pupils studied the growth of a local village. In this study, the village's many geographical features were related to its historical development, its religious aspects and its economic progress; its site, houses, shops, church and farms were studied in detail. A study undertaken by another group about the horse integrated not only subjects like geography and history, but also geology, anthropology and the concept of time.

The Staff

In a system as flexible as I.D.S. the teacher has to be equally flexible. In the Dunsmore experiment the organization that was necessary demanded team teaching. Every week — usually a Friday lunch break — the team of teachers involved met with the team leader to discuss the progress of the past week and the day to day details of the following week. Outstanding interdepartmental understanding and co-operation was therefore a large and essential element in the structure. Another vital element was the teacher's role as 'adviser' to the pupil in her studies and school social life. In the free enquiry method used at Dunsmore there was an emphasis on personal contact between the individual pupil and the individual teacher. This was particularly the case with the four members of the team who were also the group tutors.

Report back

An essential part of the year's programme was the organization and presentation of the 'report-back' material. At the end of every half-term, or period appropriate to the subject studied, the cluster gathered together its accumulated work. Members of the cluster would take it in turns to present aspects of the ground they had covered in the period to other clusters. The report-back session took many different forms. Illustrated and demonstrated talks were the commonest method. Pupils used as appropriate carefully prepared blackboard diagrams, pictures, models, rock samples, film-strips, slides and the tape-recorder. Notes were carefully prepared by the report-back group and were duplicated and distributed to the other clusters. Drama was also used to show certain historical aspects of the subject studied. For example, one report-back group dramatized, with costumes, an ancient Greek market-place, and activities which might be seen in a typical gymnasium, including boxing, wrestling, javelin-throwing and the private debates of the leisured Athenian gentleman. General discussion on the reports was always encouraged. They were not passive affairs. The tutors were involved in that they helped the reporting cluster to prepare and to produce the material. In particular the subject specialist was involved to check on accuracy and depth of content, while the English specialists gave guidance on manner of presentation.

The 'audience' group made notes for their report-back folders, checked samples, asked questions and answered specially prepared questionnaires. In fact the report-back period meant, on the one hand, collating, consolidating and making sense of weeks of work, and on the other disseminating experiences in a vital and interesting manner.

Visits to the surrounding villages were an integral part of the year's work. They provided both stimulus and source material on the historical, religious and geographical beginnings of environmental studies.

The year's studies finished with an exhibition of models, materials, charts, maps and written reports.

Conclusions
One of the most important lessons learned from the experiment was that it is *possible* to organize such a project in a secondary school of traditional architecture (it was opened in 1952), with ordinary staff-pupil ratios, with mixed ability groupings (IQs ranged from 70 to 140+), with no extra equipment, and no more than the normal growth of the school library. At least two major aspects had to be borne in mind. First, the need for willing co-operation by the IDS team (at Dunsmore the experiment centred on the humanities although other subject teachers were consulted from time to time), and second, the necessity for a very clear view of the *need* for enquiry methods, and the objectives thought to be desirable. From both points of view the Dunsmore experiment, though limited in its subjects and scope, was a success.

World Studies at Walworth Comprehensive School

D. HOGAN, 1972

Closely associated with proposals for using school courses to promote citizenship have been suggestions for furthering international understanding through the curriculum. For geography teachers the international arena is an integral part of their daily work. As a recent D.E.S. publication states: 'If geography can reduce an apparent chaos of unstable spatial distributions into some recognizable order it will have played a significant part in helping pupils to understand their world' (Department of Education and Science 1972). But an earlier publication had warned over-enthusiastic geography teachers who might seek to promote international harmony, correct 'wrong' prejudices and change pupils' attitudes to foreign peoples and places: 'International goodwill is not likely to be fostered by direct teaching. Goodwill is generally an attitude of mind induced by religion and social philosophy and nurtured through study in many branches of the humanities' (Ministry of Education 1960).

Teachers, often encouraged and supported by an array of agencies, have designed courses which may focus on single countries, continents, international groupings, or global themes and problems, and these appear under a variety of titles. Frequently these courses are of an integrated kind and in this article Hogan describes how such a course, in this case entitled 'World Studies', can be arranged so that it is studied by pupils throughout a comprehensive school.

Some Driving Forces behind the Innovation

As is often the case, the reasons for considering a major curriculum change probably sprang from a variety of sources which manifested themselves as an unconscious attempt to relieve pressure rather than as a conscious effort to improve the learning performance of the pupils — though, obviously, in the long run those two go hand in hand.

For example, the physical appearance of the area is that of a run-down working-class ghetto — old two-storey terraces are being bulldozed to leave vast areas of devastation on which an eleven million pound housing scheme apparently better designed for battery hens than human beings is being reared. Moreover, the old proletarian skills of docker and printworker are quickly being destroyed and with them a sense of identity. No member of staff — because of the enormous waiting lists and the total absence of rented accommodation — has any chance of living in the catchment area of the school and the immediate impression one gets of the district often gives rise to feelings of panic and despair in new staff. There are two possible responses: one is to run away; the other is to stay and try to do something dramatic about it — so far as it is within a teacher's power to do so. In these circumstances, curriculum reform may be seen as social reform manqué, especially when it is directed to personalizing and making 'relevant' the learning experience.

Again, we were very aware of the frightful jolt which children suffer when moving from primary to secondary school — made worse when the secondary draws from more than 30 'feeder' schools. Any curriculum change which helped to create areas of stability in timetable and school (i.e. uninterrupted blocks of time with familiar teachers) would be desirable.

As a last example, it was long a source of irritation to both history and geography specialists that the original allocation of two periods per week each was totally inadequate, and its more recent replacement by four periods of 'social studies' equally unsatisfactory in that it tended to lead to the swallowing up of geography altogether in an inadequately conceptualized curriculum. English, too, had long felt the need to be associated with other subjects in important areas of its work so that language could be developed right across the curriculum in a unified way.

Some Essential Pre-requisites

In practice, I do not believe, looking back, that the changes which ensued ever seemed very noteworthy, mainly because the school atmosphere was one of continual experiment in every major area. This not only reduced inter-departmental friction to a minimum but actually led to positive feed-back — for example between science and World Studies. Moreover, whereas one would normally expect to go through hard periods of conversion of key teachers resisting change because it seemed to diminish subject autonomies — and, therefore, their own, hard-won, competencies — we enjoyed a remarkable consensus both in respect of broad aims and also detailed curriculum units.

The other potential area of opposition — from Head and Inspectorate — also not only failed to materialize but, in both cases they showed every enthusiasm so that we all felt that we were 'swimming with the tide' and drew much encouragement.

Lastly, subject integration with team teaching and individualized learning can hardly take place where the learning spaces do not permit reorganization. It is very well worth stressing, for the encouragement of others, that our oldest buildings — dating from, and unchanged since 1888 — proved quite the most flexible that one could reasonably hope for, due to their light internal partitions and lack of load-bearing internal walls. Here the ILEA Architects Department were extraordinarily helpful, even to the extent of following a class around for a whole week to plot movement patterns.

The Integrated Syllabus

A. We began by agreeing that, as we saw it then, the major stumbling block at the outset would be to agree a content which would satisfy both history and geography while, at the same time, offering opportunities to English. In fact, history and geography agreed at once that geographical factors were in all societies in the past and in most today, a determinant of the form and the development of a culture. We should, therefore, select societies and periods which would allow the working out of these factors to become manifest. Furthermore, a successful course of this type in the first 9 terms in the School would be an excellent foundation for the subsequent Certificate work which every pupil is involved in: this includes the normal geography work as well as British social and economic history since 1750 and Social Studies (MREB) in Years IV and V, leading to history, sociology and economics in VI.

Lastly, by studying whole societies in their environment — albeit, highly selectively — we would give English a wide choice of material, not only in the development of specific language skills relating to the history/geography tasks, but also in imaginative and creative writing of all types.

The Departmental organization which emerged, then, was as follows:

Years I—III: World Studies (Eng. + Geog. + Hist., with co-operation from R.I. and Art) 11 periods.

IV—VI: Eng. + Geog. + Hist. + Soc.   Studies + Sociology + Economics + VI Gen. Studies — all to be *co-ordinated* under the umbrella of 'Liberal Studies' (i.e. with subject autonomy still, temporarily at least, retained).

B. *Syllabus: Year I, Terms 1 and 2: Foundations of Geography* — an introduction to the main terms and skills in the subject, together with a study of the main contemporary physical environments and their impact on their inhabitants (deserts, grasslands, forests, the seacoast, climate, etc.). This intensive geography input has the additional useful affect of ironing out disparities of previous learning arising from the range of feeder schools.

Term 3: Birth of civilization — a study of the probable environments and causes of the shift from hunting to agriculture leading to a specific study of the agricultural base of Nile Valley civilization and the consequent growth of technology, art, religion and government.

Year II: Term 1: The foundations of Hindu society;
   2: The birth of Chinese civilization;
   3: The civilizations of pre-Columbian America.

leading to . . .

Year III: Term 1:   The U.S.A. — a study of the roots of some of the main
characteristics of contemporary America;

       2:   The U.S.S.R — as for the U.S.A;

       3:   An urban field study of the origins, growth and present
form of London.

The approach throughout is to encourage the pupils to discover how
techniques, beliefs, customs, etc., grow out of Man's experience of earning his
living in an environment which changes him, and which he changes. This
latter aspect is particularly strongly developed in the IVth Year and above
and links across to science with its study of the environment.

Teaching/Learning Methods

We have aimed to create a spectrum of learning situations associated with a
range of learning skills. Four classes of 30 pupils come together for a weekly
lecture on a Monday morning when the work for the week is introduced in
outline by the team member responsible for the curriculum unit. This
provides a key common learning experience for all the pupils (we would give
it to the whole year of 240 but are limited by accommodation) as well as a
briefing for the rest of the teacher team. Moreover, it represents an important
element of ritual where all pupils know exactly what they are expected to do
and where common standards of behaviour are reinforced. Next, the classes
(they retain their separate identity at first in order to give security to pupils
trying to adjust to the 'confusion' of a large school with multiplicity of
teachers) return to a Form base for a period of planning and follow-up. They
then spend one whole morning and one afternoon working in a cluster of
spaces arranged around a resource centre: here they will form functional
groups, ranging from a large number for, say, a film or discussion, down to a
solitary individual working on a structured assignment in a carrel. The work is
increasingly structured into programmes, work suggestions and set work cards
with increasingly specific objectives: for example, we aim to improve not
only recognition and recall of facts but also problem solving, data handling,
various psychomotor skills and, perhaps as important as any, social
interaction skills which we feel to be vital in the world of today and
tomorrow.

An interesting spin-off of these developments has been the identification
of the teams with 'their' course since they decide the objectives and share the
material preparation work — a feeling which is beginning to heal the
'them-and-us' division between staff and hierarchy because more and more
important decisions are being devolved. On the other hand, it would be wrong
to disguise the immense strain that unsupported developments of this type
involve.

Modern Studies: A Growth Area in the Curriculum of Scottish Secondary Schools

MICHAEL T. WILLIAMS, 1970

In post-1945 Scotland there were two main types of state secondary school — the selective academy or senior secondary school and the non-selective junior secondary school. The former had a subject-based curriculum orientated towards the external examinations of the Scottish Certificate of Education and the matriculation requirements of the Scottish universities. Without the constraints of external examinations the junior secondary school was able to develop a more flexible curricular structure. The pattern of having a single head of department with responsibility for geography, history and English meant that the introduction of integrated courses was relatively easy. Not surprisingly the Scottish schools experienced a social studies movement comparable to that in the secondary schools of England and Wales. However in devising an Ordinary grade course labelled 'Modern Studies' the Scots introduced an integrated course at a time when the social studies movement was running out of steam in the south. In this article the growth of Modern Studies in the decade 1960 to 1970 is reviewed. It distinguishes between courses of Modern Studies taught at Ordinary grade, Higher grade and to non-examination pupils. Since the publication of this article two important developments in the field of Modern Studies have taken place. Firstly, a curriculum development centre for the social studies subjects in Scotland has been established in Glasgow, and secondly, a Modern Studies Association has been formed to provide a forum for discussion of Modern Studies.

Introduction

The expression 'Modern Studies' was coined in 1960 when a syllabus was published by the Scottish Education Department under this title. After a brief introductory note the syllabus was outlined, followed by a Specimen Question Paper at Ordinary grade of the Scottish Certificate of Education. That the course might have been called 'Social Studies' is indicated by the statement in the introductory paragraph, 'The title "Modern Studies" has been given to this alternative course as being a more accurate description of its content than the phrase "social studies" ' (Scottish Education Department 1960).

The most distinctive feature of this new course is its lack of precise definition. Ten years have elapsed since the course was introduced; the number of candidates presented for the annual examination has increased steadily; a Higher grade course has been introduced and a report has been published which introduces courses for non-certificate pupils. The end of the first decade in the history of this curricular innovation is a suitable time to describe some of the features of its growth.

The Origins

To place Modern Studies in its curriculum context it is necessary to understand the place of the teaching of history and geography in Scottish secondary schools prior to 1960. The division of the secondary schools into selective six-year schools, referred to as 'academies' or 'grammar schools', and non-selective, or three-year junior secondary schools, is fundamental to this understanding. In the former, pupils aged twelve started their secondary education by following a basic course composed of many subjects, including geography and history. At the end of the second year pupils generally chose between history and geography; the majority chose history and this subject was then studied up to the Higher grade examination taken in the fifth or sixth year.

Some history teachers were concerned that, although the pupils studied history for six years, they rarely studied any aspects of the twentieth century. Geography teachers were concerned that only a small proportion of pupils studied geography beyond the second year of the secondary school.

In the non-selective schools a single teacher was usually responsible for the organization of courses in history, geography and English, throughout the school. In some schools, courses for school leavers entitled social studies, current affairs, civics or citizenship were devised for the third year, i.e. the final year of the junior secondary school, and these replaced history and geography. Courses in civics and current affairs were sometimes found in the final years of the selective schools. These courses suffered from the same defects found in similar courses south of the border and these weaknesses have been discussed by Cannon (1964) and Williams (1963).

A group of teachers and HM Inspectors was anxious to end the tradition of loosely defined, unstructured terminal courses, generally called social studies, in Scottish secondary schools, and it was their successful experimental work and their pressure on the Scottish Education Department which resulted in this statement appearing in the report of the Working Party (1959) on the secondary curriculum, 'While we consider that all pupils should include history and geography in their course, we realize that for many it will not be possible to continue the study of both subjects to the Ordinary grade level. There is therefore a place for an alternative course in social studies including something of both history and geography, the emphasis being placed on what would be useful for a man or woman to know as a background to present-day affairs.' The structural weakness in the traditional curriculum of the secondary school combined with the need to produce 'useful' courses for school leavers led to the introduction of Ordinary grade Modern Studies.

Modern Studies at Ordinary Grade

The persons who framed the syllabus published in 1960 recognized the difficulties in delimiting the new course. Further, they stated: 'Not only is the potential material vast in quantity but much of it could involve considerable difficulty for the teacher, partly because of its controversial nature, partly because of the uncertainty that inevitably surrounds the interpretation of recent happenings, and partly because suitable source-books may not always be easily available' (Scottish Education Department 1960). With these difficulties in mind a syllabus divided into three sections was constructed. The sections were based on this division:

'Section A deals with Great Britain and gives the pupil the opportunity to become thoroughly familiar with the constitution, customs and ways of life of the homeland.

Section B aims at giving him some understanding of the peoples of the countries overseas which exert major political influences in the world today, and to introduce him to the facts and problems of international affairs.

Section C contains two parts: (i) a study of the British Commonwealth, (ii) study of selected topics of particular interest and importance which it would be difficult to fit into a syllabus of any normal pattern.'

In 1968 the syllabus was recast to 'cut out some items which are now out of date, and to change the emphasis given to certain topics'. Thus Section C consisted only of special topics, and Commonwealth topics were moved into Section B. Overall the scope of the syllabus was significantly reduced.

The Ordinary grade syllabus is impressive in its length and comprehensive coverage of social, economic and political issues on local, national and international levels. In its design the syllabus follows a concentric approach similar to that described by Dray and Jordan (1950). The syllabus framers emphasized that the arrangement of the subject matter was not intended to indicate the sequence in which topics should be taught. Any teacher attempting to follow the published syllabus topic by topic would soon discover the impossibility of the task. Some criteria for the selection of topics to be studied must be adopted for the effective teaching of the course.

Some of the criteria which have been adopted are these: the teaching qualifications of the teacher or teachers responsible for the course; the needs of the pupils; the interests of the pupils; the published material, textbook and other materials, available; the topics dominating the contemporary scene at the time of teaching; the topics most easily taught to meet the requirements of the conventional essay examination (Williams 1968).

An important determinant of the nature of the course has been the amount of teaching time available in any particular school. Thus Ordinary grade Modern Studies may be a one year course taken by pupils in the fourth, fifth or sixth years in selective schools. In such courses the pupils are taught Modern Studies for four periods per week for little more than two terms. In some of these schools, two of the weekly periods may be taken by a geography teacher while the others are taken by a history teacher; in other schools all four periods are taken by the same teacher. Modern Studies at Ordinary grade may be a two year course for pupils in the third and fourth years who intend to leave secondary school when they have taken Ordinary grade examinations. Usually four periods are allocated for each week in these courses.

The fact that the topics in the syllabus can be divided neatly into geography, history and 'other' sections, plus the easy recognition of examination questions biased towards these conventional subjects, has led to the growth of courses described as Modern Studies, which are hardly different from conventional geography or history courses. Because of this it is possible to distinguish two separate types of Modern Studies courses at Ordinary grade and these can be explained briefly by Figure 1(a) and (b).

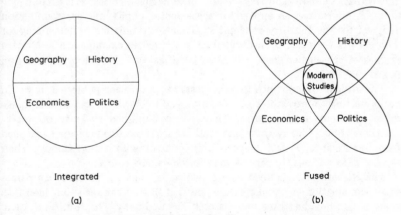

Fig. 1. Two forms of Modern Studies course organization.

The distinction is shown here between courses constructed from two or more separate disciplines, in which the values of disciplined study are retained, though sufficient co-operation between the teachers representing the disciplines exists for an integrated course to emerge, and those courses in which a degree of fusion, or synthesis, is achieved, so that the distinctive contribution from any individual discipline may be difficult to detect (Williams 1969). The integrated course permits specialist teachers of history, geography, economics or politics to contribute to the teaching of Modern Studies, sometimes as a formal team, though more usually in a more informal co-operative way. The fused course is usually the responsibility of a single teacher. Both of these arrangements have advantages and disadvantages. Suffice it to say here that no attempts have been made to assess experimentally the effectiveness of either arrangement. The dichotomy expressed in Figure 1 is clearly reflected in the 'Big Four' Scottish colleges of education which are responsible for the pre-service and in-service education of Modern Studies teachers: at Jordanhill (Glasgow) and Aberdeen Colleges of Education there are Departments of Modern Studies; in Moray House (Edinburgh) and Dundee Colleges of Education lecturers from the Departments of History, Geography, Economics or Commerce contribute to the education of Modern Studies teachers.

Modern Studies at Higher Grade

The case for introducing a new course of Modern Studies at Higher grade of the Scottish Certificate of Education was stated simply and briefly in 1966: 'Modern Studies at Ordinary grade has found increasing acceptance among pupils, parents and teachers since its introduction. The number of candidates has steadily increased and continues to grow. There is evidence, however, that many pupils find it a positive drawback that they are unable to pursue the course beyond the Ordinary grade. Furthermore, the number of candidates drawn from the fifth and sixth years continues to increase. It is encouraging that the course has an appeal for these senior pupils, but an examination designed for the fourth year is not sufficiently stimulating or demanding for them. It has therefore been decided to introduce an examination in Modern Studies at the Higher grade' (Scottish Certificate of Education Examination Board 1966).

The evidence upon which this case rests has never been published. It would be interesting to learn the methods employed to measure parents' acceptance of an Ordinary grade course. There is no published evidence of pupils' reactions either. Clearly these observations are subjective judgements gleaned from the reports of HM Inspectors in contact with many schools. Their reports were sufficiently persuasive to initiate a new course.

The Higher course is divided into two parts, each examined by a separate essay examination paper. Paper I is entitled 'Britain' and is subdivided into Section A, which has three sub-sections: The Economy, The Political System, and Social Change; and Section B, 'Nominated Topics' containing two topics: Regional Development and British Political Parties. Paper II is also divided into two sections, under the general title 'World Affairs.' Section A is divided into three sub-sections: The Major Powers, Western Europe, and International Organizations and World Problems. In Section B, Race Relations and Australia constitute two nominated topics.

The course was designed, as are all Higher courses, to cover two years of work. Compressing two year courses into a single year is a common feature of Scottish secondary schools. To cover Paper I of the course in the winter term and Paper II in the spring term requires intensive formal teaching in which the accumulation of facts in a form suitable for regurgitation under examination conditions is the leading priority. The inadequacies of a senior school structure in which pupils study four or five unrelated subjects for the Higher grade examinations is one of the reasons for the introduction in 1967 of a Certificate in Sixth Year Studies in selected school subjects, and in these courses, reminiscent of Scholarship level courses south of the border, the emphasis is placed upon the individual's intellectual development resulting from thorough study and dissertation writing on a narrow range of topics. Modern Studies is not one of the subjects in which pupils can be presented for this Certificate.

It is contended that the number of candidates being presented for Modern Studies at Higher grade would increase dramatically if the older Scottish universities were to recognize the course as an acceptable entrance requirement for their faculties. Although it has been accepted by the new universities, such as Strathclyde, Stirling and Heriot Watt, it is not recognized by the Universities of Aberdeen, Dundee, Edinburgh, Glasgow and St. Andrews. Only when this recognition is accorded will Modern Studies become academically respectable.

Modern Studies for Non-certificate Pupils

By 1965 Modern Studies as an Ordinary grade course was established in the curriculum of many secondary schools. (In the same year a Department of Modern Studies was formed at Jordanhill College of Education to prepare Ordinary and Honours graduates to teach the new course in the secondary schools.) The introduction of Modern Studies was achieved with the minimum of literary debate and its progress was not noted in any educational publication. Its development was achieved through the co-operative efforts of a small number of HM Inspectors, college of education lecturers and enthusiastic teachers. In-service courses, held mainly at Jordanhill College of Education, were the occasions for exchanges of opinions and ideas between interested parties and these courses continue to be the meeting place of persons interested in the teaching of Modern Studies.

In 1965 the Scottish Education Department Consultative Committee on the Curriculum set up a Working Party to 'consider the place of Modern Studies in the curriculum of secondary pupils following non-certificate courses; to report to the Department on the approaches to the subject and on the kind of syllabuses which might be recommended to schools.' The Working Party's report was published in 1968. It is a document characterized by hazy thinking: it begins with a failure to define Modern Studies in operational, or indeed in any educational terms, and proceeds to describe 'experimental' situations in an unscientific way (Musgrave 1969).

In paragraph 2 of the report it is stated that Modern Studies is 'the study of various aspects of contemporary society by means of courses drawing mainly from subjects such as geography, history and economics, and also from other subjects having a direct bearing on particular social questions.'

The ambiguities of a 'study' based on 'courses' are clear; such ambiguities are emphasized in paragraph 4: 'The successful introduction and continued development of Modern Studies as a certificate subject showed that, in spite of past failures, integrated courses could work well, if suitably constructed and well taught. At the same time advances in methods of teaching geography and history revealed fresh merit in the subject approach. The lesson seemed to be that the approach should be determined by what was most suited to the needs of the pupils and the nature of the material being studied at a given time.' Such statements can produce this kind of response: 'Heavy commitment to "usefulness" or "needs" as a principle of motivation has not been supported by evidence. The pupil treated in this way is not appealed to as a thinking, aspiring, free person, but as a behaving animal' (King and Brownell 1966). Similarly: 'Too often reformers pass from the undeniable truth that the present subject-centred curriculum is often boring, to the conclusion that it should be abandoned and a topic-centred one substituted for it. They do not consider sufficiently seriously the less radical suggestion that the more traditional type of curriculum could be both more imaginative and more realistically interpreted' (Peters 1969).

The authors of the Working Party report sit on the fence in this debate. They recognize the value of subjects but wish to promote an alternative arrangement of the curriculum. The bulk of the report consists of descriptions of course arrangements relevant to five main areas of study: community studies, vocational studies, economic studies, mass communication and world affairs. Two additional elements, clearly integral to the Working Party remit were mentioned, namely leisure and personal relations, but the authors felt that Modern Studies could offer only general guidance in these areas. They were too personal and too individual for teachers concerned with contemporary society.

It is on this matter of not teaching personal relations that Modern Studies is most open to criticism. The tone of the Working Party report echoes that of the Scottish Education Department memorandum, 'Raising the School Leaving Age'. In paragraph 19 of this publication we read, on the subject of personal relations: 'It is sometimes said that only a teacher in regular contact with the pupils could know them well enough to undertake these discussions; it is also said that only someone who is not associated with the class-room and its atmosphere of praise and blame could win the confidence of the pupils. The same answer will not apply in all schools and there is as yet too little evidence to make any judgement possible' (Scottish Education Department 1966). That teachers of Modern Studies can cope with a study of contemporary and political matters there is no doubt, especially if they have followed relevant university courses. The tendency towards triviality and dullness associated with school courses based on these matters is always present. Until persons engaged in the teaching of Modern Studies are ready to engage in a genuine detailed study of the role of the individual in contemporary society, Modern Studies will remain a ghost of its true potential.

Conclusion

Modern studies has emerged as an undefined area of the secondary school curriculum. Despite its lack of definition it has achieved increasing popularity for certificate and non-certificate pupils. Each school approaches the courses in its own individual way. Any uniformity of approach has been achieved through the work of the Inspectorate and the colleges of education who are the agencies responsible for promoting the courses. In the space of a decade Modern Studies courses at Ordinary grade, Higher grade and for non-certificate pupils have been devised. Recent developments in the field have been the planned introduction of non-examinable sixth year Social Studies courses in Glasgow secondary schools and the formation of groups of teachers sponsored by local education authorities to formulate courses for non-certificate pupils. In the colleges of education and colleges of further education, the term Modern Studies is being used for courses formerly called General Studies or Liberal Studies. There is always a danger that all these courses will revert to the poor social studies courses which existed prior to 1960.

European Studies and the Study of Europe

C. V. JAMES, 1973

It would appear that most subjects in the curricula of secondary schools could be integrated with geography to produce new courses. In the first reading in this collection Mackinder discussed the integration of geography and history, and, elsewhere, one finds suggestions for integrating geography with history, religious education, English, science subjects and the social sciences. The substantive components of geography to be utilized in integrated courses are partially determined by a rough division of the subject into its scientific and human sides. A relatively new feature to emerge in secondary schools is the initiation of courses labelled European Studies and in these courses geography frequently figures. For the geographer these courses pose a new problem, the relationship between geography and modern languages. In this article by James integration is viewed from the standpoint of the teacher of modern languages. In discussing the place of modern languages in European studies he utilizes a number of diagrams to illustrate possible course arrangements which could be applied in secondary schools and which have their origins in institutions of higher education. Geography is a major element in his models. The article is of interest not only for the insight it gives into European studies but also because the principles embodied within it can be applied to area studies in general, whether they be American studies, Asian studies or Latin American studies. By pointing out the growth of area studies in higher education James also pinpoints the importance of looking at the curricula of secondary schools in the broader perspective of education in general and this is something which we find stressed in the opening reading in this collection.

Several contributors have already pointed out the ambiguity of the term European studies when applied at school level, and in the introductory paper it was suggested that possibly the confusion of nomenclatures was indicative of thought that was similarly confused. Whether this is true or not, it is certainly undeniable that European studies mean very different things to different teachers, and whereas none can claim copyright it is obviously in all our interests to clarify what we do in fact mean and to agree on a common terminology. The object of this paper is to highlight some of the issues and suggest some tentative solutions and descriptors.

(1) Two main factors have assumed importance in the schools in the last few years and have now begun to override all others for the language teacher, and though not basically related, they have impinged so extensively on each other that they are in danger of obscuring the true nature of the problems arising from them. The two factors are:

- (i) the necessity, for social reasons, to solve the pedagogical problem of teaching foreign languages across the ability range;
- (ii) the necessity, for political reasons, to solve the curricular problem of ensuring that the pupil's studies are conducted in a wider European setting than formerly they were.

The main problem engendered by the first of these demands arises from a realization that the biggest proportion of the school population (a commonly quoted figure is 80 per cent) lacks the motivation and/or ability to learn a foreign language beyond a certain very limited extent. A solution has been sought in the inception of 'language' courses taught in English and consisting of:

—general knowledge of the country whose language it is (becoming, at its worst, a continuous quiz show of the sort against which warnings were issued in the CSE *Examinations bulletin no. 1*, 1963);

—some rudimentary speech habits in the foreign language, providing what is quaintly termed a 'survival' knowledge (*Le cabinet n'est pas très gai . . .*).

The problem engendered by the second demand and exacerbated by British entry into the European Economic Community — the problem of the Europeanization of the school curriculum — has led to attempts to invent or discover a new 'subject' called European studies to take a place in the timetable alongside such familiar and proven items as history and geography, and one pioneer states as a 'first principle' his 'article of faith' that a course in this subject should have a language input.

In practice, the two solutions become identical: European studies are adopted as the pedagogical solution of the social problem, and in so doing assume a role in the curriculum which leaves the political demands unsatisfied. As a language course, European studies are in fact concerned only with one country (or, in what one contributor piquantly called 'conventional courses of the Nuffield-Schools Council type', one linguistic community) and do not therefore contribute toward a broadening of the curriculum. If European studies claim a separate existence outside the other subjects in the timetable, then they become irrelevant defeating their own object. On neither count do they contribute towards a broader European orientation, nor merit the appellation European.

It is hardly surprising that the British are sometimes called insular; they do, after all, live on an island! But if the concept of Europe is to mean anything, and if European studies are to mean what they say, then the centre of the pupil's awareness must be shifted from a national to a European basis. This will hardly be achieved by setting aside a few lessons per week if for the rest of the time the pupil proceeds exactly as he has always done. To achieve such an object, in the words of our Norwegian contributor, 'the European concept must permeate the entire curriculum' (Sirevåg 1973).

(2) The relationship between language and non-language elements in various kinds of course is determined in such circumstances according to similarly conflicting sets of criteria and results in a similar degree of imprecision of common nomenclature. Here, too, some attempt to agree on a terminology might also help to clarify thinking.

A basic element in the study of a language, arising from purely linguistic causes, is a consideration of the deeper meaning of, for example, certain lexical items (to explain the Russian *kolkhoz* as 'collective farm' is insufficient for a student to whom the concept of collectivized agriculture is unfamiliar). Such knowledge, the scope of which is dictated by the linguistic material to which the learner is exposed, might perhaps best be called *background information*.

Of a rather different order, however, is what is often known as 'background studies', comprising a more systematic study of various aspects of the society whose language is being learned. The course remains a language course, but the language is studied within the context of a consideration of the society. An appropriately unambiguous label for this non-language element might therefore be *contextual studies*.

In a third stage, such a study of the society becomes the object of the course, fed by a number of subjects, one of which is language. Such courses are commonly termed *area studies*, and it is into this category that both types of course discussed above ('language' and 'European studies') will in fact fall. One structural problem, to which several contributors have drawn attention, is that of the design of the language input.

However, as the proportion of non-language content increases, two other problems become more acute — one structural and one political. They pertain both to the comparatively elementary *civilization/Landeskunde/ stranovedeniye* level of the contextual studies and to the more serious demands of the area studies, since in each case the basic principles are the same. The first concerns the need to integrate elements of different subjects into a coherent whole, avoiding the fragmentary and superficial nature of the quiz show approach. This is usually tackled by concentrating the teaching/learning around a series of 'topics', each of which is approached from several points of view. The second problem is that of preserving some degree of objectivity, avoiding, for example, both francophilia and francophobia — equally unfitting to teachers whose desire is to inform rather than instruct and to pupils whose aim is to learn rather than be taught. It is certainly disquieting that certain teachers and administrators openly declare their objective to be the instilling into their pupils of certain 'desirable' attitudes — which to an outside observer might look very much like simply passing on prejudices, and which has some frightening implications only too visible in recent history. In fact the teacher's role is to enable the pupil to form his own attitudes, not to mould them into pre-determined shapes. In this sense the whole concept of European studies is highly dangerous and should be approached with extreme circumspection.

(3) Harold Macmillan wrote of General de Gaulle that when he said Europe he in fact meant France. It is quite certain that when most of our teachers and some of our administrators say European studies they mean French studies and this is a direct result of the confusion of the two basic problems as outlined in our opening paragraph. As long as European studies are in practice an offshoot of language teaching or a replacement for language teaching to the less able pupil, it will naturally reflect the proportions of the language scene and be overwhelmingly French oriented. To many this may seem a somewhat limited vision of Europe. Indeed, it was that same General de Gaulle who spoke of Europe as stretching from the Atlantic to the Urals, but the vision of the architects of European studies courses hardly extends beyond the Rhine, let alone the Oder-Neisse line. Moreover, preoccupation with the EEC excludes also the Iberian peninsula, as well as subjecting to vivisection the Scandinavian community. Such a myopic view of Europe can do nothing but harm, and this is perhaps the most powerful argument in favour of divorcing the study of Europe from the teaching of languages. In its present guise 'European studies' not only fails to propagate the concept of Europe, it impoverishes and impedes it.

(4) The school situation, still very much in a state of flux, may perhaps be illumined by a consideration of the tertiary level — universities and CNAA courses — which are subject to not dissimilar pressures. A number of types of course may be isolated:

Model 1: Language

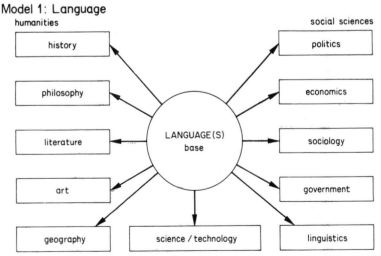

Language is the central factor of the course, providing access to all aspects of the life of the linguistic community or country by use of materials from those contexts. Each aspect (or any combination) is studied in general in English, followed by a more detailed study of *one*, and a period of residence in the country, culminating in a dissertation or project in the foreign language.

Model 2 : Service courses

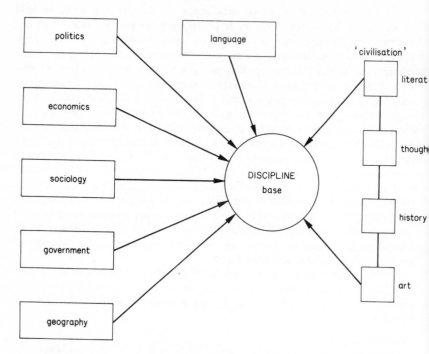

The organizing factor is the study of social science disciplines etc., consisting of general courses in English, followed by specialization in *one* social science. The language input is continued throughout the course and may be accompanied by a background 'civilization' course taught largely in English. In the final year the chosen discipline is applied to a specific linguistic area and materials are used in the foreign language. A further variant intercalates a year in the foregn country, culminating in a dissertation or project in the foreign language.

Model 3: Area studies

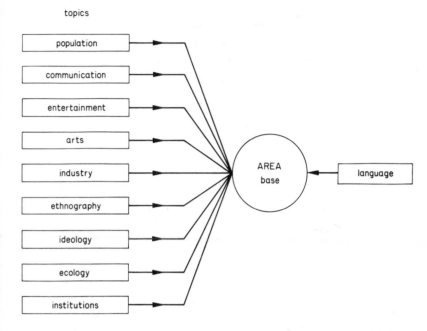

An area, defined in terms of one or more linguistic communities, is studied via a series of cross-disciplinary and inter-disciplinary topic-based courses, with specialized work in one or several of these as special subjects, and a language input which varies in extent according to the interests and aptitudes of the student.

All three types of course include an element of foreign language, but in each course the role of language is different:

Model 1 is a language course, leading to a high standard of performance in all skills, usually with some functional training in translating, interpreting etc;

Model 2 is a course in another discipline, in which the foreign language is a tool for the expert in the field;

Model 3 considers the foreign language as an aspect of the foreign culture; the input may be quite small and limited.

Courses bearing the title European studies may also vary in structure and organization:

Model 4 : European studies (core/context model)

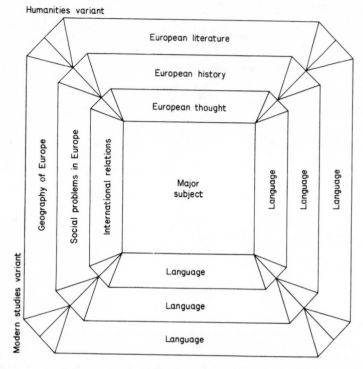

The major subject is studied within the context of courses of European literature/history/thought (Humanities variant) or European economics/sociology/geography/government (Modern studies variant). The language input is a contextual course lasting throughout the overall course. There is a year abroad, during which a dissertation is written, either in English (for major courses other than a foreign literature) or in the foreign language.

The following models concern the organization of courses rather than their content:

Model 5 : European studies (umbrella model)

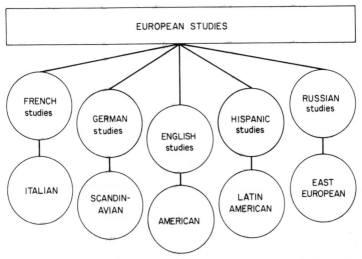

The study of Europe is sub-divided into that of a number of areas, defined in terms of linguistic communities, each of which may also include an element of a second, related linguistic community. Each component is in fact an area studies type course (Model 3). In some degree courses more than one area may be studied, sometimes with obligatory residence in one or both.

Model 6 : European studies (Cold War model)

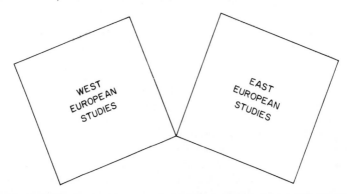

Europe is considered to consist of two distinct parts, one of which may be studied without reference to the other. West European studies have a French/German input; East European studies have a Russian and other slavonic language input.

Model 7 : European studies (Common Market model) 1973

Western European studies are further sub-divided into EEC countries and the Iberian peninsula.

(5) For the school situation, models 3 and 4 have an obvious relevance — Model 3 if European studies is to be inserted as a separate course, Model 4 if the concept of Europe is to 'permeate the curriculum'. But the implications for language teaching are very different.

Model 3: Area studies. In these courses the definition of the area is subject to a number of possible variations in both space and time. Though at school level the time factor is rarely discussed, it can be safely supposed that the historical span with which the course is concerned is the modern, contemporary period. It should, however, be noted that the approach is equally applicable to earlier periods and that there is nothing inherent in the structure of such courses that dictates a preoccupation with the current scene.

In the courses already discussed in paragraph 1 the area is, as we have seen, a country or linguistic community — hence the inappropriateness of the title European studies as opposed to, say, French studies, German studies, or Russian studies. And since the courses tend to be designed to replace language teaching proper (Model 1) for the below average learner, the language input is degraded to the 'survival' level of a *son et lumière* phrasebook. It must be open to question whether at this level it can really be considered language teaching, and it is extremely doubtful whether it has any educational value whatsoever. None of this, however, is inherent in the design of the course, into which it is perfectly possible to insert a rigorous and demanding language component, rather more relevant to the pupil for the great proportion of the time that he spends at home than for the odd week which he may or may not pass in the company of a gang of his English-speaking fellows during a school trip abroad. If the object of the course is to deepen the pupil's understanding of a foreign culture, there are surely more intellectual demands to be put upon him than ordering his vino or locating the loo. Yet it is to such lowly considerations, more fitting to travel agent than pedagogue, that many teachers in such courses now direct their attention and time. A question that must therefore be asked is whether a language input of this type is preferable to the absence of language altogether.

Area studies, however, need not be concerned with only one linguistic community; the area involved may indeed be Europe. In this case, the only one in which the title European studies is entirely fitting, the topics will cut across national frontiers as well as subject delimitations. The language input, however, will be of a special sort. French alone will not do, but to put in courses in French, German and Russian — a minimal coverage of Europe — will hardly be possible (unless this is done on a module basis). It may therefore be thought wisest to design a course on *language* rather than of languages, on a comparative philology basis which is particularly well suited to audio-visual presentation, with recorded samples and overhead projector transparencies. Such an input would in fact be a direct parallel of the other topics, illustrating the unifying as well as dividing factors at work in Europe. Language subject specialists could each make their contribution; it is assumed that a European studies course of this type would not be a replacement for language teaching but run parallel with normal Model 1 language courses. Rather than attempting to teach any one language it would give the pupil an overview of what a title such as 'the languages of Europe' might suggest.

Model 4: Core-context. A Model 3 course of either type does, however, claim a separate existence in the timetable, with the drawbacks suggested in paragraph 1. In essence it need contribute very little to the Europeanization of the curriculum as a whole. Of more direct assistance is the core-context concept, Model 4, when applied to all (or nearly all) the subjects in the timetable. If consideration of any historical period in any country is first made on an all-European background; if the geography of any area is first placed in an all-European context; if the art, music, literature of any nation are related to that of the others; if — in the words of the Ealing Technical College CNAA course in Modern European Studies — the pupil is enabled, even at a humble and primitive level, to sense 'the interplay of geographical, historical, economic and political factors in shaping a modern multi-national society', then he cannot but become a better and fuller citizen of the society to which, for better or worse, we now all belong, of Europe and of the world.

References

Abler, R., Adams, J. and Gould, P. (1972). *Spatial Organisation*, Prentice-Hall International.

Association for Education in World Citizenship (1935). *Education for World Citizenship in Secondary Schools.* O.U.P.

Association for Education in World Citizenship (1949). *Sixth Form Citizens.* O.U.P.

Bale, J., Graves, N. and Walford, R. (Eds.) (1973). *Perspectives in Geographical Education*, Oliver and Boyd.

Ball, J., Steinbrink, J., and Stoltman, J. (1971). *The Social Sciences and Geographic Education — A Reader*, Wiley.

Banks, L. J. (1969). 'Curriculum Development in Britain 1963—1968', *J. Curriculum Studies*, 1, 3.

Bartz, B. (1970). 'Maps in the Classroom', *The Journal of Geography*, 69, January.

Berman, L. M. (1968). *New Priorities in the Curriculum*, Merrill.

Bernstein, B., Elvin, H. L. and Peters, R. S. (1966). 'Ritual in Education', *Philosophical Trans. of the Royal Society of London*, B 251 (772).

Bernstein, B. (1967). 'Open Schools, Open Society?', *New Society*, September 14th.

Bloom, R. S. (1956). *Taxonomy of Educational Objectives; Cognitive Domain*, McKay.

Board of Education (1927). *Report of the Consultative Committee, The Education of the Adolescent (Hadow Report)*, H.M.S.O.

Board of Education (1931). *Report of the Consultative Committee, The Primary School*, H.M.S.O.

Board of Education (1938). *Report of the Consultative Committee on Secondary Education (Spens Report)*, H.M.S.O.

Board of Education (1943). *Report of the Secondary Schools Examinations Council, Curriculum and Examinations in Secondary Schools (Norwood Report)*, H.M.S.O.

Bolam, D. (1972). 'Integrated Studies', *New Era*, 53, 6.

Bolam, D. (1971) 'Integrating the Curriculum — A Case Study in the Humanities', *Pedagogica Europaea*, 1970/1971.

Bramwell, R. D. (1962). 'Social Studies', in Burston, W. H. (Ed.), *A Handbook for History Teachers*, Methuen.

Brimble, L. J. F. and May, F. J. (1943). *Social Studies and World Citizenship*, Macmillan.

Broudy, H. S., Smith, B. O. and Burnett, J. R. (1964). *Democracy and Excellence in American Secondary Education*, Rand McNally.

Brown, M. (1971). *Some Strategies Used in Primary Schools for Initiating and Implementing Change*, unpublished M.Ed. thesis, University of Manchester.

Bruner, J. S. (1960). *The Process of Education*, Vintage Books.

Bruner, J. S. (1966). *Toward a Theory of Instruction*, Harvard University Press.

Bruner, J. S. (1970). *The Relevance of Skill or the Skill of Relevance*, a lecture in the Encyclopaedia Britannica International Conference, London, January.

Bull, G. B. G. (1968). 'Inter-disciplinary Enquiry: A Geography Teacher's Assessment', *Geography*, **53**.

Burston, W. H. (1954). *Social Studies and the History Teacher*, Teaching of History Leaflet No. 15, Historical Association.

Burston, W. H. (1967). 'The Study of the Curriculum', *Bulletin of the University of London Institute of Education*, 13.

Cannon, C. (1964). 'Social Studies in Secondary Schools', *Educational Review*, **17**, 1.

Carson, S. McB. (1973). *Environmental Studies*, N.F.E.R.

Childe, G. (1942). *What Happened in History*, Pelican Books.

Chorley, R. and Haggett, P. (Eds.) (1965). *Frontiers in Geographical Teaching*, Methuen.

Corbett, P. (1965). *Ideologies*, Hutchinson.

Council for Curriculum Reform (1945). *The Content of Education*, University of London Press.

Council of the Geographical Association (1919). 'The Position of Geography', *The Geographical Teacher*, **10**, 55.

Crozier, M. (1964). *The Bureaucratic Phenomenon*, Tavistock Publications.

Dale, P. F. (1971). 'Children's Reactions to Maps and Aerial Photographs', *Area*, **3**, 3.

Department of Education and Science (1972). *New Thinking in School Geography*, Education Pamphlet 59, H.M.S.O.

Dewey, J. (1910; rev. edn. 1932). *How We Think*, D. C. Heath.

Dewey, J. (1938). *Logic: The Theory of Inquiry*, Henry Holt.

Dewey, J. (1946). *Democracy and Education*, Macmillan.

Dray, J. and Jordan, D. (1950). *A Handbook of Social Studies*, Methuen.

Durkheim, E. (1933). *The Division of Labour in Society*, trans. G. Simpson, The Free Press.

Elliott, G. G. (1974). 'Integrated Studies — Some Problems and Possibilities for the Geographer', *General Education*, 23, Autumn.

Everson, J. (1969). 'Some Aspects of Teaching Geography through Fieldwork', *Geography*, **54**.

Fairgrieve, J. (1926). *Geography in School*, University of London Press.

Farquharson, A. (1950). 'Social, Local and Field Studies', *J. Education*, November.

Fereday, E. L. (1950). 'Social Studies in the Secondary Modern School', *J. Education*, November.

Fleure, H. J. (1919). *Human Geography in Western Europe*, Williams and Norgate.

Fleure, H. J. (1935). 'Geography', in Association for Education in Citizenship (Ed.), *Education for Citizenship in Secondary Schools*, Oxford University Press.

Fromm, E. (1956). *The Sane Society*, Routledge and Kegan Paul.

Geikie, A. (1892). *The Teaching of Geography*, Macmillan.

Geographical Association (1949). *Local Studies*, rev. edn.

Geographical Association (1962). 'Memorandum Submitted to the Central Advisory Council for Education, November 1961', *Geography*, 47.

Geographical Association (1970). *Geography in the Primary School.*

Graves, N. J. and Simons, M. (1966). 'Geography and Philosophy', *Bull. University of London Institute of Education*, 9.

Graves, N. J. (Ed.) (1968). 'Geography, Social Science and Inter-disciplinary Enquiry', *Geographical Journal*, 134.

Graves, N. J. (1972). *New Movements in the Study and Teaching of Geography*, Temple Smith.

Greenhough, A. and Crofts, F. A. (1949). *Theory and Practice in the New Secondary School*, University of London Press.

Hamilton, E. (1940). *Mythology*, Mentor Books.

Happold, F. C. (1928). *The Approach to History*, Christophers.

Happold, F. C. (1935). *Citizens in the Making*, Christophers.

Hartshorne, R. (1948). 'On the Mores of Methodological Discussion in American Geography', *Ann. Association of American Geographers*, 38.

Harvey, C. (1969). *Explanation in Geography*, Arnold.

Hemming, J. (1949). *Teaching of Social Studies in Secondary Schools*, Longman.

Henry, N. B. (ed.) (1958). *The Integration of Educational Experiences*, 57th Yearbook of the National Society for the Study of Education, University of Chicago Press.

Herbertson, A. J. (1905). 'The Major Natural Regions: An Essay in Systematic Geography', *Geographical Journal*, 25.

Hewlett, M. (1971). 'Urban Environmental Studies', *General Education*, 16, Spring.

Hirst, P. H. (1965). 'Liberal Education and the Nature of Knowledge', in Archambault, R. D. (Ed.), *Philosophical Analysis and Education*, Routledge and Kegan Paul.

Hirst, P. H. (1966a).'Educational Theory', in Tibble, J. W. (Ed.), *The Study of Education*, Routledge and Kegan Paul.

Hirst, P. H. (1966b). 'Language and Thought', *Proc. Philosophy of Education Society*.

Hirst, P. H. and Peters, R. S. (1970). *The Logic of Education*, Routledge and Kegan Paul.

Hogan, D. F., Hore, P. S. and Tucker, M. (1969). 'Integrated Studies at Walworth School: A Pragmatic Approach by English, History and Geography', *Bull. University of London Institute of Education*, 19.

Hogan, D. F. (1972). 'World Studies at Walworth Comprehensive School', *General Education*, 18, Spring.

Honeybone, R. C. (1953). 'Field Studies', *National Froebel Foundation Bulletin*, 84.

Honeybone, R. C. (1954). 'Balance in Geography and Education', *Geography*, 34, 184.

Hubbard, D. N. and Salt, J. (Eds.) (1969). *Integrated Studies in the Primary School*, University of Sheffield Institute of Education.

Hubback, E. M. (1936). 'Education for Citizenship in the United Kingdom', in *The Yearbook of Education*, Section V., Ch. 1, Evans.

Hunt, A. (1969). 'The Tyranny of Subjects', in Rubenstein, D. and Stoneman, C. (Eds.), *Education for Democracy*, Penguin.

IAAM (1967). *The Teaching of Geography in Secondary Schools*, Cambridge University Press.

Illife, A. (1968). *The Foundation Year in the University of Keele*, Sociological Review Monograph 12, University of Keele.

James, C. (1968). *Young Lives at Stake*, Collins.
James, C. V. (1973). 'European Studies and the Study of Europe', in *Modern Languages and European Studies*, Centre for Information on Language Teaching and Research, June.

King, A. R., Jr. and Brownell, J. A. (1966). *The Curriculum and the Disciplines of Knowledge*, Wiley.
Kirk, W. (1963). 'Problems of Geography', *Geography*, 48.

Lamm, Z. (1968). 'Teaching and Curriculum Planning', *J. Curriculum Studies*, 1, 2.
Lawton, D. (1967). 'Social Studies and the Social Sciences', *Ideas*, 4.
Lawton, D. (1969). 'The Idea of an Integrated Curriculum', *Bull. University of London Institute of Education*, 19.
Lawton, D., Campbell, J. and Burkitt, V. (1971). *Social Studies 8—13*, Schools Council Working Paper 39, Evans/Methuen.
Lawton, D. and Dufour, B. (1973). *The New Social Studies*, Heinemann Educational Books.
Livingstone, R. (1941). *The Future in Education*, Cambridge University Press.
Livingstone, R. (1943). *Education for a World Adrift*, Cambridge University Press.
Livingstone, R. (1946). *Some Tasks for Education*, Oxford University Press.
Long, M. (1971). 'The Interests of Children in School Geography', *Geography*, 56.
Lunnon, A. J. (1969). *The Understanding of Certain Geographical Concepts by Primary School Children*, unpublished M.Ed. thesis, University of Birmingham.

Mackinder, H. J. (1887). 'On the Scope and Methods of Geography', *Proceedings of Royal Geographical Society*, Vol. IX.
Mackinder, H. J. (1913). 'The Teaching of Geography and History as a Combined Subject', *The Geographical Teacher*, 7, 35.
Maclean Carey, W. (1909). 'The Correlation of Instruction in Physics and Geography', *The Geographical Teacher*, 5, 25.
McCellan, J. C. (1951). 'The Logical and the Psychological: an untenable dualism?', in Smith, B. O. and Ennis, R. H. (Eds.), *Language and Concepts in Education*, Rand McNally.
McNichol, H. (1946). *History, Heritage and Environment*, Faber and Faber.
Mander, J. (1948). *Old Bottles and New Wine*, Newnes.
Mannheim, K. (1943). *Diagnosis of our Time*, K. Paul, Trench, Trubner.
Mannheim, K. (1951). *Freedom, Power and Democratic Planning*, Routledge and Kegan Paul.
Miel, A. (1971). 'Reassessment of the Curriculum — Why?', in Hooper, R. (Ed.), *The Curriculum — Context, Design and Development*, Oliver and Boyd.
Ministry of Education (1947). *School and Life*, Central Advisory Council, H.M.S.O.
Ministry of Education (1949). *Citizens Growing Up*, Pamphlet No. 16, H.M.S.O.
Ministry of Education (1952). *History in Relation to Civics and Social Studies*, Pamphlet No. 23, H.M.S.O.
Ministry of Education (1960). *Geography and Education*, Pamphlet No. 39, H.M.S.O.

Ministry of Education (1963). *Report of the Central Advisory Council for Education (England): Half Our Future (Newsom Report)*, H.M.S.O.

Mitchell, P. (1972). 'The Humanities Programme in Thomas Bennett School', *Forum*, 15, 1.

Moore, E. R. (1957). *Report of an Investigation of the Teaching of Social Studies in English Schools and Teachers' Colleges in 1955*, unpublished Associateship Report, University of London Institute of Education.

Musgrave, P. W. (1969). 'Boundaries of the Subject', *Times Educational Supplement*, (Scotland), January 24th.

Musgrove, F. (1968). 'Curriculum Objectives', *Journal of Curriculum Studies*, 1, 1.

Musgrove, F. (1971). *Patterns of Power and Authority in English Education*, Methuen.

Musgrove, F. (1973). 'Power in the Integrated Curriculum', *J. Curriculum studies*, 5, 1.

Naish, M. C. (1970). 'New Curriculum Developments in Geography', *New Era*, 51, 8.

Naish, M. C. (1972). 'Geography in the Integrated Curriculum', in Graves, N. J. (1972).

National Education Association (1962). *Scholars Look at the Schools*, N.E.A.

N.U.T. (1952). *The Curriculum of the Secondary School*, N.U.T.

Nicholls, A. D. (1973). 'Environmental Studies in Schools', *Geography*, 58.

Nicholson, F. J. (1949). 'Some Suggestions for Teachers of Social Studies in Post-primary Classes', Le Play House Press.

Nicholson, F. J. and Wright, V. K. (1953). *Social Studies for Future Citizens*, Harrap.

Oliver, S. P. (1954). *The Scope and Presentation of Social Studies in England*, unpublished Associateship Report, University of London Institute of Education.

Peters, R. S. (1967). 'A theory of Classical Education', *Didaskalos*, 2, 2.

Peters, R. S. (1969). *Perspectives on Plowden*, Routledge and Kegan Paul.

Phenix, P. H. (1964). *Realms of Meaning*, McGraw-Hill.

Pring, R. (1970a). 'Curriculum Integration', *Bull. University of London Institute Education*, Spring.

Pring, R. (1970b). 'Philosophy of Education and Educational Practice', *Proc. Philosophy of Education Society*.

Pring, R. (1973). 'Curriculum Integration: the Need for Clarification', *New Era*, 54, 3, April.

Reich, C. A. (1971). *The Greening of America*, Allen Lane, The Penguin Press.

Reisman, D. (1958). *Constraint and Variety in American Education*, Doubleday.

Reynolds, J. (1971). 'Schools Council Curriculum Development Project: Geography 14—18 years', *Geography*, 56.

Rhys, W. T. (1966). *The Development of Logical Thinking in the Adolescent with reference to the Teaching of Geography in Secondary Schools*, unpublished M.Ed. thesis, University of Birmingham.

Rink, F. T. (Ed.) (1802). *Immanuel Kant's Physische Geographie*, Konigsberg.

Rogers, V. R. (1968). *The Social Studies in English Education*, Heinemann Educational Books.

Rooper, T. G. (1901). 'Methods of Teaching Geography', *The Geographical Teacher*, Vol. I.

Royal Geographical Society (1950). *Geography and 'Social Studies' in Schools*, a memorandum prepared by the Education Committee, R.G.S.

Schon, D. A. (1971). *Beyond the Stable State*, Temple Smith.

Schools Council (1967a). *Curriculum Development*, H.M.S.O.

Schools Council (1967b). *Forward from Newsom*, Manchester University School of Education.

Schools Council (1967c). *Society and the Young School Leaver*, Working Paper 11, H.M.S.O.

Schools Council (1969). *General Studies 16—18*, Working Paper 25, Evans/ Methuen.

Schools Council (1970). *Project on Environmental Studies*, Cartrefle College of Education brochure.

Scott Keltie, J. (1886). *Report to the Council of the Royal Geographical Society*, R.G.S. Supplementary Papers, Vol. 1, 1882—1885.

Scott Keltie, J. and Howarth, O. T. R. (1913). *History of Geography*, Watts and Co.

Scottish Certificate of Education Examinations Board (1960). *Modern Studies for the Ordinary Grade.*

Scottish Certificate of Education Examinations Board (1966). *Modern Studies: Higher Grade.*

Scottish Education Department (1959). *Report of the Working party on the Curriculum of the Senior Secondary School.*

Scottish Education Department (1966). *Raising the School Leaving Age.*

Scottish Education Department (1968). *Modern Studies for the School Leaver*, Consultative Committee on the Curriculum, Curriculum Paper 3.

Sealey, J. (1971). 'Interdisciplinary Studies', *Forum*, 13, 2.

Shaplin, J. T. and Old, H. F. (1964). *Team Teaching*, Harper and Row.

Sharma, C. L. (1963). *A Comparative Study of the Process of Making and Taking Decisions within Schools in the U.K. and U.S.A.*, unpublished Ph.D. thesis, University of London.

Shipman, M. (1971). 'Curriculum for Inequality', in Hooper, R. (Ed.), *The Curriculum*, Oliver and Boyd.

Sirevag, T. (1973). 'A Mainland Viewpoint', in *Modern Languages and European Studies*, C.I.L.T.

Skilbeck, M. (1970). 'Man: A Broadcast Series', *Trends in Education*, 19.

Skilbeck, M. (1972). 'Forms of Curriculum Integration', *General Education*, 18, Spring.

Sloman, A. E. (1964). *A University in the Making*, BBC.

Smith, B. O., Stanley, W. O. and Shores, H. J. (rev. ed. 1957). 'Fundamentals of Curriculum Development', Harcourt, Brace and World.

Smith, D. (1971). 'Radical Geography — the Next Revolution', *Area*, 3, 3.

Stenhouse, L. (1968). 'The Humanities Curriculum Project', *J. Curriculum Studies*, 1, 1.

Stewart, W. A. C. (1950). 'Social Studies: A Résumé, *J. Education.*

Stewart, W. A. C. (1968). *The Educational Innovators 11: Progressive Schools, 1881—1967*, Macmillan.

Taba, H. (1962). *Curriculum Development*, Harcourt, Brace and World.

Taylor, W. (1963). *The Secondary Modern School*, Faber and Faber.

Tibble, J. W. (ed.) (1970). *The Extra Year: The Raising of the School Leaving Age*, Routledge and Kegan Paul.

Toffler, A. (1970). *Future Shock*, The Bodley Head.

Towler, J. (1970). 'The Elementary School Child's Concept of Reference Systems', *J. Geography*, 69, January.

Welton, W. P. (1914). 'The Educational Outlook of Geography', *The Geographical Teacher*, 17, 39.

Wheeler, D. K. (1967). *Curriculum Process*, University of London Press.

White, J. (1968). 'Instruction in Obedience', *New Society*, May 2nd.

Wilensky, H. J. (1964). 'Mass Society and Mass Culture: Interdependence or Independence', *American Sociological Review*, April.

Wilkinson, F. J. (1901). 'Recent Examination Papers in Geography', *The Geographical Teacher*, Vol. I.

Williams, A. (1973). 'Integrated Studies Project', *Forum*, 16, 1.

Williams, M. T. (1963). *The Teaching of Social Studies in the Secondary Schools of England and Wales*, unpublished M.A. thesis, University of Reading.

Williams, M. T. (1968). 'Difficult to Teach, are Modern Studies Worthwhile?', *Times Educational Supplement*, (Scotland), September 6th.

Williams, M. T. (1969). 'Integration-*v*-Fusion', *Times Educational Supplement*, (Scotland), January 24th.

Williams, M. T. (1970). 'Modern Studies: A Growth Area in the Curriculum of Scottish Secondary Schools', *Education and Social Science*, Vol. 1.

Wooldridge, S. W. (1949). 'On Taking the "Ge-" out of Geography', *Geography* 24.

Wooldridge, S. W. and East, W. G. (1951). *The Spirit and Purpose of Geography*, Hutchinson University Library.

Wright, V. K. (1950). 'Social Studies in the Classroom', *J. Education*, November.

Young, M. F. D. (ed.) (1971). 'An Approach to the Study of Curricula as Socially Organized Knowledge', in *Knowledge and Control*, Collier, Macmillan.

Index